THE MIND AND METHOD
OF THE ECONOMIST

To George L.S. Shackle

The Mind and Method of the Economist

A Critical Appraisal of Major Economists in the 20th Century

Brian J. Loasby

Emeritus Professor of Economics, University of Stirling

EDWARD ELGAR

Published by
Edward Elgar Publishing Limited
Gower House
Croft Road
Aldershot
Hants GU11 3HR
England

Gower Publishing Company
Old Post Road
Brookfield
Vermont 05036
U.S.A.

British Library Cataloguing in Publication Data
Loasby, Brian, J. (Brian John), *1930–*
   The mind and the method of the economist:
   a critical appraisal of major economists
   in the 20th century.
   1. Economics. Theories, 1900–1986.
   330.1

ISBN 1 85278 124 6

Printed and bound in Great Britain at
The Camelot Press Ltd, Southampton

Contents

v

Preface

The economist's problem is insoluble. The complexity of the systems to be studied, and the interdependencies, not merely of its natural elements but also of human choices, are far beyond the bounds of human rationality. Yet we have both a psychological and a practical need to understand, and where possible to predict, the behaviour of these systems. How economists have set about this ultimately impossible task is the theme of this book. The particular examples discussed are placed in a context of the quest for knowledge by the methods of science, and the organization of that quest. The mixture of collaboration and competition which characterizes science has some notable, but little exploited, similarities with the mixture of collaboration and competition which characterizes what are loosely called competitive economies. These similarities are noted in several of the following chapters, but I have not included any of my work which is centred on them. The final chapter, however, provides a link for those who might like one.

The substance of Chapters 1, 2, 3 and 6 have previously appeared in print, and Chapter 4 uses material from two published articles; permission to republish is acknowledged in the appropriate places. Chapter 5 is also being published separately. The remainder have not appeared in print before, although several have been issued as discussion papers. All have been revised – some very extensively.

In preparing these essays for publication I have tried to bear in mind the interests both of those who wish to read about only one topic and those who are seeking a coherent presentation; thus, each chapter is intended to be capable of independent existence, but deals as briefly with issues more fully treated elsewhere as seems to me compatible with that objective. The sequence has been chosen to provide as much continuity as I could contrive.

At my publisher's request, I have added a personal introduction. Although I do not believe that biography is relevant to the appraisal of anyone's ideas, it may help to understand them; and the understanding of other people's ideas is, in my view, an underrated skill among economists. Understanding ideas is not equivalent to replacing them by formal models. Since the theme of this book is the variety of perceptions and analyses of economic issues, and the evolution of ways of dealing with them, it seems most appropriate to concentrate on the origins of my own perceptions. Appropriately enough, it is a story of unintended consequences rather than of rational choice.

A few specific acknowledgements are indicated in appropriate chapters; but I could not possibly list all the people whose ideas, comments, and criticisms I have made use of – not always, I am sure, in ways they would approve. I am conscious of a particular obligation to past and present members of the Economics Department at the University of Stirling: most of the chapters were presented in some form to departmental workshops, and I have had many individual and group discussions on many of the issues. My final thanks must go to the Economics Departmental Secretary, Ann Cowie, who has processed and reprocessed this material, more often than either of us would care to remember, but always with speed, skill, and cheerfulness beyond reasonable expectations.

Introduction

Kettering Grammar School provided an excellent academic education, and in the process equipped its pupils, who were mostly from working-class homes, for middle-class occupations. By the time I reached the sixth form, it was becoming very efficient at getting them into university.

I applied for entry to Emmanuel College, Cambridge, on the advice of the headmaster, who was himself a graduate in English of that college. This was not the only reason for his choice: Emmanuel was particularly well disposed to applicants from grammar schools, and offered a multi-subject entrance examination to counter the advantages which public school candidates were likely to have in the traditional specialist examinations. I was successful in this examination; and it left me free to choose my own course of study. I chose economics partly because of some political interest, and partly because I hoped to understand better how the world worked. I still do.

Edward Welbourne, Senior Tutor and later Master of Emmanuel, is as unforgettable to those who were at the College in his time as he is unknown to others. A historian by profession, he published almost nothing, and read almost everything; he would weave ideas and evidence into a monologue – for hardly anyone managed a conversation with him – which was designed to test the grounds for his hearer's beliefs; he attacked second-hand opinions, and especially those whom he thought were trying to foist second-hand opinions on others. Above all, he opposed what Hayek (1975) was later to call the pretence of knowledge.

Welbourne's critical attitude no doubt helps to explain why I gradually became, and still remain, critical of Cambridge economics. The Economics Faculty did not lack famous figures, nor those (such as Harry Johnson) who were to become famous. But it was not a harmonious place – although it became much worse later, as the number of factions multiplied – and I could not help noticing that criticisms of other people's views were usually based on a presumption of the critic's own unquestionable knowledge. One characteristic which the Cambridge factions have had in common, despite fundamental differences on both theoretical and policy issues, has been intellectual arrogance; and my Welbourne-educated reaction has been scepticism about both theories and policies.

By the end of my undergraduate course, in 1952, this scepticism was focused on two issues. I accepted the basic Keynesian analysis, but saw no reason why this should exclude the revival of monetary policy; so the denunciation of this revival by the Cambridge Keynesians – who at that time included Harry Johnson – raised more doubts in my mind about the quality of their thinking than about the wisdom of the policy. Nor could I agree that Dennis Robertson's objections to Keynes's analysis should be disregarded; for example, if savings were equal to investment by definition, why did we need a theory to explain that they were brought into equality by changes in the level of output? Yet Keynesians appeared to claim that it was precisely because of this definition that the equality needed to be explained. Nowadays this seems to me an understandable confusion on the part of Keynes and his supporters (perpetuated by Harrod as late as 1969); for a theory which seeks to explain how an economy can get stuck is not likely to be very good at explaining movement – as the *General Theory* assuredly is not. The maintenance of an accounting identity by unintended investment, through the accumulation of unsaleable goods, though helpful in constructing what Hicks calls a 'continuation theory', is an embarrassment to a theory of unemployment equilibrium.

On the whole, I thought Dennis Robertson was more wrong than right; but he was more willing than most to admit the possibility of other views, and I had more sympathy with his attitude, if not his analysis, than with any other of the Cambridge principals. I was disconcerted by his tendency to rely on metaphor at crucial stages in his argument; it was many years before I came to realize that rigorous models are also metaphorical. Robertson's metaphors at least had the advantage of signalling the need for translation, whereas some very distinguished economists still seem to believe that it is translation into the modelling metaphor that is both necessary and sufficient for understanding.

Coming from a manufacturing town, I was always primarily interested in what Marshall (1961, p.1) called 'the study of mankind in the ordinary business of life'; and once we had left Marshall behind (which meant quite early in the second year) the treatment of what is now called microeconomics did not satisfy that interest. I was, and remain, very grateful for Hicks' *Value and Capital* (1939), not least for Hicks' care in explaining what he was doing and why; but I was a little worried at his declared willingness to assume away imperfect competition in order to develop his theoretical structure. This worry I now mark as the beginning of my recognition that the methods of economic analysis are both important and problematic.

Imperfect competition was a major source of difficulty. Of secondary, though substantial, importance was the dispute between Joan Robinson and Chamberlin about the core of their theories (usually, if inadequately, characterized as the 'tangency solution'); by the time I graduated I was beginning to understand why the theories were different, but not why the dispute made no progress towards a resolution. However, the central problem was that the theory of imperfect competition clearly did not correspond in any relevant way to business practice, either as it was or as it ever could be; yet it seemed logically impregnable. That was how businessmen must behave; yet they could not possibly do so, because they could not possibly know what the theory required them to know. Of course, this was a false dilemma. Price theory had already parted company from business behaviour, and the theory of imperfect competition, far from being impregnable, is incoherent, as Andrews (1964) – who was scorned in Cambridge – was to demonstrate.

However, at the time I could see no way out; nor did I realize that the question of what people could know when they made decisions was a fundamental issue, and a challenge to the standard methods of analysis. Hayek was not recommended at Cambridge; but even if I had read his papers (1937, 1945) on knowledge in economics, I doubt that I would have seen how they could help. So when, to my surprise – for I was engaged in a series of interviews with firms seeking management trainees – I was offered the chance to stay at Cambridge, I turned for my research topic to economic history. Another economist at Emmanuel, one year ahead of me, abandoned the prospect of an academic career at least partly for the same reason. When I met him again, a few years later in Birmingham, he gave me a copy of a paper that he had been giving on the use of economic ideas in business, in which he had written that 'some new ideas need to be worked out in the theory of the firm, as revolutionary in their way as the ideas of Keynes'. But economists, like economies, can get stuck.

For my research topic, I turned to the history of my home town, Kettering, in the later nineteenth century. Its population had grown slowly from 3,000 at the 1801 Census to 7,000 in 1871; it then quadrupled within 40 years, but its growth came to an abrupt halt at the beginning of the twentieth century. Here was a well defined problem situation. The first stage of the explanation was easy. Rapid growth was attributable to the localization of shoemaking which accompanied the mechanization of the industry; but, since the productivity increases brought by mechanization were converted into reduced employment as well as greater output, once the localization was complete, the growth of the shoe towns was bound to stop. This pattern was confirmed by the population statistics for other shoe manufacturing centres; the more specialized they became, the more rapid the acceleration and the more abrupt its end.

The next stage was to examine the transformation of the industry, and any particular factors which applied to Kettering. The key technology was machine sewing, and this was predominantly American. Major innovations were adapted, but did not originate, in Britain. The development of the industry in Britain was Marshallian, rather than Schumpeterian, although I was not clever enough to make the distinction at the time: indeed, since I did not realize that there was a viable alternative to imperfect competition as a theory of the firm, and since that theory was clearly inapplicable to a competitive oligopoly some way from static equilibrium, I did not attempt a formal analysis. This was the major missed opportunity of my career – and it was missed, like so many opportunities, because I did not realize that it existed.

However, what did result was an enhanced sense of historical process, especially of the importance of timing and of sequence, not least of unintended consequences. I have never since been satisfied with equilibrium models as explanations of how the economic system works; and how the system works is my conception of an economic problem. I believe it was Adam Smith's too, but I have a strong impression that many modern theorists find the question either uninteresting or unanswerable – and therefore best avoided.

After three years in Aberdeen, two of them teaching economic history, I moved to Birmingham in 1958 to undertake a study of industrial location. I decided to investigate location decisions by interviewing senior managers of firms in the Birmingham area. The original objective was to find ways of discriminating between those which had moved to Development Areas, as they were then called – areas of high unemployment (by the standards of the time) such as South Wales, Merseyside, and what is now Strathclyde – those which had moved to towns outside, but close to, the West Midland conurbation, and those which had moved within the conurbation. Such an analysis, it was thought by those who had created the research project, would help policy. I was interested in policy, but I was also interested in business decisions; and the first conclusion from early interviews was that an explanation of a location decision had to begin with an explanation of how location became a subject for decision. In modern terminology, a theory of optimal choice does not explain what is to be optimized – and that may be more important than the optimization itself.

Among the firms which I visited, by far the most frequent initiator of a location decision was the pressure of increasing business on present facilities, which could not be expanded either because of physical constraints or (less often) because the firm was denied an Industrial Development Certificate, which was then a prerequisite for planning permission. However, as many of the people whom I interviewed took care to point out, once the decision to seek a new site was made, the problem began to change, and the principal focus of attention thereafter was on improving efficiency. Most of the firms which had decided to move because they required more capacity saw the main advantage of the move, in retrospect, as greater efficiency; and some of them acknowledged that the prospect of greater efficiency would not have been sufficient to induce a move.

In the late 1960s, I was invited to report on the relocation of W.H. Smith's book and stationery warehouse from London to Swindon and found a similar story. Business was growing at a rate which would soon outstrip the capacity of the London warehouse, and this was the problem which forced the move. However, the company recognized from the outset that a move would provide the opportunity to tackle what had long been acknowledged as inefficient ways of handling distribution. The reform of the system (especially the ordering and delivery cycle, which was not crucially dependent on either the location or structure of the warehouse) would actually have made it possible to continue in the old warehouse for several more years, yet, as everyone realized, this reform would never have been undertaken without the decision to move.

By the time that I moved to Bristol University in 1961 I was convinced that business decisions should be analysed as processes. Conventional equilibrium models could be very helpful in elucidating parts of the problem, but they could not encompass it all: in my view, they assumed too much that needed to be explained. At Bristol I worked in the newly created School of Management Studies – a failed innovation for the classic reason that the University assumed a ready-made market. However, I learned something from most of the managers I encountered, and perhaps most from the Director, D. K. Clarke. David Clarke had been Director of the Conservative Research Centre from 1945 to 1950 (the years in which R. A. Butler was primarily responsible for reshaping Conservative policy), and then on the Directing Staff of the Administrative Staff College at Henley until moving to Bristol. He introduced me to organization theory, by way of Chester Barnard and Simon, and to his own concept of a decision cycle, which fitted the pattern of my own investigations so well.

While I was at Bristol, Cyert and March (1963) published their

Behavioral Theory of the Firm: here I thought were the beginnings of the revolutionary new ideas which my fellow-student, quoted earlier, had been asking for. The development of these ideas has been very disappointing to me, but so too has been the lack of response to them within the economics profession. Why should economists continue to prefer a method of analysis which has very little to tell us about the process of management to one which provides usable categories? I believe I now understand why. This was the problem which aroused my interest in the development of economic theory and method.

In 1965 I was one of a group of British academics sent to America for a year by the Foundation for Management Education as part of their efforts to promote business schools in Britain. The others became full members of the International Teachers Program at Harvard Business School, but I was chosen for an experimental Fellowship, which combined half-time working with Arthur D. Little Inc. (ADL) and half-time study at Harvard or the Sloan School at the Massachusetts Institute of Technology (MIT). I believe I was the first person to be a student at those two management schools simultaneously. This was a very important year, and not only because of what I learned in the classes I attended and in my consulting assignments. ADL was a fascinating organization, and I set out to understand the way it worked, using as my principal key Burns and Stalker's (1961) analysis of mechanistic and organic systems. My attempts were well received within the company, and resulted in a (suitably expurgated) article in *Management Today* (1967).

Harvard Business School and the Sloan School also offered an illuminating contrast in styles. The Sloan School developed analytical skills within fairly conventional subject boundaries; Harvard avoided conventional subjects, emphasized problems, and (in accordance with its model in the Harvard Law School) encouraged persuasive argument. Harvard graduates generally made more successful business careers. This experience reinforced my belief that a dominant emphasis on the analysis of well defined choice was misguided as a means of understanding and ineffective as the basis of management education (Loasby, 1966). Yet it was the Dean of the Sloan School, W.F. Pounds, who had just written what, for me, was an invaluable paper on the process of problem-finding (published in 1969). He had come from Carnegie.

The Adviser to Foreign Students at MIT, Eugene Chamberlain, noticed from my registration form that I had a business visitor's visa and invited me to explain this anomaly. (He had found a problem.) The explanation, of course, was my attachment to Arthur D. Little Inc. After a very pleasant conversation, he invited me to help in entertaining some of the visitors from British industry who were seeking to recruit staff from MIT graduates. This I was very happy to do. Among those I met as a result were two managers from ICI, one of whom shared my interest in the recognition and specification of problems, and invited me to visit him when I returned to Britain. This was my introduction to Charles Suckling, at that time a research manager in Mond Division of ICI. By the time I visited him at Runcorn, he had become Divisional Research Manager, and one of his colleagues, Frank Bradbury, had been appointed Professor of Industrial Science at the newly approved University of Stirling, with the primary remit of developing courses in Technological Economics – a title invented by two other ICI people. So I went to Stirling in 1967 as an unintended consequence of applying for a business visitor's visa.

The development of Technological Economics at Stirling was heavily conditioned by the problems of research management. We were thinking of a sequence of decisions and discovery, which David Clarke's concept of a decision cycle fitted perfectly, and in which success depended on the timely identification of important problems. My experience of different ways of thinking at Arthur D. Little, Harvard and MIT, and at W.H. Smith, was now organized by the concept of a paradigm, to which I was introduced by one of our first research students. He was using a group of ICI case histories as the basis of an analysis of barriers to innovation and had identified the need to switch paradigms as an important obstacle in some of these cases. Of especial interest to me was the story of the inhalant anaesthetic halothane, which was most strongly resisted by the very distinguished anaesthetist who had pioneered the supersession of the old inhalant anaesthetics by carefully controlled barbiturate cocktails. Thus I have never thought of paradigms as exclusively, or even mainly, applicable to intellectual history.

However, I did see that this provided a novel framework for analysing the development of imperfect and monopolistic competition, and explaining economists' lack of interest in the work of Cyert and March. My article (1971) has been republished (Caldwell, 1984), and much of it was also used in my book, *Choice, Complexity and Ignorance* (1976); so it is not included in this volume. Some of its topics, however, do appear.

From Kuhn I worked my way into the theory of the growth of knowledge, the potential scope of which seemed continually to expand. It encompasses (along with much else) both the development of economic theory and decision-making within organizations. Gradually the idea grew of trying to put them together in a single book and, with the aid of a sabbatical leave spent at the Oxford Centre for Management Studies (now Templeton College), the book appeared in 1976. During this long process I rediscovered both Shackle (to whose ideas I had been introduced at Cambridge by Charles Carter) and Richardson, who unintentionally provides some answers to the generally pessimistic tone of Shackle's *Epistemics and Economics* (1972), as O'Brien (1974) pointed out in a review of Shackle's work. But Shackle's insistence on the problems of knowledge certainly reinforced my conviction that, whatever their intentions, the topic addressed by Arrow and Debreu was the coherence of economic theory, not the coordination of economic activities.

Choice, Complexity and Ignorance excited some highly selective enthusiasm. What I had not expected was a welcome from some members of the Austrian school, understandably tempered by my failure to make any reference to them. This failure I now regard as a serious deficiency: my explanation, like Dr Johnson's for an error in his *Dictionary*, is pure ignorance – which I have tried to remedy. I have continued to work on the development of economic ideas and on the way an economy – especially its constituent businesses – operates, trying to apply the same concepts in both fields, for reasons which Adam Smith would have well understood. In 1984 I formally retired, under the terms of what turned out to be a generous scheme for allowing hard-pressed universities to reduce their salary costs. Most of the following chapters have been written, and all have been revised, since then: I will leave them to speak for themselves.

1 George Shackle's history of economic theory*

Professor George Shackle has discussed topics in the development of economic thought – especially the evolution and interpretation of Keynes's theory of unemployment – on many occasions. In this chapter, however, we shall consider only his systematic attempt in *The Years of High Theory* 'to cut a few sods in aid of an eventual theory of the origin of theories' (1967, p.3).

Theory as imposed order: Smith and Shackle
It will be observed that Shackle's ultimate objective is more ambitious than is normally claimed by historians of economic thought, and we should begin by examining his embryonic theory of theory development. In doing so, we cannot fail to draw on Skinner's (1979) comparison between Shackle's views and those of Adam Smith – the latter to be found, not in the *Wealth of Nations* but in a much earlier piece, the purpose of which is clearly indicated by its full title: 'The Principles which Lead and Direct Philosophical Enquiries; Illustrated by the History of Astronomy'. (This was first published, after Smith's death, in 1795; references are to the Glasgow Edition of 1980.) The following paragraphs are substantially derived from Skinner's article.

Adam Smith's explanation of the development of theories is psychological: theories are created to assuage the mental discomfort of the unexpected and the unaccountable. When objects or events seem to fall into some recognized class, or to follow in some familiar order, then

> . . . the thought glides easily along them, without effort and without interruption. They fall in with the natural career of the imagination. . . . There is no break, no stop, no gap, no interval. The ideas excited by so coherent a chain of things seem, as it were, to float through the mind of their own

*This chapter is a revised version of 'G.L.S. Shackle as a historian of economic thought', in W.S. Samuels (ed.), *Research in the History of Economic Thought and Methodology*, 1, pp.209–21, and is reproduced by permission of J.A.I. Press, Inc. I wish to acknowledge my debt to Andrew Skinner for his analysis of Adam Smith's theory of the development of scientific theories, and the very helpful comments on a previous draft by Mark Blaug and Denis O'Brien.

accord, without obliging it to exert itself, or to make any effort in order to pass from one of them to another. (Smith, 1980, p.41)

But if we observe something which does not match our notions of coherence, then the easy progress of the imagination is interrupted and we experience the unpleasant emotion of surprise. If the gap cannot easily be filled by a plausible supposition, we pass, according to Smith, into the yet more disturbing state of wonder: there are objects or events which we cannot account for, and our ideas are thrown into confusion.

The only remedy for this confusion, Smith asserts, is the invention of a new system of thought which will supply the missing connections and thus soothe the disordered imagination. If such a new system is indeed invented, it is then admired for its ability to restore tranquillity; and the greater the disorder which it subdues, the greater that admiration will be. Admiration will be still further enhanced if the new theoretical system appeals to the imagination through the elegance and beauty of its construction, especially its economy in explaining apparently diverse phenomena by a few general principles. The new system will then continue to soothe the imagination until such a time as new gaps appear, and a new cycle of theory creation begins.

Such, in briefest summary, is Smith's account of the psychological principles which lead and direct philosophical inquiries. In his words:

> Philosophy is the science of the connecting principles of nature. . . . [It] endeavours to introduce order into this chaos of jarring and discordant appearances, to allay this tumult of the imagination, and to restore it . . . to that tone of tranquillity and composure, which is both most agreeable to itself, and most suitable to its nature. Philosophy, therefore, may be regarded as one of those arts which address themselves to the imagination. (Smith, 1980, pp.45–6)

Smith then illustrates his thesis by tracing the sequence of the four great cosmological systems – those of the concentric and eccentric spheres, and those of Nicolaus Copernicus and Sir Isaac Newton. He emphasizes the supreme appeal of the Newtonian system in its ability to account for the widest range of appearances by the smallest number of principles; but he is very careful to warn us that even this system is not to be regarded as a description of 'the real chains which Nature makes use of to bind together her several operations' (1980, p.105) but as the product of Newton's imagination. Newton did not discover the laws of nature; he invented them. Such a view of science, and especially of Newtonian science, may be thought somewhat unusual for the eighteenth century. As Skinner (1979, p.116) observes, it raises fundamental questions about Smith's conception of political economy; but that is not directly our concern.

Let us compare Smith's psychological theory with what Shackle has to say, noting that he knew nothing at the time of this work by Smith. Shackle's very first sentence is as follows: 'If the activities of men were arranged in sequence according to the degree in which he shares them with other parts of the animal creation, theory-making would surely rank amongst the most exclusively human' (1967, p.1); and this opening paragraph ends by invoking 'the claim, by which all theory ultimately stands or falls, of imaginative splendour lifting thought above itself'. The appeal of theories as intellectual constructions is a recurrent theme in the book.

In his final chapter, Shackle offers his own sketch of a theory of theory development. He begins by denying, like Smith, that theory describes reality:

> Insight into the *thing in being* of which we form a part, whether we attend chiefly to its non-human or its human aspect, cannot consist in a knowledge of its nature or meaning in any ultimate, absolute sense. All we can seek is consistency, coherence, order. The question for the scientist is what thought-scheme will best provide him with a sense of that order and coherence, a sense of some permanence, repetitiveness and universality in the structure or texture of the scheme of things, a sense even of that one-ness and simplicity which, if he can assure himself of its presence, will carry consistency and order to their highest expression. (1967, p.286)

It is possible, he admits – but no more than possible – that in the material sciences successive theories approximate more closely to the truth. (Smith does not deny this: he is content with the claim that they encompass a greater number of 'appearances'.) Shackle continues (1967, p.288): 'But in the sciences (so-called) of men and their affairs, the investigator may be said to impose rather than discover the orderliness which constitutes knowledge.'

What, then, is the purpose of theory? Shackle's answer is astonishingly similar to that given by Smith:

> The chief service rendered by a theory is the setting of minds at rest. So long as we have a satisfying conceptual structure, a model or a taxonomy which provides for the filing of all facts in a scheme of order, we are absolved from the tiresome labour of thought, and the uneasy consciousness of mystery and a threatening unknown . . . Theories by their nature and purpose, their rôle of administering to a 'good state of mind', are things to be held and cherished. Theories are altered and discarded only when they fail us. (1967, pp.288–9)

Failure, according to Shackle, may take two forms: inability to account for observed facts (in Smith's terminology, the opening up of a gap in the connecting chain) or the perception of internal inconsistency. The latter may well become apparent from an attempt to modify a theory in order to account for recalcitrant observations, but it might also be brought to light by continuing endeavours to refine the theoretical structure; for what appears coherent to the layman may fail to soothe the imagination of a professional in the field. Whichever form it takes, failure stimulates efforts to restore order and to remove discomfort through the invention and imposition of a new theoretical system. It is the tracing of these efforts, and of their unintended consequences, which occupies most of Shackle's book.

In one important respect, Shackle extends Smith's explanation of the stimulus to construct theories. 'A sense of order and consistency is needed, not only to satisfy a detached curiosity, but also to make practical life possible' (1967, p.286). 'Detached curiosity' is an odd phrase, since, for Shackle as for Smith, the imagination is deeply engaged in the quest for coherence and composure: no doubt it was chosen to emphasize, by contrast with this desire for tranquillity, the need for some scheme of order to permit something which might be called rational decision. One would not expect to find any discussion of the connection between theory and action in an analysis exemplified by the history of astronomy; but this additional function of theory as a guide to action does not seem in any way inconsistent with Smith's account. It is entirely consonant with Shackle's own theory of human decision.

Shackle's description of the content of theory is an unconscious paraphrase of Smith's. Theory offers us

> recurrent configurations of particular circumstances, configurations involving both simultaneous association and temporal sequence, and . . . we ascribe to this recurrence a permanence, a power of survival, a claim to belong to the nature of things, a guarantee of future as well as past validity. (1967, p.286)

Thus, in Smith's words:

> As its ideas move more rapidly than external objects, [the imagination] is continually running before them, and therefore anticipates, before it happens, every event which falls out according to this ordinary course of things. (1980, p.41)

While it does so we are protected from the discomforts of surprise;

moreover, Shackle adds, we can base our decisions on what we take to be established patterns. Since many of the stimuli to the development of new theories in the period under study are located by Shackle in the collapse of configurations which were embodied in received theory, this unconscious extension of Smith's theory to include action as well as understanding is clearly appropriate.

Shackle does not fail to observe that his account of 'the mode of making inventions and discoveries, including the invention of theories' (1967, p.287) is itself an example of the imposition of order by theory which he is discussing. It is then more than a little surprising (in Smith's sense) to note that, before beginning his detailed consideration, Shackle declares: 'We cannot formulate our questions in advance. Questions and answering hypotheses must arise together from the material' (1967, p.12). As Skinner has observed (1979, p.116), Smith's theory is not compatible with the view that Newtonian theory is derived from the evidence although, on this view, it is certainly a result of the urgent need to devise a scheme which would impose order on that evidence. Similarly, Shackle's own explanation of the development of theories is inconsistent with his apparent belief that this explanation emerges from his own detailed study. He has not done justice to his own originality.

The testing of theories

Shackle leaves us, however, with a major problem, which can perhaps be most clearly stated in the terms used by Sir Karl Popper. Popper's analysis of the progress of science through bold conjecture and attempted refutation links together two very different kinds of activity. The English title given to Popper's original work – *The Logic of Scientific Discovery* (1972) – is not entirely appropriate, for the logic is that of the testing of ideas, not of their emergence; indeed it is a fundamental principle of his argument that the hypotheses to be tested cannot be derived from the evidence by any logical scheme of induction. Although he has himself repeatedly emphasized the role of imaginative conjecture and, like Smith, extols Newton as the creator of a superb theoretical structure (the eventual falsification of which Smith was careful not to exclude), Popper has attempted no systematic treatment of the process of theory creation. So it is possible to regard Shackle's analysis (like Smith's) as complementary to Popper's. But would Shackle in return accept Popper's sophisticated falsificationism as complementary to his own analysis? In *The Years of High Theory*, it is not clear that he would.

If what is required is 'a model or a taxonomy which provides for the filing of all facts in a scheme of order' (Shackle, 1967, p.288), then this requirement is best met by a theory which is comprehensive and non-falsifiable, such as a theory of choice which depends on the maximization of the chooser's subjective utility but which imposes no prior restrictions on either preferences or perceptions. For this purpose, the power of a theory is judged by what it can accommodate; but for Popper, its power is judged by what it forbids. Now, Shackle's lifework has been driven by the desire for a body of economic theory true to the human condition, yet he has never been a strong advocate of the rigorous and systematic testing of theories against evidence.

One possible reason for this coolness toward testing may be the influence of F.A. Hayek's arguments against the assimilation of the social to the natural sciences. What restrains Shackle from a firm commitment to such methodological dualism is not a belief in the value of natural science methods for economists, but a suspicion that natural science may share more of the difficulties of the social sciences than some of its methodological propagandists may care to admit (1967, p.288). Those difficulties receive their most extended treatment in his *Epistemics and Economics* (1972), which exhibits a fundamental pessimism about the possibilities of predictive knowledge of human action in human society. Probability distributions as a technique for handling uncertainty, he argues, are misleading fictions; and it appears to follow that no effective testing procedure is possible. Yet Popper is hardly more sympathetic than Shackle towards probabilistic assessments of knowledge; and it is not clear that recognition of the fallibility of knowledge must inevitably lead to the conclusion to which Shackle seems to feel himself driven: that theories must be judged by their ability to soothe the imagination, not by their correspondence with the truth.

The disintegration of the Great Theory
Shackle's history begins, in a sense, where Smith left off. The Great Theory, as he calls it, which was constructed between 1870 and 1914, is compared more than once with the Newtonian system; it was, of course, to a considerable extent, consciously modelled on it. Its universal gravitational principle was self-interest, working through a complete system of markets; thus the configuration of prices and outputs throughout an economy could be explained as a general equilibrium between the subjective factors of human wants and the objective constraints of resources and technology. The conflict between self-interest and scarcity was resolved through the impersonal mechanism of the market. Such a theory had great intellectual and aesthetic appeal – not least, as Shackle omits to mention, because it seems to abolish any

need for direct human rivalry in economic matters, whether between individuals, groups, or nations. But whereas Smith had shown the history of astronomy culminating (though not necessarily terminating) in the grand Newtonian scheme, what Shackle records is the disintegration of the economists' Great Theory. The developments of indifference-curve analysis and of input–output analysis (which are carefully explained) are developments within that theory, but in the analysis of competition, and what we now call macroeconomics, the work was one of destruction.

Shackle traces in great, though selective, detail the struggle to adapt existing theory. In none of the case histories which he studies, except that of input–output analysis, does a new scheme emerge from a single person's thought. Amendment is added to amendment, some are withdrawn and some modified, until the hesitant steps accumulate into what, in retrospect, seems to have been a leap across a chasm. Shackle argues that this is how it must normally be. If the development of a discipline is a collective activity, each practitioner must make continual reference to what is familiar to his colleagues. Whether a particular suggestion is of major importance or a detour may thus not become clear until much later – and, indeed, either verdict may be reversed by a later generation. In Lakatosian language, once-progressive research programmes may start to degenerate, but apparent degeneration does not preclude later recovery (Lakatos, 1970).

Shackle traces this process with great sympathy and understanding, explaining the confusions of the pioneers. Thus, we see Sir Roy Harrod introducing the concept of marginal revenue in a paragraph which veers from the individual firm to the industry and back again, and misleadingly deriving marginal revenue from the industry demand curve (Shackle, 1967, p.24). Then, with this concept in his hand, he still worries how a firm with falling average costs, and therefore with marginal costs below average costs, can avoid making a loss on every unit sold (1967, p.32). We see Keynes defining savings and investment as identically equal, and then insisting on the need to explain how this definitional equality is established (Shackle, 1967, p.237). We then observe his failure to understand the significance of the distinction between *ex ante* and *ex post*, which would have clarified so much of his analysis, even when Bertil Ohlin had explained it to him: Keynes assumes that the *ex ante* view is appropriate to investment plans for a future date, and thus to the 'finance motive' for liquidity (Shackle, 1967, p.241). Readers' reactions will no doubt be divided between reassurance that even such giants are subject to the ills with which we are too familiar and despair that, if these can go so wrong, we could ever go right.

Theories of unemployment

The two principal groups of chapters deal, respectively, with the development of imperfect competition theory and the theory of unemployment. The former group fairly closely follows a chronological path, whereas the latter, after a long and enthusiastic chapter on Gunnar Myrdal, principally works back from what Shackle claims to be Keynes's ultimate meaning: that the impossibility of foreknowledge makes investment non-rational and unstable, fit to be handled only by an economics of disorder. On this view, the very attempt to formulate a macroeconomic model is a denial of Keynes's message. It is here that Shackle's own perception of the problems of human knowledge are most intimately entwined with the content of a specific theory; thus we should not be surprised that he is clearly concerned to argue his case, whereas his treatment of imperfect competition is more detached. The chapters on macroeconomics, although occupying more than half the book, are not much less concerned to persuade than to explain. This duality of purpose may account for some surprising omissions.

Although the publication of *Banking Policy and the Price Level* is given as one reason for starting the study in 1926 (the other reason being Piero Sraffa's famous article published in the same year), Sir Dennis Robertson receives no more than four passing mentions in this section of the book; yet he saw the basic paradox of money as clearly as anyone. If we are concerned to show how an exchange system can converge on an equilibrium without recourse to such implausible fictions as an auctioneer or recontracting, it is essential that initial exchanges at non-equilibrium prices should have little effect. But, as Marshall (1961, pp.791–3) points out in his Appendix on barter, if all exchange is by barter, then an initial transaction at a non-equilibrium price may affect too high a proportion of the traders' initial stocks of the commodity traded for us to have any confidence that this requirement will be met. If goods are exchanged for money, the risk is much reduced. It is not eliminated, as Marshall (1961, pp.334–6) also observes – especially, and significantly, if money is exchanged for labour.

This incomplete solution also creates a new difficulty. When someone chooses to accept money in exchange for goods and to hold that money in stock, he gives no indication of what he later intends to buy with it. Indeed, he probably does not know himself. The holding of financial assets to provide for future consumption is a claim on future production which cannot easily be prepared for, since the composition of that claim cannot be known; some investment is clearly needed, but no one can be sure what it will be. This difficulty could not exist if assets were held only in the form of dated claims on specified goods, and it would be far less serious if capital goods were less specific.

This, then, is the paradox: a market system without money has no very sure means of arriving at the equilibrium which our moneyless theory predicts, but the introduction of money into a market system entails risks of serious coordination failures. Money destroys knowledge. In Shackle's words: 'Money enormously enlarges the hurtful power of uncertainty at the same time as it enormously facilitates the beneficent power of specialization' (1967, p.137). Sir Dennis Robertson pioneered the exploration of the dangers and of possible remedies, and the mutual influences of Keynes and himself are nowadays well recognized. He seems to deserve a place similar to that accorded to Sir Roy Harrod in the story of imperfect competition.

Shackle looks to Stockholm rather than Cambridge for the development of monetary theory. It was in attempting to elucidate Knut Wicksell's analysis – to refine an established answer which seemed still serviceable, not to find a way of bridging a newly opened gap in the chain of events – that Myrdal produced, as a by-product, a 'radical and momentous' innovation (1967, p.116). Although Keynes is the dominant figure in Shackle's history, Myrdal is its hero; for it was Myrdal who introduced the distinction between the *ex ante* and the *ex post*, thus requiring economic agents to peer into the future and allowing them sometimes to make mistakes. In commenting on the significance of this development, Shackle makes a natural, almost inevitable, comparison with astronomy:

> Myrdal released economic theory from the tacit, imprisoning assumption that the economy moves like the planets, in paths each known as a whole irrespective of the point in it which a given planet happens to be at when we do our calculation of its orbit. The future is not known to those whose decisions, in their combined effect and interplay, determine it. (1967, p.116)

Myrdal certainly saw this lack of certainty as a source of disturbance. Shackle draws attention to a passage in which Myrdal observes that shifts of expectations can influence real variables:

> The fact that the size of our current income available for purposes of consumption or saving is in this way ultimately dependent upon our own subjective calculations, relating the present to the future periods by imputation, deserves increased attention in the explanation of booms and slumps.

> Thus it comes about that in certain conditions a sudden fall or rise in people's available incomes and consequently their consumption and savings can occur, although the so-called objective circumstances do not justify the change. (1967, p.125)

But Myrdal, like Wicksell, was concerned with fluctuations of prices, and with the misallocation of resources which might thereby be induced, rather than with unemployment. Indeed, as Shackle observes (1967, pp.118–20) Myrdal follows Wicksell in assuming full employment. Yet, what others might regard as a fatal defect is, for Shackle, of minor account in comparison with Myrdal's formal incorporation into economic theory of the need to take decisions in the face of an unknown future. It is the explanation of unemployment in terms of inescapable human ignorance, given powerful leverage by the otherwise beneficent human invention of money, which forms the theme of Shackle's macroeconomic chapters. That will surprise no-one who has any familiarity with his substantive contributions to economics.

Shackle points out that the concept of liquidity preference depends on a division of opinion between 'bulls' and 'bears' about the future course of bond prices: since both parties cannot be right, the present balance of opinion, and the price which it supports, must destroy itself by the mere passage of time. That a given set of facts can give rise to diverse opinions seems to impose severe limits on the scope of monetary theory, as it was described by Sir John Hicks in 1935:

> . . . the whole problem of applying monetary theory is one of deducing changes in anticipations from the changes in the objective data which call them forth. Obviously, this is not an easy task, and, above all, it is not one which can be performed in a mechanical fashion. . . . When once the connection between objective fact and anticipations has been made, theory comes again into its rights. (Hicks, 1935, p.13)

Shackle (1967, p.226) comments: 'Keynes would, I think, have declared [the task] utterly impossible.' Nevertheless, there is no shortage of economists proposing formulae for deriving expectations from data (objective data, if such are available, but in extremity any data will do) in order to preserve the rights of theory. It is only fair to say that Hicks is not of their number.

Shackle is no doubt saddened by this, but he surely understands. For he draws attention to the insistent grip of equilibrium, and its connotations of knowledge, on the minds of Harrod and of Keynes himself. Both are inclined to use the continuous present tense; and Shackle (1967, p.267) records that, when Harrod was asked (one infers by Shackle himself) whether his expression 'output is increasing' was to be interpreted 'has been increasing' or 'is expected to increase', he declined to accept the distinction. Shackle (1967, p.258) explains this reluctance on the part of either Harrod or Keynes to distinguish between plans and outcomes by a deep desire to preserve the appearance of rationality. The multiplicity of conjectures do somehow issue in a single set of events and, if we focus on the events, we can forget the conflict of conjectures and the falsification of many of them. As many economists have discovered, expectations are a threat to order; Keynes had to imprison them to obtain an unemployment equilibrium. Thus, even when analysing unemployment – the economics of disorder – there remains a deep instinct to impose order.

Here we must note another omission. Shackle makes no reference to the attempt by his own admired teacher, F.A. Hayek, to explain unemployment as the consequence of false conjectures which are based on a rate of interest driven below the natural rate by excessive monetary expansion. Hayek's theory was very different from that of Keynes, but it does depend on the likelihood of entrepreneurial mistakes – even if those mistakes result from misleading information rather than entrepreneurial ignorance. Hayek's world cannot be one of perfect knowledge; but Shackle's (1967, p.92) passing reference to Hayek's 1937 essay 'Economics and knowledge' fails to comment on Hayek's recognition that the mutual compatibility of plans by which he defines equilibrium is something that needs to be attained through a process of discovery. Is it not natural to enquire whether that process might fail? Hayek did not so enquire, for he was a believer in spontaneous order. Nevertheless, his insistence on the need for a discovery process had the unintended consequence of providing the basis for an economics of uncertainty and disorder. One would very much like to hear Shackle's explanation as to why that basis remained unused.

There is perhaps a clue in his final comment on the attachment of both Keynes and Harrod to formal models of equilibrium:

> There is a most curious psychic twist of unconscious argument in all this. Theories give knowledge, and so (it is unconsciously felt) knowledge must be ascribed to the people who play a part in our theories. It is almost as though the writers said to themselves: We cannot theorize rationally about conduct which is not completely rational. (1967, p.270)

On reading those sentences, does any reader not immediately think of the modern enthusiasm for theories embodying 'rational expectations'? But we may observe in the work of so thoughtful a modern follower of Hayek as Kirzner (1973, 1985a) the same reluctance to accept fundamental uncertainty. The market process is a discovery procedure, the detailed working of which cannot be known but which, in the absence of governmental interference, can be relied on to overcome the problems of dispersed and incomplete knowledge: certainty is thus preserved at the system level. By some means or other, we are determined to impose order. Lachmann (1986) appears to be the only Austrian economist who is prepared to take seriously the possibility that market processes may break down: it is no coincidence that he is much the closest to Shackle.

Imperfect and monopolistic competition

Since Shackle emphasizes the effects of uncertainty, it is rather surprising that he makes no attempt to interpret developments in the theory of value in these terms. Indeed, he follows the convention of treating value theory and macroeconomics as quite separate and, in so doing, he is in the very best of company. But Kalecki, the quality of whose work is acknowledged but not discussed (Shackle, 1967, p.127), did build market imperfections (though not imperfect knowledge) into his theory of unemployment, and it is still a good question why the distinction between micro- and macroeconomics persisted. If I may venture a tentative answer, it is because the question of macroeconomic stability was seen as a problem of money, not goods, and because uncertainty, as it came to be acknowledged, was attached to money and to those objects – financial assets, then investment goods – which were not immediately associated with the commodities of value theory. Thus, the goods markets could remain suffused with perfect knowledge. Shackle gives proper credit to Hugh Townshend (1937) for extending the implications of uncertainty to all commodities, with the consequence that convention becomes the basis of valuation throughout the economic system (1967, pp.228, 246–7) – a view which is so subversive that it has been ignored throughout the economics profession. Thus, microeconomics has remained well ordered.

Shackle's patient and perceptive exposition of the emergence of the theory of imperfect competition cannot be faulted, save in one very important respect – namely, the assimilation to imperfect competition of the core of E.H. Chamberlin's (1933) argument, an assimilation which was standard doctrine in 1967 but which Shackle would now reject. Its persistence as standard doctrine, despite Chamberlin's continual protests, poses a key question for the historian of economic thought and has been thoroughly examined by O'Brien (1984b), but lies outside the present discussion. The power and pedagogic convenience of the (apparently identical) graphic representation of the equilibrium of the firm in monopolistic and in imperfect competition was probably a major factor.

What can be observed is that the interpretation of Chamberlin, offered by Romney Robinson (1971, pp.33–4), of a theory in which suppliers have to discover what customers want and inform them of what they have to offer, is another challenge to the assumption of sufficient knowledge. Shackle himself comments (1967, pp.133–4): 'The world in which *enterprise* is necessary and possible is a world of uncertainty. . . . Enterprise is risk, risk is ignorance, and equilibrium, by contrast, is the effective banishment of ignorance'; but this comment occurs in his discussion of Keynes, with no hint of its possible relevance to Chamberlin. According to Robinson, Chamberlin's theory was one of enterprise, but he does not add that it is set in a world of uncertainty. Yet Chamberlin chose to cast all his formal arguments (although certainly not the whole of his text) in terms of equilibrium – in order, presumably, to engage the attention of equilibrium-minded theorists. At least he thereby avoided the fate of P.W.S. Andrews and G.B. Richardson – though at the cost of persistent misinterpretation. It must be a matter for great regret that Shackle's acceptance of the orthodox view, in this instance, deprived him of a theme which he is uniquely fitted to develop – a theme which accords so well with his central concerns.

Destruction and restoration
Robinson (1971, pp.56–7) points out that Chamberlin and Keynes have both been seen as threats to the fundamental principle of scarcity on which economic theory has rested: Keynes because he purported to show how valuable resources could remain unused; Chamberlin because expansion of output was constrained not by rising costs but by falling demand. Both replace supply constraints by demand failure. Robinson's view, though less emphatic, appears very similar to that of Shackle, who leaves us, at the end of his period of study, to contemplate the consequences of so much brilliant constructive endeavour – the disintegration of the Great Theory. As Hicks (1939, pp. 83–5) warned, in a much quoted passage, imperfect competition threatened to wreck 'the greater part of economic theory' – a theory which claimed to explain the persistence of involuntary unemployment, especially if founded on the impossibility even of probabilistic foreknowledge, seemed to undermine economists' central concept of rational choice.

As the implications were realized, the gaps and intervals opened up in the structure of economic theory by this 'landslide of invention' were widely felt to be unacceptable. Imperfect and monopolistic competition theory were banished to the pen formerly reserved for monopoly, and perfectly competitive general equilibrium was restored, in a much improved form. The neoclassical synthesis provided a serviceable temporary repair to the Keynesian rent by denying that Keynes's work had any theoretical significance; nevertheless it was realized that something better was needed, and we are now well on the way to proving that involuntary unemployment is a logical impossibility. There is no denying the intellectual quality of much of this work, and Shackle and Adam Smith would both very well understand its appeal to the imagination. Of the original Great Theory, Shackle wrote:

> In its arresting beauty and completeness this theory seemed to need no corroborative evidence from observation. It seemed to derive from these aesthetic qualities its own stamp of authentication and an independent ascendancy over men's minds. (1967, p.5)

Adam Smith observes (1980, p.77): 'how easily the learned give up the evidence of their senses to preserve the coherence of the ideas of their imagination.' In a world which seems frighteningly irrational, our confused imaginations seek desperately for order. What few have acknowledged is that Shackle's theory of the development of theories is part of a general theory of knowledge which seems capable of very wide application: in particular it can help us to interpret economic processes. Shackle's lifework suggests to us the possibility of a scheme of order far wider even than the Great Theory, and it challenges us to build a new synthesis.

2   On scientific method*

The attempt to base economic theories on rational choice requires careful specification of the knowledge which is deemed to be available to the chooser. If the specification is to be complete, it also requires some explanation of how that knowledge could be acquired. The failure of theorists to explain how economic agents can know what they are presumed to know has been at the heart of Shackle's (1972) criticisms of conventional theory; and it is to the credit of some rational expectations theorists that they have taken up the challenge. Unfortunately, their claim that agents learn the relevant true model through experience relies on an inductive theory of knowledge, the inadequacy of which was demonstrated by Hume more than two centuries ago. Post-Keynesians are unlikely to lament the logical discomfiture of rational expectations theorists: yet Keynes's (1973b) own attempt, in the *Treatise on Probability*, to establish a basis for degrees of rational belief depends on a probabilistic version of the same unjustifiable principle. In this chapter we shall examine a less ambitious approach to the problem of knowledge, which is associated primarily with the work of Sir Karl Popper.

Knowledge and evidence
Inductive methods attempt to derive knowledge from evidence. But no logical derivation is possible: no matter how many instances one has observed of a particular phenomenon, one is never justified in concluding that it is certain to recur. Just because the sun has risen every day, that is no proof that it will rise again tomorrow.

This is no idle example. In the first place, until recent years it has never been possible to observe the sun every morning; for some mornings are cloudy. Thus the statement that the sun has risen every day in Stirling cannot itself be a fact, but an inference, resting on certain assumptions about the behaviour of the sun on cloudy mornings. By flying above the clouds, the inference can be confirmed. However, sending instruments above the clouds merely substitutes a different inference, which needs its own justification: Galileo's telescope

*This chapter is a revised version of 'On scientific method', *Journal of Post Keynesian Economics*, **6**, pp.394–410, and is reproduced by permission of M.E. Sharpe, Inc.

provided evidence only for those who could accept Galileo's theory of optics, which was less well established than the hypotheses it was required to support. In the second place, the statement that the sun rises every day is simply not true – and not just because the phenomenon which we call sunrise is due to the rotation of the earth: it is not true of all places within either the Arctic or the Antarctic Circles. Many generations of men had observed the sun rising day after day, except when obscured by cloud, and until one of them ventured into the far north no-one would fail to observe it. We could hardly hope for a greater degree of rational belief. Yet the belief was not rational; and it was wrong. Repeated demonstrations cannot prove a general rule beyond the possibility of refutation.

Since the time of Hume, no philosopher has been able to overthrow this conclusion, and it has made many of them unhappy. For, if the principle of induction is not logically defensible, what then is our criterion of objective truth? Bertrand Russell, not surprisingly, was particularly exercised by this problem, for if there is no way of establishing the truth then 'the lunatic who thinks he is a poached egg is to be condemned solely on the ground that he is in a minority, or rather – for we must not assume democracy – because the government does not agree with him' (Russell, 1946, p.699). Given the Russian practice – now apparently modified – of certifying those who do not agree with the government as lunatics, one can understand Russell's concern. And yet he could find no better remedy than the proposal that if only we could all agree to pretend that the principle of induction was valid, we could thereafter use it in a thoroughly logical way. But, although morally superior, this is logically no better than agreeing that the Party is infallible. There is a tone of desperation in Russell's discussion which clearly indicates his recognition of a weakness which might prove fatal to rational enquiry.

Falsification

When two hundred years of effort by the world's greatest thinkers have failed to produce an answer to a question, it may be a good idea to change the question. That is what Popper did. For the problem of verification he substituted the problem of falsification. 'There is no criterion of truth at our disposal. . . . But we do possess criteria which, *if we are lucky*, may allow us to recognise error and falsity' (Popper, 1969, p.28). The qualification will need to be considered shortly. But, first, let us observe what has been done. The logic of science, says Popper, is not a logic of verification, but a logic of refutation. No matter how many million times the sun is observed to rise, we cannot thereby prove that it rises every day; but a single negative observation is enough to prove that it does not.

We should notice two things about Popper's view. First, although it still enjoins us to search for truth and to search for truth by means of evidence, it warns us that we can never reach certainty. All knowledge is provisional; even if the 'final truth' in some area of science has been reached, we can never know. There is thus no model which can justify rational expectations. Nor has the government any means of proving that it is correct: the provisional nature of knowledge is a much more defensible argument against authoritarianism than the most impassioned assertion of the principle of induction, and has been used in this way by Popper (1966). Second, it transforms one's conception of the progress of science. Instead of accumulating facts on the basis of which one tries to formulate a proposition which they will support (and a very large number of propositions can be contrived to fit previously accumulated facts) one starts with conjectures and then seeks evidence which might refute them. Thus, a good theory is not confirmed by supporting facts, but is corroborated by the failure of attempts to refute it.

Popper's position has been widely misunderstood. He has not argued that truth is an illusion; indeed, he has argued strongly in favour of the objectivity of knowledge. What he has done is to distinguish between truth and our knowledge of the truth. This misunderstanding is associated with a confusion perpetuated by the philosophers of the logical positivist school, who attempted to demonstrate that there were only two kinds of meaningful statement: tautologies and verifiable statements. They thought that Popper was merely substituting falsifiability for verifiability as the only test of non-tautological meaningful statements. But falsification was devised as a demarcation criterion for science, not as a criterion of meaning, or even of truth. Unfalsifiable statements, in Popper's view, may well be true, and very important (one of his own examples is 'God exists') and myths may be very important even if not true – they have even been very important in the development of science by suggesting hypotheses to be tested. Popper denies the logical positivist claim that metaphysics is nonsense: he simply asserts that it is not science.

Conjectures

Now, if the method of science is induction, then hypotheses may be expected to arise naturally out of the accumulation of evidence. But if hypotheses must precede the evidence by which they are tested, their origin is problematical. The two components of Popper's method are sharply contrasted: conjectures are the product of imagination; attempted refutations are guided by strict logical rigour and methodological rules. Most of his attention is concentrated on the latter, for this is amenable to analysis; but he does remind his readers quite frequently of the enormous importance of the former. There is no doubt that one of the most attractive features of Popper's view for working scientists is that it provides scope for both discipline and imagination (see Medawar, 1982, pp.73–114). A scientific hypothesis may be as great a creative achievement as a novel or a painting. Hence the great value which Popper places on 'metaphysical' statements as spurs to creativity.

How to test hypotheses is the problem of scientific logic. Before examining that question, however, it is important to consider what happens when a hypothesis is refuted. Two courses of action are possible. One is to attempt to rephrase it in a narrower way – for example, 'the sun rises every day except within the Arctic and Antarctic Circles'. The other is to seek for a more general underlying explanation – in this instance, of the relative movements of earth and sun. There is no doubt that Popper advocates the latter as the preferred way to the truth – indeed, as the only way to increase understanding, as distinct from recognizing the limitations of understanding. It is here that Popper would part company, decisively, with Friedman (1953). Theories of the firm were once thought, and intended, to be approximately descriptive of business behaviour; as such the formal models of perfect and imperfect competition have been refuted. Justification of such theories on the basis of predictive success, while conceding – indeed emphasizing – their descriptive falsity, represents precisely such a narrowing of the scope of theory as Popper condemns.

The reason for Popper's objection is clear: this procedure in effect rules out the behaviour of firms as a proper subject for economic enquiry, as Machlup (1974, p.273) has made plain. The argument that 'there is no need for these hypotheses to be true, or even to be at all like the truth; rather, one thing is sufficient for them – that they should yield calculations which agree with the observations' was made by Osiander in his preface to Copernicus's *De Revolutionibus* (Popper, 1969, p.98). That argument would have kept Galileo out of trouble; but for him, as for Popper, it set unacceptable limits to scientific inquiry. It is essential to Popper's view that existing theories should be regarded as inadequate in the sense that they are liable to be superseded; it is equally essential not to regard them, like Friedman (1953, p.14), as necessarily inadequate in the sense of descriptively false, and therefore in no need of improvement in this respect. The job of science is indeed to predict, but also to understand; it is to widen, not to contract, the scope of predictions, and to do this it is necessary to pay attention also to the structure of the theory.

Hypothesis testing

The testing of theories is not a simple matter. It is impossible to test one hypothesis without taking a very great deal for granted. As Coddington (1975a, p.543) has noted, acceptance of an apparently refuting observation requires a decision that

> . . . the blame will *not* be placed on the observer, the equipment, the data, the calculations, the theories on the basis of which the equipment is designed, the theories on the basis of which the data were interpreted, the unspecified background knowledge which has guided the investigation or the concepts in terms of which the theory is expressed.

In Popper's own words: 'observations, and even more so observation statements and statements of experimental results, are always *interpretations* of the facts observed; . . . they are *interpretations in the light of theories*' (1972, p. 107). Thus 'every corroboration is relative to other statements which, again, are tentative' (1972, p.280).

Now if, in order to test one hypothesis, we are compelled to assume the validity of many others, which themselves must remain for ever liable to falsification, then there can be no guaranteed test procedure. This Popper has himself emphasized: no test can be decisive – not even one which appears to refute the hypothesis under test – because it is always possible to argue that what has actually been refuted is one of the many other hypotheses which have had to be assumed in order to make the test possible. The assertion that 'other things were not, after all, equal' is perhaps not much less popular among natural scientists than social scientists; and it may indeed point the way to a major new discovery. Thus, the failure to isolate his apparatus against unexpected effects provided the opportunity for Roentgen to discover x-rays. As an example of a (fanciful) refutation which everyone would now reject, consider the use of the Michelson–Morley experiment to decide between Ptolemaic and Copernican astronomy (Polanyi, 1958, p.152).

Refutations and frameworks

If scientific method entails testing fallible hypotheses by a fallible procedure, how should we behave? Any hypothesis which apparently conflicts with evidence can be saved by *ad hoc* explanation – an explanation which excuses that particular result. Although *ad hoc* explanations are always possible, and may be correct, they are clearly hopeless as a general method, since we would be continually breaking up general laws into loosely related collections of facts. So Popper's recommendation is to be wary of *ad hoc* explanations.

However, this advice is not intended to apply to every apparent refutation of a hypothesis. Experimental failures need to be checked; and there are sufficient examples of refutations which have subsequently been overthrown by improvements in experimental techniques or redefinitions of the (inevitable, even if only implied) *ceteris paribus* clause. New theories, in particular, may justifiably survive the failure of some of their predictions. Thus, as counterpoint to his insistence on a critical approach, Popper (1970, p.55) has repeatedly 'stressed the need for some dogmatism: the dogmatic scientist has an important role to play. If we give in to criticism too easily, we shall never find out where the real power of our theories lies.' Unfortunately, Popper thereby leaves open the question: at what point should a theory be abandoned in the face of contrary evidence?

However, before considering that question, we must turn to a second problem. If we accept that experimental failure requires an amendment to be made somewhere in the body of scientific knowledge, then the injunction to construct a new general hypothesis leaves us with a very wide choice of possibilities. Moreover, if we accept Popper's characterization of human knowledge, we shall not expect our amendment to bring us to the truth (although we would hope that it would bring us slightly nearer to it); and greater truth may be sought – and may be found – in very many different directions. And yet, for the most part, science appears to have the characteristics of a systematic, rather than a random process.

Another way of posing this problem is suggested by Kelly (1963), who, from the basic assumption that the universe is an interdependent system, the interconnections of which are far beyond human comprehension, concludes that to act in a scientific manner entails the imposition on the phenomena to be studied of man-made patterns which are necessarily incomplete, and therefore in some measure false. Science, like any other thoughtful human activity, is characterized by what Simon has called bounded rationality. Since any pattern is incomplete, it is subject to replacement by other patterns, which will be incomplete in different ways. Thus, in principle, it might be possible to respond to any refutation of any hypothesis by choosing a different scientific framework. But such behaviour would hardly be called scientific.

Popper himself has emphasized that a scientist working in a particular field has the inestimable benefit of an established framework. 'A structure of scientific doctrines is already in existence; and with it, a generally-accepted problem-situation' (1972, p.13). He has also argued (1970, p.56) that 'if we try, we can break out of our framework at any time. Admittedly, we shall find ourselves again in a framework, but it will be a better and roomier one; and we can at any moment break out of it again.' But such break-outs are much more difficult, and happen less frequently, than Popper seems to imply; and that is not entirely a matter for regret. For, although Kelly asserts (1963, p.15) that 'there are always some alternative constructions available to choose among in dealing with the world', nevertheless for a scientist as for a human being simply engaged in the process of living (and like Popper, Kelly sees scientific activity as a special case of human problem-solving behaviour), the effective interpretation of experience, including experimental evidence, requires some consistency in the use of these constructions. Frameworks may either be revised or replaced; but effective learning depends on the predominance of revision. The obvious corollary is that the accepted framework should be of a kind that lends itself to correction. In Kelly's terms (1963, p.79), it should be permeable to new elements.

But there is a further corollary. Science is necessarily a social activity. Popper's notion of objective knowledge depends on a process of inter-subjective criticism within a scientific community, and the history of science shows clearly enough the importance of both collaboration and competition. Now, for this process to take place it is not enough for each scientist to accept a framework; these frameworks must be sufficiently similar to allow constructive communication. Thus, there should be general agreement that, when faced with a convincing refutation of a particular hypothesis, only a small subset of the possible alternative hypotheses will be considered – that is, that the next hypothesis will belong to the same family as the one rejected. Within economics, the most striking current example of such agreement is to be found within the school of general equilibrium theorists; and it is no accident that general equilibrium theory is almost solely responsible for whatever theoretical prestige is currently possessed by economics.

However, our argument seems to have gone too far. Science now appears to proceed by rather timid conjectures and attempted refutations within an agreed framework, which is necessarily inadequate (as is any single framework) for investigating all the phenomena of interest to science. From time to time it is necessary to change frameworks to enable other sets of problems to be effectively tackled. Science, it appears, requires two kinds of activity: work within an agreed set of rules, and work to change the rules.

Paradigms and research programmes

It is the demarcation of two kinds of scientific activity, designated as 'normal science' and 'revolutionary science', which marks the contribution of T.S. Kuhn (1962; 1970a) to this problem. Kuhn dramatized his case (and thus attracted much attention, both eulogistic and condemnatory) by claiming that it was precisely the dominance – at least the quantitative dominance – of work within an unchallenged framework which accounted for scientific progress. Kuhn called this framework a 'paradigm'; the alternative of 'disciplinary matrix', proposed in his second edition, conveys a much better sense of his argument, but (partly for that reason) lacks the provocative power of the former label.

In its first presentation, Kuhn's thesis seemed a direct (though not intentional) attack on Popper's position. The basic conjectures of science, it appears, are never tested, but are accepted without question by all scientists in an area of study as guides to work on those anomalies which the conjectures, in their original form, leave unexplained. Scientists then proceed to force scientific phenomena into the conceptual boxes provided by the paradigm, and any failure to solve such 'puzzles', as Kuhn calls them, is attributed to the scientist's lack of skill, not to any defect in the paradigm. But Kuhn is neither seeking to revive inductivism nor any notion of verifiability; for him, quite as much as for Popper, the basic conjectures on which all this activity is based cannot be verified. Indeed, in due course, they are likely to be abandoned. For, although individual failures are still attributed to the individual scientist (or scientific team), a rising proportion of failures eventually precipitates a crisis, resulting in the acceptance of a new set of basic conjectures as a guide to future work. The former conjectures are not refuted; they are simply rejected as no longer capable of supporting a successful programme of 'normal science'. Hence the insistence that it is 'puzzle-solving' which is 'normal' in science.

Since paradigms are accepted because they offer an attractive series of puzzles to be resolved, the persistence of unsolved, but apparently soluble, problems is, on Kuhn's argument, a necessary condition for the persistence of a paradigm. Furthermore, the more perplexing the puzzle, the greater the personal satisfaction – and the scientific credit – derived from its solution. Thus there is never a clear sign that it is time for a paradigm to be abandoned; and it does one's professional reputation no good to give up a puzzle-solving tradition which one's more assiduous colleagues later demonstrate to be still fruitful in their hands. Moreover, argues Kuhn, any new paradigm necessarily begins in a poorly articulated form, and, although offering new ways of attacking some recalcitrant problems, it also suggests that others should simply be given up; worse, some solutions which give much credit to the old paradigm may have to be abandoned (as, for example, must the Paretian welfare criteria in satisficing theories of the firm). There is therefore no generally acceptable algorithm for choosing between paradigms. Logic may rule within a paradigm but it cannot determine within which paradigm it shall rule. For these reasons, periods of paradigm change are considered by Kuhn to be quite different in character from periods of 'normal science'.

In Kuhn's analysis, the practice of normal science is not sufficient to ensure continued scientific progress: a sequence of revolutions is indispensable to provide the appropriate frameworks within which progress can be achieved. Now, Kuhn's revolutions, as he has made clear, are Popperian. Moreover, as he has emphasized (1970a; 1970b), his concept of revolution is not confined to such upheavals as are associated with Newton and Einstein. More local and limited changes occur fairly frequently. There are sub-paradigms in his scheme, just as there are subordinate constructs in Kelly's. We shall return to this very significant point later.

First, however, it is important to consider, if only briefly, the contribution by Lakatos (1970), who is held by some (notably Blaug, 1976) to have taken what is of value in Kuhn's analysis and developed it in a more fruitful way. Lakatos is much exercised by the problems of falsifiability, concluding, like Popper, that falsification must depend on a methodological decision to exclude certain kinds of excuses (contamination of the sample, measurement error, a wrongly specified functional form, and so on) for disregarding apparently refuting instances. But such excuses are often justified. So, if we wish to retain the criterion of falsifiability (as Lakatos certainly does), it must be applied not to a single experiment, or indeed to a single hypothesis, but to a family of hypotheses. Refutation of a single variant is not adequate; refutation of all the variants that one can think of is conclusive.

By this route Lakatos arrives at the concept of a 'scientific research programme', in which the notion of refutation is still further modified. Such a research programme consists of a 'hard core' of basic assumptions which, by implicit methodological decree are, for the present, not to be tested. Popper's recognition (1972, p.104) that 'every test of a theory . . . must stop at some basic statement or other which we *decide to accept*', and his advice that these should be 'statements about whose acceptance or rejection the various investigators are likely to reach agreement' foreshadow Lakatos's scheme. What is to be tested is each member of a series of hypotheses in a 'protective belt', which is formed by applying the basic assumptions according to the research programme's 'positive heuristic' – a 'partially articulated set of suggestions or hints on how to change, develop the "refutable variants" of the research-programme, how to modify, sophisticate, the "refutable" protective belt' (1970, p.135). If these successive variants lead to the prediction of new facts, which appear to be corroborated, then the programme exhibits 'progressive problem-shifts'; if they require more and more saving qualifications, the programme is degenerating. Thus, one may aim to apply critical standards to what Kuhn (1970b, p.256) has himself recognized as an analytical apparatus very similar to his own.

Kuhn is, however, far from convinced that judgement of a research programme can be based entirely on agreed critical standards. As Lakatos himself points out, the verdict that a research programme is degenerating is always subject to appeal on the production of new evidence. Moreover, Lakatos does not deny Kuhn's assertion that the scope of a new candidate research programme will not, in general, simply include all that was once 'progressive' in the old; any choice between them must therefore include some assessment of what are the more important phenomena to explain – within microeconomics, for example, the behaviour of firms and single industries, or the coherence of an economic system.

Kuhn's critics have claimed that his analysis leaves theory-choice irrational; his own version is that, although good logical arguments can be employed, the evidence is not beyond dispute and no single preference system is likely to suit all choosers (Kuhn, 1970b, p.262). Some of Kuhn's critics seem to be looking for proof of the validity of theories; it would surely be very curious, and quite at variance with a Popperian rejection of determinism, for the choice of theory to be fully programmable. That, at best, our research programmes relate to subsystems artificially isolated from the rest of the universe should warn us against being too optimistic about their range of convenience. Economists, above all, should appreciate the dangers of making inferences from subsystems to systems – even when the subsystems are models of the economy.

An economist's view

It is not surprising that paradigms and research programmes have been welcomed by some economists as convenient concepts for organizing histories of economic thought. The analytical structure, too, should have its own appeal, since it corresponds to a familiar economic distinction between the categories of short and long run (the former recently revived in the guise of temporary equilibrium). From experience in the methods of his own subject, an economist might make a suggestion to the philosophers of science. Just as the short-run/long-run distinction is a very crude representation of a series of possible 'runs', distinguished by the particular set of forces to be regarded as variable for a specific piece of analysis, so one might suggest that the distinction between 'hard core' and 'protective belt' is not independent of time, nor of analytical viewpoint. Thus 'profit maximization' might be regarded as the hard core of a market theory which itself serves as part of the protective belt of equilibrium theory. In Remenyi's (1979) terms, imperfect competition forms a demi-core. Yet, as this example shows, the relationship between core and demi-core is often ambiguous: what to some is a progressive problem-shift is to others a mortal threat. Managerial optimizing theories likewise serve to protect the concept of equilibrium by extending the range of phenomena to which it can apparently be applied, but they create a new anomaly because of the difficulties in specifying any general equilibrium of the system in terms of managerial objectives. Thus it is far from clear whether the introduction of such theories constitutes a progressive or a degenerative problem-shift.

Part of the difficulty here is that frameworks cannot, in general, be uniquely ordered. Such an ordering would be possible if both the universe and our understanding of it formed a single completely decomposable system in which the elements of any subsystem interacted only with each other. If the universe, and our knowledge of it, were indeed so ordered, then any hypotheses about interactions within one system, at any level, could never be invalidated by observations at either a higher or a lower system level. On the other hand, if knowledge were not ordered at all, then it would be very difficult to produce any hypotheses at one particular level which could survive exposure to any other level.

It is the ordering of knowledge which makes science possible, for otherwise no framework could be expected to apply to more than a handful of cases. Indeed, without such an ordering, rational behaviour could scarcely exist. But because the ordering is incomplete, no single framework will do for all problems, or for all time. A working assumption of decomposability licenses both normal science and work in the protective belt of a research programme; the inevitable eventual breakdown of that assumption is the factor that precipitates paradigm crisis or the degeneration of a research programme. That the universe is nearly decomposable, but that this decomposability depends upon a limited range of environments and is likely to fail in critical instances, has been argued by Simon (1969) in the context of artificial systems; I have elsewhere applied this argument to human decision making (Loasby, 1976).

But just because these frameworks are not uniquely ordered, it may not be at all clear at what level any necessary revision should take place. Since they formally treat all paradigms or research programmes on a single level, neither Kuhn nor Lakatos discusses this question. One paradigm, or one research programme, simply replaces another. The relationship betwen successive paradigms is obscured by Kuhn's original overemphasis on the difficulties of comparing them, but some of his discussion – and that of Lakatos too – could be more sharply pointed by analysis in terms of an incompletely specified hierarchy of paradigms, which in time of crisis leads to disputes both about the proper ordering and the level at which to propose changes. Certainly, such an amplified structure of analysis promises to make more sense of theoretical developments in economics. For example, does the attempt to produce a model of unemployment by removing market clearing from general equilibrium represent a relatively minor modification, or does the imposition of such a constraint, which is not derivable from any of the basic parameters of the model, represent a challenge to the axiomatic procedure which to some people constitutes the hard core of microeconomic theory? This question is considered further in Chapter 11.

One further important modification to the Kuhn and Lakatos schemes may be proposed. Both authors are concerned with the temporal succession of frameworks, and Kuhn, at least, seems to believe that, between crises, scientists in one field must accept a single paradigm. But it is neither obvious in principle nor observable in practice that they should be so restricted. The argument that a group of scientists – or managers, or any group of people – will find progress difficult if each member uses a different framework does not necessarily imply that they must confine themselves to one; still less does it exclude the possibility of other groups employing different schemes. Alternative frameworks may be contemporaneous, and not simply overlapping at periods of crisis, as Kuhn argues. Kuhn lays great emphasis on the importance, in crises, of a diversity of judgement within the relevant scientific community in allowing that community to hedge its bets; but may not a little hedging be appropriate at other times too – if only (within Kuhn's scheme) to facilitate the production of a better thought-out new paradigm when the old enters its crisis? Some diversity of frameworks is an asset. Here too, it appears that Kuhn's own attempt to force the whole of scientific activity into only two boxes, labelled 'normal science' and 'revolutions', has led him astray.

An economist might regard the group of scientists working on a particular kind of problem as members of an invisible college bound voluntarily by the terms of an imperfectly specified contract. The fundamental reason why the contract should be imperfectly specified is identical to that leading to the unspecified contracts which characterize the firm: ignorance of future circumstances, and of the precise ways in which it might be best to cope with them, make the formation of a whole series of contingent contracts at best wasteful, at worst quite inadequate. Since the terms of the contract are not defined, they are open to conflicting interpretation and to amendment (often claiming to be interpretation) at any time; and it cannot necessarily be foreseen which attempts at interpretation or amendment will lead to a breakdown of the contract. Unintended disintegration was Shackle's (1967) theme.

Although Popper has not so argued (and indeed, to judge from his attitude to Kuhn, he might not find the argument congenial), the idea that scientists necessarily work within a framework, but one which is imperfectly specified, seems to follow from the Popperian conception of science. The expectation that existing hypotheses will need to be discarded and replaced by new conjectures hitherto unthought of, makes it essential for scientists to have some rough measure of agreement about how to proceed, but makes it absurd to specify that agreement in any detail. Even a Bayesian approach will not do; since an essential feature of science is the creation of novelty, it is impossible in principle to specify all the relevant possibilities in advance.

It should be clear that Popper, Kuhn and Lakatos are not 'modernists', in the sense used by McCloskey (1983). As Popper is the most likely to be misinterpreted by those not well acquainted with his work, four of its principles may deserve summary emphasis. First, falsification is simple only in its deductive logic, which is an insufficient guide to practice. Second, in addition to its predictive success, a scientific theory may also be judged by its internal consistency, its logical form, and its potential in comparison with available alternatives (Popper, 1972, pp.32–3); indeed, such appraisals constitute a major part of Popper's own writing. Third, progress requires the replacement of refuted hypotheses by novel conjectures, which cannot be produced to order. Finally, scientific knowledge is not the only kind of knowledge, although it is the kind which offers the best opportunities for an analysis of its growth.

Knowledge and equilibrium
None of these authors, therefore, would claim any exclusive rights either over the methods by which economic knowledge may be

improved or over the treatment of knowledge within economic theory. Even timeless equilibrium models may furnish a kind of knowledge. But they do provide a fundamental objection to a general reliance on models which require perfect – even probabilistically perfect – knowledge. 'There is no criterion of truth at our disposal' (Popper, 1969, p.28). Any economic model which assumes that agents have a correct model of the economy cannot itself be a correct model. It may nevertheless have its uses, but should be treated warily. The growth of knowledge is a continuing process, with no recognizable end; it therefore requires a process analysis. The state of knowledge at any particular time is to be explained by its history up to that time, and Popper, Kuhn and Lakatos all draw freely on history for evidence. (Indeed, Lakatos draws too freely, in Kuhn's (1970b, p.256) view.) But history cannot be written in advance: knowledge changes, and its changes are not predictable, since it is logically impossible to foresee when a presently accepted hypothesis will be refuted, still less when a still unimagined conjecture might replace it.

Hahn (1973; 1984, p.59) has proposed a general equilibrium of knowledge, in which the economy 'generates messages which do not cause agents to change the theories which they hold or the policies which they pursue'. Such a definition is compatible with a great deal of error, both in agents' theories and in the messages which they receive. Indeed, the preservation of equilibrium may depend on the absence of accurate signals: organizational coalitions, for example, can often stand only a limited amount of truth. But accurate signals, even about the past, are hardly consistent with the theories of knowledge discussed in this chapter. 'Observations . . . are always interpretations . . . in the light of theories' (Popper, 1972, p.107), and even present unanimity of interpretations may not be 'correct', as judged by later theories at a later date. Moreover, the record of the past may be irretrievably entwined in expectations about the future: it is impossible to calculate profit for any period without valuing the assets carried over to the next period; and that value depends on anticipations of future events.

However, Hahn's definition is perhaps more useful in characterizing disequilibrium, which is not only more interesting but a precondition of improvement. In disequilibrium there are unreconciled and incompatible conjectures, and therefore unreconciled and incompatible decisions. Like the testing of scientific hypotheses, the 'testing of plans in the market' (Kirzner, 1973, p.10), and in other places, leads to a mixture of corroboration and refutation, to the resolution of old anomalies and the creation of new – and thus to some degree of (provisional) equilibration and also to new perceptions of disequilibrium which provide scope for fresh conjectures and revised plans. It is because this process is, for the most part, carried on within a shared framework that it usually produces a tolerable degree of coordination.

Shared paradigms or research programmes facilitate compatible trades, in goods or ideas, and probably contribute far more to the working of an economy, or a scientific community, than theorists who rely on individual preferences imagine. The Chicago prescription 'de gustibus non est disputandum' (Stigler and Becker, 1977) is an effective analytical device just because it imposes a single paradigm on the agents to be studied. Marshall's incrementally progressive firm practises the equivalent of Kuhn's normal science; indeed (as we shall see in Chapter 4) Marshall's theory of the firm is a theory of the growth of particular kinds of knowledge, and therefore gives reasons for the predictive value of some equilibrium models. Established practices, by setting bounds to conjecture, may encourage convergence.

But research programmes can degenerate, and paradigms face increasing anomalies; then scientific communities fall into growing disarray, and economic decision making becomes increasingly incoherent – as can also be seen in organizations and industries where a well-tried formula for success has broken down. Another possible cause of breakdown is the juxtaposition of incompatible research programmes or paradigms which have hitherto been confined to separate subsystems (for example, through the merger of previously independent organizations): if each has hitherto been successful in its own sphere, the reconciliation or supersession of these programmes may be particularly difficult. So although short-term predictions may be safer than long-term, any prediction may prove a spectacular failure; the potential for surprise cannot be excluded.

Discontinuous change may also arise from major (Schumpeterian) innovation. Imagination may outsoar reason to create a new conjecture. If corroborated, this conjecture will inevitably entail the refutation of some other hypotheses and the failure of many production and trading plans, and there may be severe coordination failures in parts of the economy. But successful innovation, in theory or the economy, redefines the scope of normal science or incremental change, and offers fresh prospects for the growth of knowledge and economic welfare.

3 Public science and public knowledge*

We have come to rely on the modern sciences as the major sources of our knowledge; yet there is a growing realization that the epistemological basis of scientific inquiry is problematic. It is not surprising then to find increasing interest in the study of science, both as an intellectual enterprise and as a social form. The significance of the social organization of the sciences was emphasized by Kuhn's (1962, 1970a) highly influential work, which appeared to show that any adequate explanation of the growth of scientific knowledge depended perhaps as much on sociology as on epistemology.

Kuhn's unitary treatment of the sciences also reinforced the general tendency to assume a single ideal pattern (which, by no accident, resembles an idealized version of physics) and to treat departures from this as signs of immaturity – inevitable or regrettable according to taste. This assumption makes both epistemological and sociological analysis much simpler, but it does not necessarily make it more helpful. Indeed, the proposition that attempts to assimilate the social to the natural sciences are misguided has a fairly long history, although it has never been generally accepted. That proposition Richard Whitley (1984) does not mention; his purpose is much more ambitious in that he seeks to expound and illustrate a comprehensive scheme for differentiating scientific fields, and the kinds of knowledge which they produce, on the basis of an extensive development and application of the contingency approach to work organization.

Attempts to replace universal principles of effective organization with contingency theories of various kinds have become so common that the application of this idea to scientific fields may seem rather obvious – once it has been done; but it is Whitley who deserves full credit not only for seeing the obvious (which is so often remarkably obscure) but for working out his analytical scheme with such care. (It is to be regretted that similar care was not given to the proofreading; the inci-

*This chapter is a revised version of 'Public science and public knowledge: a review of Richard Whitley, *The Intellectual and Social Organization of the Sciences* (Clarendon Press, Oxford University Press, New York, 1984) in W.S. Samuels (ed.), *Research in the History of Economic Thought and Methodology*, **4**, pp.211–28, and is reproduced by permission of JAI Press Inc. I have received helpful comments on an earlier draft from A.W. Coats.

dence of misprints in this book is beyond reasonable bounds.) Since this chapter contains much which may be judged critical, it is important to emphasize at once that Whitley has not only given us much to think about, but also very substantial help in organizing our thoughts.

Public science

Whitley's analysis is focused on the 'public science' of universities and research institutes. The reason he gives (1984, p.8) for thus dismissing industrial and state science is that public science is what people have in mind when they associate science with truth and knowledge. That reason is valid enough, but the primary justification must surely be that public science offers a sufficient but manageable challenge to the analyst. This restriction allows Whitley to associate the production of knowledge with reputational systems of production and control, which are treated as the defining characteristics of scientific work organizations. State science intrudes increasingly as the book progresses – and indeed appears to be primarily responsible for the loss of autonomy by some reputational organizations which Whitley notes – but it is primarily treated as part of the environment which conditions the organization of scientific fields. It seems very likely that an analysis of state science (and perhaps of industrial science too) will need to be accorded a high priority in the research programme that Whitley is developing, since it may prove impossible to deal adequately with some features of contemporary public science without investigating the impact of these other forms; but we can agree that the analysis of public science provides quite enough to be going on with.

What every field of public science has in common, Whitley asserts, is the production of knowledge through collectively organized work. Since the production of knowledge requires individual contributions of novel facts and ideas, which can then be appropriated and used by others, there is a necessary tension between innovation and conformity to established patterns; and, since each scientist's reputation depends on individual efforts which others subsequently put to effective use, there is a similar necessary tension between competition and collaboration. The uncertainty which is inseparable from innovation entails substantial discretion for the individual scientist or working group, and control depends less on formal employment relationships than on the approval and recognition of colleagues who may be working in different organizations, and indeed in different countries. This control is made possible by an elaborate communication system, notably by publication and citation in specialist journals. Within each scientific field, this reputational control system is strengthened by the standardization of research techniques and of communications. Control is also easier if both techniques and communications are differentiated from those employed in other scientific fields, since it is then more difficult for a scientist to appeal to another jurisdiction.

Influences on forms of work organization

From this basis, Whitley proceeds to analyse the factors which influence the structure of each field. These factors he categorizes into two groups, which, though interrelated, he believes deserve separate treatment. The first, considered in his Chapter 3, is the degree of mutual dependence between scientists within a field. This dependence is of two kinds: *functional dependence* denotes the extent to which each is constrained to use the ideas, results, and procedures of others; *strategic dependence* denotes the extent to which the problems on which each works must be demonstrably integrated into a unified research strategy. Physics and chemistry are alike in possessing a highly standardized set of methods and concepts, but, whereas physics has a clear hierarchy of problem significance, in chemistry major areas develop more or less on their own terms, with little concern over their relative priority within the field. (Within each area of chemistry, strategic dependence is presumably high; but Whitley pays little attention to the organization of subfields, which he leaves to subject specialists.) German psychology before 1933 is offered as an example of a field in which high strategic dependence (general agreement on what were the most important issues) was combined with low functional dependence (a diversity of views on the appropriate concepts and techniques with which to tackle them), and management studies exemplifies low dependence in both dimensions, with no more than local agreement either on the significant problems or on methods.

Whitley indicates some of the consequences of increasing dependence (1984, pp.95–104), and three sets of contextual factors which, he claims, primarily influence this dependence (1984, pp.104–12, 220–38): the ability of members of a scientific field to specify and judge skills, determine what is important, and define the field; the degree of concentration of control both within the field and each employment unit; and the diversity of audiences and their relative importance – factors which economists might recognize as barriers to entry, industrial concentration, and market differentiation. But just as industrial economists have begun to consider whether causation might run in the opposite direction from that traditionally assumed, one may ask whether these contextual factors might sometimes be influenced by the scientific structure, and whether some of the supposed consequences of dependence might sometimes contribute to its development or decay.

For the present, however, let us continue with the exposition. In his Chapter 4, Whitley turns to the second group of factors which influence the structure of scientific fields: the degree of uncertainty. Since the purpose of public science is the production of new knowledge, it is clearly impossible to know in advance what will be the outcome of any scientific activity; but if a scientific field is to be highly organized, then uncertainty must be constrained. Two dimensions of uncertainty, which parallel the two dimensions of dependence, are considered. *Task uncertainty* is a measure of the reliability of the procedures and results (and presumably, although this is not discussed, the precision of the concepts) which are employed; *strategic uncertainty* reflects a lack of agreement or of continuity in the formulation of problems and in the assessment of their relative importance.

Physics, it is asserted, shows little uncertainty in either dimension; and chemistry is here classed with physics since, although (as has been noted) strategic dependence is low, the relevant problems in each sub-field are well agreed and the relationship between fields is not on the agenda. Biology exemplifies the combination of low technical task uncertainty (methods are agreed and reliable) with high strategic uncertainty (there are various and changing opinions about the issues to which these methods should be directed), while ecology displays high uncertainty in both dimensions. Economics is singled out as an – apparently unique – example of the potentially unstable combination of low strategic but high technical uncertainty: wide agreement on the definition of important issues is somehow maintained despite the recognized inadequacy of the technical means for dealing with them. How it is maintained we will consider later. Some of the organizational implications of these various combinations are next discussed (pp.130–9), and then the contextual factors, which, not surprisingly, turn out to be those which were invoked to explain the degrees of mutual dependence (pp.139–47).

The organizational structure of scientific fields
In his Chapter 5, Whitley uses the degrees of functional and strategic dependence, and of technical and strategic uncertainty, to define the range of organizational forms. If each of these four factors is allotted the simplest binary scale, sixteen combinations are possible. However, because nine of these are inherently implausible (for example, high functional dependence on methods which are acknowledged to be unreliable), we are left with seven possible types of scientific field. High

technical and strategic task uncertainty, together with low functional and strategic dependence produces a *fragmented adhocracy*, such as management studies or British sociology, in which individuals are relatively free to choose both problems and techniques but have difficulty in producing results which carry more than sectional assent. If strategic dependence is imposed on such a system (which can only be through the centralization of employment in a few units), we have a *polycentric oligarchy*, in which each unit has its own research programme, as in British social anthropology.

Where functional dependence is high and task uncertainty low there are four possibilities. Low strategic dependence and high strategic uncertainty give rise to a *professional adhocracy*, such as biomedical science, in which reputational groups cluster around different and changing problem formulations, although the basic skills and methods are developed and certified within well defined disciplines. Where the range of alternative problem formulations is externally restricted, through the designation of centres and control of funds, we have a *polycentric profession*, such as experimental physiology: this tighter and more stable structure (by comparison with a professional adhocracy) permits much easier transfer of specific results between research programmes and some measure of agreement about the value of the programmes themselves. If strategic task uncertainty diminishes to the point where the range of research programmes is much more complementary than competitive, and they are linked by highly standardized concepts and skills, we move to a *technologically integrated bureaucracy*, as exemplified by chemistry. If a unified theoretical structure is added, we reach the extreme case of maximum dependence and minimum uncertainty, labelled a *conceptually integrated bureaucracy*, and there we shall not be surprised to find physics.

One anomalous category remains. It might be expected that a combination of high strategic dependence and low strategic uncertainty would be unable to coexist long with low functional dependence and high technical uncertainty, since the agreed problems could not be effectively handled by the means available and there would be no way of preventing the introduction of other concepts and techniques, which would undermine the strategic agreement and open up routes to other reputational systems (as the textile industry was invaded by chemical firms, and ocean liners eclipsed by long-distance aircraft). Yet it is this combination that Whitley attributes to economics, which is stabilized by its unique structure as a *partitioned bureaucracy*: control is maintained by segregating the less controllable empirical studies from the theoretical core, which, being thus insulated, maintains both its coherence and its superior status.

After considering the organizational features of these seven kinds of reputational system (1984, pp.164–205), Whitley returns, in Chapter 6, to an examination of the changing contexts of these fields, and the links which he sees between these contexts and their internal structures. Then, in the final chapter, he invokes the general category of science as another level of organization, and seeks to analyse the relationships between scientific fields as subsystems of science, preserving the unity of his analytical scheme by focusing on the relationships of functional and strategic dependence between fields. Thus, Whitley applies a range of contingencies to public sciences which share common features.

It is an interesting question to what extent these supposedly common features appear to be derived from some particular science: is physics commonly taken as an ideal science, or is it perhaps that science is commonly construed as an ideal physics? If the latter, then other sciences must exhibit some dependence on physics, while physics may be strategically dependent on no other field. It remains, of course, functionally dependent on mathematics. Aided, Whitley (1984, pp.285–7, 295–7) argues, not only by its own successes in public science but by the practical evidence of its fruitfulness in peace and war, physicists have not only maintained a tight control of their own field, but have invaded other fields, and stepped forward as organizers of science. In contrast, the increasing dependence of scientists on extra-university sources of funds, and in particular the development of state science, which is oriented towards problems rather than knowledge, has reduced the power of reputational organizations in some other fields – most notably in biology.

As physicists move into areas in which their ability to deliver is more doubtful, the status of physics is becoming less secure than Whitley seems to believe. It has been alleged, for example, that the physicists' monopoly of the design of the British Advanced Gas-cooled Nuclear Reactor led to unnecessarily complex engineering problems, and was partly responsible for the lengthy construction delays; and the attempt to determine the expected cost of nuclear accidents by multiplying economists' dubious estimates of the value of human life by physicists' probability estimates (which are no better-founded) is unlikely to yield convincing results.

Whitley's double argument that there are important differences in intellectual and social organization between scientific fields, and that the organization of any field is subject to change in response to changing circumstances, is both persuasive and significant. His propositions are clearly amenable to empirical inquiry, which would need to be under-taken by those familiar with particular fields. (The choice of appropriate scalars is, however, likely to produce some task uncertainty.) Whether he has accurately characterized the different patterns of organization, and whether he has appropriately allocated scientific fields to them, I do not have the expertise to judge.

He does appear to be largely, though not entirely, correct in his description of economics as a partitioned bureaucracy, and partly correct in the reasons which he gives for the existence of this structure. Those working within the theoretical core are neither so united nor so powerful as Whitley seems to think; quite apart from the presence of dissidents, traditional general equilibrium theorists are not notably enthusiastic supporters of the new classical macroeconomics. A more detailed consideration of the structure of economics, which entails some modification of Whitley's analysis, will be made later. Before that, however, I would like to consider an approach to these issues which Whitley dismisses at the outset.

Scientific organization and scientific knowledge
A major reason why we might be interested in differences between the patterns of work organization in different sciences is the claim that, contrary to the assumption of a single epistemic rationality for all scientific knowledge, 'different patterns of work organization and control lead to different types of knowledge' (Whitley, 1984, p.10). What these different types of knowledge are (and whether any or all of them are 'true') is never discussed – except for the partitioning of economics into assured theory and insecure applications.

Whitley's lack of focus on the outputs of these organizations may be justified by his desire to concentrate on the determinants of their struc-ture, but it is matched by a deliberate refusal to consider differences of subject matter as a cause of organizational differences (1984, p.6). To support this refusal we are offered no more than the assertion that 'historically contingent variations which alter with changing circum-stances and contexts' provide a better, and implicitly sufficient, para-digm. Historically contingent variations are important, and the signifi-cance of the development of the German university system in the nineteenth century is well displayed. But, as a consequence of this exclusion, we are left to contemplate, for example, varying degrees of task dependency and task uncertainty without any adequate explanation of the origins of such variations. An agreed set of methods facilitates training and certification by a reputational organization; but might not a reputational organization create and impose an agreed set of methods? Indeed, it is suggested that this has happened in economics.

To what extent the characteristics of scientific fields at any one time reflect the characteristics of their subject matter, and to what extent they are determined by other influences, is a question which could stand much detailed investigation; to rule it out of order perhaps reflects a tendency among sociologists (and shared by economists) to give inadequate attention to the content of the activities to which they seek to apply their constructs. To exclude from a study of the intellectual and social organization of knowledge any explicit consideration of the fundamental problems of knowledge does seem a little odd – yet no doubt susceptible to a sociological explanation. I propose to offer a brief discussion of these problems.

Public knowledge through public science

If 'true knowledge' (a question-begging phrase from the second sentence of Whitley's book) were obtainable by following appropriate rules of induction, then individual inquiry would be sufficient to attain it. Collaboration might well be more effective, by permitting the faster accumulation of data from which valid inferences could be drawn, but there would be no general argument for excluding any competent amateur from any scientific field. But there is no such route to valid knowledge; there is no logical basis for induction. Any personally constructed knowledge may be an illusion.

It was to escape from this impasse that Popper proposed 'to replace the question of the sources of our knowledge by the entirely different question: "How can we hope to detect and eliminate error?"' (1969, p.25). Theories must be exposed to severe, but fair, criticism: they must be confronted with argument and with evidence. But these theories cannot be derived from data; they must be invented. Now, an individual is not likely to be the most effective critic of his own conjectures and, even if he were, it is most unlikely that he could think of all the relevant criticisms or of all the relevant tests. The elimination of error must therefore be a collaborative process.

However, as we have seen in Chapter 2, there is a deeper problem with the critical approach. If there is no way by which the truth of any synthetic statement about the world can be established beyond question, so that any piece of presumed knowledge must remain forever subject to refutation, then even an apparent refutation may be false. No conclusion whatever can be drawn from any confrontation between theory and evidence unless we are prepared to accept, for this purpose, the truth of a great many propositions, all of which nevertheless remain forever subject to falsification. This difficulty, usually referred to as the Duhem–Quine problem, is well known to Popper, who has always emphasized the need for a set of conventions if any coherent falsificationist programme is to be followed. In general, the search for knowledge must always proceed within a framework; and if the process of conjecture and criticism is to be efficient, then this framework must be generally accepted – although not more than provisionally, and not in every detail – by those who wish to participate in the search. Moreover, as knowledge increases, frameworks are likely to become more elaborate, and the requirements for collaboration more restrictive.

Any knowledge which might be a public good according to the usual economists' definition must also be public in another sense: it is produced by an orderly social process of conjecture and criticism. It is in the latter sense that Ziman (1968, p.8), to whose writings Whitley makes no reference, defines science as public knowledge. It is not surprising, then, to find that this public knowledge is predominantly the production of a system which Whitley terms public science – a feature which he does not attempt directly to explain. The best way we have yet found to establish knowledge which may be treated as reliable – although its truth cannot be proved – is through the search for open agreements, openly arrived at, and sought within an agreed, but permeable, framework, using concepts, methods and language which are, as far as possible, accepted by all participants. Not all frameworks are equally useful, and Whitley's analytical scheme (which is itself, of course, such a framework) can help in explaining how and why they differ between fields.

As Ziman argues, before a consensus can be reached, the subject of the desired consensus must become consensible; and the attempt to achieve, and to preserve, consensibility is a social process which is carried on within, and helps to shape, the structures which Whitley desires to analyse. The social institutions of science reflect not only characteristics such as dependence and uncertainty, which may be shared in various degrees with other forms of work organization, they also reflect the necessary characteristics (as far as we can tell) of the search for knowledge. The search for 'a *consensus* of rational opinion over the widest possible field . . . *is* the scientific method itself' (Ziman, 1968, p.9); the scientific method is a social institution.

Competition and control

Many economists have professed to analyse information; relatively few have considered carefully the problems of knowledge. Among those who have, Hayek is pre-eminent, and he has emphasized the value of a market system in providing encouragement to individuals to find and make use of knowledge, while simultaneously affording checks on its misuse. Competition, he has argued (Hayek, 1978, pp.179–90), should be regarded as a discovery and control procedure – a proposition obviously related to Popper's advocacy of an open society. A scientific field in which most people share the objective of gaining new knowledge embodies this kind of competition. Just as the market rewards knowledge which enables someone to offer goods or services which customers wish to acquire, so the reputational system rewards those who produce new ideas which others can put to use: and if the goods or ideas are unwanted or defective, they will be ignored or criticized. In both contexts, value is determined by the recipient.

The knowledge thus produced, Ziman (1978) argues, is better regarded as intersubjective than objective (which is Popper's preferred adjective) since it rests on such subjective elements as the acceptance of the relevance of a particular logical argument to a set of phenomena, the recognition of patterns in the phenomena or in the data which purport to represent them, and the assumption that others who are accepted as colleagues can be regarded as equivalent observers. The control system is not impersonal, but interpersonal.

Whitley's treatment of this issue is not always clear. 'Organization' and 'control' are terms of ambiguous, almost contrary meaning, sometimes referring to interacting systems, sometimes to hierarchical structures, and sometimes to a combination of the two. In some passages there is no doubt that Whitley is describing a market in which the ideas and reported results of each individual or team are evaluated and criticized by other individuals or teams scattered through many formal organizations, and that the hierarchical status of both contributor and critic count for little or nothing in relation to the quality of what they write or say. In others, references to authority and leaders suggest that assessments are hierarchically based.

Part of the problem is that, within a scientific field, some people (who may be of equal rank but elected or appointed to a committee) will usually be required to make judgements about salary or promotion, or about the award of research grants, and these judgements will be partly – even principally – judgements about an individual's past contribution to knowledge. But those who make such judgements do not have the power to decide whether any specific contribution or criticism is to be accepted; that will emerge, possibly over some considerable time, from the responses of those who work on the same or related problems. That is not to say that such judgements have no effect on the development of knowledge. Both directly and through the messages which they convey, these decisions will influence the activities of those within the field, and therefore also the flow of ideas, evidence and criticism. Thus, although they cannot determine the response to any contribution, they can help to determine what contributions come forward – not the choice, but the contents of the choice set.

Another difficulty is caused by Whitley's recognition that within any field or sub-field not all are equal, from which he appears to argue that leaders can exert great influence by virtue of their authority. Now we should not forget Barnard's proposition that the authority to be accorded to any pronouncement, even within a formal organization, is determined by its recipients (Barnard, 1938, p.163). Within a hierarchy, the recipient's decision is no doubt influenced by perceptions of positional status; within a scientific community, it is likely to depend primarily on experience. Some people do prove to be particularly fertile of productive ideas and some – usually they are different people – especially perceptive critics. Is it not reasonable to pay rather more attention to the latest communication from such people than to others whose previous work has not been well received, or to those whose name is unfamiliar? Within the world of commerce, customers' limited knowledge is partly compensated by the reputation which accrues to suppliers: 'the function of competition is here precisely to teach us *who* will serve us well' (Hayek, 1948, 1949, p.97). The scientist welcomes similar guidance among the torrent of publications. Anonymous competition is not the most effective in fostering progress, either in science or in business.

But the advantages of reputation are perishable. A manufacturer of quality goods may be able to sell a shoddy product for a time, and a scientist with an outstanding record may cause many of his colleagues to waste much time on an ill-considered theory; but neither can expect to get away with it for very long. As Ziman (1968, p.136) emphasizes, reputations are constantly under review: and who has not heard, within one's own field, such comments as 'that was a very disappointing performance; we shan't ask him again'; 'she's now only concerned to defend her past contribution'; 'he *was* a great man'?

One point of particular note is that arguments and evidence which seem particularly convenient for their author are likely to be heavily discounted. The resolution of macroeconomic controversies has not been helped by the almost universal tendency for evidence to favour the position strongly advocated by the group from which it came; by contrast the theoretical demonstration that the mechanism proposed by Wegener for continental drift was quite incapable of producing the postulated effects was rendered the more effective in discrediting the theory because its author, a mathematician of high reputation, obviously had nothing at stake – unlike Wegener – in reaching one conclusion rather than another. There was nothing wrong with the mathematics; a quite different mechanism is now invoked (Ziman, 1968, pp.56–7, 97).

Mathematics and physics
As that example implies, mathematics has a special status in public science. There is a twofold reason for this. First, the language of mathematics is far more consensible than ordinary languages: it does not tolerate such ambiguities as the uncertain meaning of 'organization' and 'control' noted above. Of course, even with mathematics one never gets something for nothing, and the precision of mathematics is achieved by sacrificing descriptive powers in favour of exact symbols (Ziman, 1978, p.14). The second consensible attribute of mathematics is its logical structure: it provides direct knowledge of what is entailed by a particular set of axioms. But the price of this logical power is that 'mathematics may be defined as the subject in which we never know what we are talking about' (Russell, 1963, pp.59–60): in other words, the applicability of any mathematical argument has to be established by other means. In Ziman's language, the theory is a metaphor (1978, p.27). Now, if one can find empirical relationships onto which mathematical arguments can apparently be mapped, the resulting combination of logic and evidence can be highly persuasive. It can provide no guarantee of true knowledge, for the applicability of a mathematical structure can never be proved and, as happened with continental drift, it can be applied to the wrong relationship; but it can create a pretty firm consensus.

The consensus is likely to be especially strong if a series of related mathematical arguments can be plausibly mapped onto a set of (apparently) related phenomena. The more elaborate the metaphor and the more extensive its application, the greater its power to persuade. It is this apparent isomorphism of a highly interconnected mathematical network with a highly interconnected network of experimental observation which distinguishes physics. 'The search for unity and coherence' (Whitley, 1984, p.203) which appears so characteristic of physics is not confined to that discipline; it is just much more successful there. That a set of connecting principles, or an interpretative framework, by which we can make apparent sense of our experience and predict and control our own future is a greatly desired comfort for the individual has been emphasized in various contexts by Adam Smith (1980), Kelly (1963), and Shackle (1967), as we have observed in the previous two chapters;

to those working in a scientific field it offers the prospect of widening and deepening the consensus through its rhetorical power.

We should note, however, that physics – perhaps more than most other scientific fields – is an artificial creation: the choice of phenomena to be studied is deliberately restricted to those for which mathematics is a good fit (Ziman, 1978, pp.28–30). The structure of physics as a conceptually integrated bureaucracy, in which alone there is a distinctive class of theorists at the summit of the hierarchy, is thus explicable by the character of this subject field as a branch of knowledge: the theorists determine what is to count as a research topic in physics. But they do this not by imposing their will; their role is to indicate to experimental physicists what problems are presently soluble by the accepted research strategy of mapping mathematical theory onto experimental conditions. Since no physicist will gain a reputation by attempting to solve insoluble problems, such guidance is of particular value: those who provide it are especially useful, and esteemed accordingly.

It follows from the above argument that physics is unlikely to be a good model for other sciences. If physicists have pre-empted the study of phenomena for which mathematics provides excellent metaphors, then no-one else can expect to create an equally persuasive combination of theory and evidence. It is not at all clear how changes in context could turn any other field into a conceptually integrated bureaucracy. We may just be able to imagine a reductionist strategy by which all biological and social phenomena are eventually explicable by the interaction of elementary particles, but if this were to happen we would not find every science modelled upon physics, but physics as the only science. That physics may take over (and thereby transform) some areas of knowledge at present occupied by other disciplines is perfectly possible (it has happened already); that it should attain universal dominance is a proposition which it seems safe to deny. Even if such a strategy were open to a race of omniscient beings, the bounds of human rationality compel us to partition our study, and to treat complex structures (cells, individuals, groups, scientific fields) as the basic phenomena of particular areas of inquiry. Perhaps indeed they are, in the sense that the behaviour of such structures cannot be fully explained by the study of their component parts.

The partitioning of economics
Let us briefly consider economics in this context. The influence of the physics model is obviously strong, but it would be much too simple to suggest that the field is dominated by those who have been brainwashed.

The search for consensibility is, I suggest, a better guide. The difficulty of matching persuasive logic with persuasive evidence has plagued all branches of economics, but what Whitley fails to observe is that the difficulties arise from the evidence, not logic. The 'technical task uncertainty' which he attributes to economics characterizes only empirical work: in orthodox theoretical economics, technical task uncertainty is very low indeed. Had he noted this contrast, he might have asked whether it was a coincidence; he might then have considered Ziman's (1978, pp.163–6) contention that the structure of mathematics provides rather poor metaphors for the social sciences, and that insistence on this well defined and communicable framework is therefore rather likely to lead to difficulties in empirical work. Nor does Whitley mention the failure of the attempt to bridge this gap by the development of econometrics, of which such very high hopes were once held.

Why then have so many – though certainly not all – economists, far from modifying their theoretical structure, tended to cling all the more tightly to its elaboration, closing their minds to what might appear to be empirical refutations? As we have seen, refutations are always problematic, and in economics the mismatch between theoretical and empirical (usually statistical) formulations leaves the significance of any evidence quite uncertain, and therefore of little value in building any consensus. No doubt there are good personal and psychological reasons for not abandoning a framework which gives personal satisfaction, prestige, and financial reward; but barriers to entry are not insurmountable, alternative approaches exist and, indeed, are the sources of some reputations. Herbert Simon, after all, did gain a Nobel Prize for economics, even if the citation played down his economic contribution.

I suggest that a major reason is that orthodox economic theory, with general equilibrium at its core, is consensible in a way which eclipses any rival. As public knowledge, economics is almost synonymous with this theory; by comparison, everything else is local speculation, poorly controlled even within the group which accepts it as a basis for work, and linked rather weakly (sometimes hardly at all) with other less-than-orthodox approaches. Hahn's (1984) essays (which are examined in Chapter 8) provide striking evidence of this view of general equilibrium theory as the only basis for consensible public knowledge. The rich theoretical network of neoclassical economics is the principal element missing from Blaug's (1980) survey: it provides a conceptual integration which would not be shamed by comparison with physics.

What the present structure of theoretical economics has to offer is clearly an impressive body of public knowledge, which, on the latest evidence, is still capable of considerable extension. The incursion of theorists into industrial economics is currently imposing a kind of order on a fragmented sub-field. It is public knowledge of a rather special sort, and much narrower than its proponents seem to believe; but it is not obvious that it should be simply discarded. If it is to be preserved and extended, then it has to be kept from undue contamination by apparently anomalous evidence, aided – as with physics – by the deliberate exclusion of some areas of study which are particularly recalcitrant. Theoretical rigour and precision are highly – and rightly – valued because they aid the preservation and extension of the consensus. Whitley (1984, p.184) draws attention to 'the highly restricted nature of phenomena in economics' and the encouragement of 'values of coherence, simplicity, and formalism over those of accuracy, applicability, and empirical relevance', but seems more concerned with the implications for control than with the corresponding implications for consensibility, and the promotion of that public knowledge which is the purpose of public science.

Although Whitley explains the procedures by which economics is partitioned, and the primacy and coherence of theory maintained, he does not show why the leaders are so successful in enforcing their conception of the subject. In fact, the apparent enforcement results more from deliberate choice by new entrants, whether as graduates or from other disciplines, than from any power monopolized by the leaders: the existing theoretical structure appears to offer the best chance both of winning reputations and of advancing knowledge. Let us not forget that reputation and authority are determined by those working in the field; the standing of well known theorists, though primarily judged by other theorists, is also validated by workers in sub-fields – even those who reject the dominant theory. It is relatively easy to accept an extension of recognized theory; but, even when there is agreement on the empirical skill and statistical success of, say, a study of the relationship between advertising expenditure and profitability, or of mark-up rules in a department store, the results may still not be incorporated into the body of public knowledge.

Conclusion
The difficulty of matching convincing demonstrations to the persuasive rigour of neoclassical logic imposes severe limits on the scope of the economic consensus. But, however carefully restricted, no consensus in any field can guarantee knowledge; since no unimpugnable proof is ever available, even the best-founded consensus may be wrong. Not only do we have no infallible criterion of truth at our disposal, we do not have any assured means of eliminating error. Just as the keenest

and widest competition within an economy cannot – unlike axiomatic perfect competition – guarantee optimal results, so the finest examples of scientific method, which is a competitive social process, cannot ensure that all the knowledge which it produces is reliable. Ziman's (1978, p.40) guess is that 'the physics of undergraduate text-books is 90 per cent true; the contents of the primary research journals of physics is 90 per cent false'. The encouragement of a critical attitude and the preservation of an open society in every scientific field are no less important than they ever were.

However, they may have become more difficult. The greater the extent of currently reliable knowledge, the more one needs to learn in order to become an effective practitioner and the more thoroughly that knowledge is integrated, the more deeply immersed one inevitably becomes in the current paradigm. If, as in physics, experimental procedures require expert manipulation of esoteric techniques and highly trained observation to recognize the results, then the conditioning process of research training may impart too much credibility to the established rhetoric. The steadily increasing distance to the frontiers of knowledge in economics likewise encourages a concentration on technical skills and the development of great critical power within a narrow focus. The influence of organization structure on the detection of error is a major question which Whitley ignores.

Nor does Whitley consider the most important effect of resource scarcity on the growth of knowledge. Indeed, his invocation (1984, pp.162–3) of the relative scarcity of resources in physics to explain its conceptual integration (whereas chemistry, being better endowed in relation to its more modest needs, requires no such principle of resource allocation) seems misconceived. The need to make choices does not always produce any single choice procedure. Investment decisions have to be made, but that necessity has not produced any single acceptable decision rule for the purpose. If resources are scarce, choices will be made by some means or other.

What matters for the growth of reliable knowledge is the effect of restricting competition. The dominance of a comprehensive paradigm may have some unfortunate effects, but it should not be confused with denial of access, any more than market dominance should be confused with statutory monopoly. Resource scarcity may lead not to agreement on a single conceptual framework, but to the exclusion of rivals through the denial of funds. It is important that one researcher should be able to conduct delicate and expensive experiments to identify gravitational waves despite apparent theoretical proof that they are undetectable, and that, when he reports an apparent success, other groups throughout the world should not only scrutinize both the theory and the experimental methods, but also set up their own experiments (Ziman, 1978, pp.67–8). It is correspondingly dangerous to rely on a single piece of apparatus (such as a particle accelerator of great size and cost) as the sole source of evidence, especially if access to it is tightly controlled, perhaps on the grounds of avoiding wasteful duplication of effort (Ziman, 1978, pp.63–4). The search for economy may prove very expensive. State science is especially prone to such dangers. But, although Whitley's principal argument for the significance of his study is that different systems of organization and control lead to different types of knowledge, he does not seem to be aware that they also influence its reliability.

If epistemology leads to the conclusion that what we call scientific knowledge is necessarily the product of a social process, then the study of the growth of knowledge is a scientific field which is open to sociologists and also to organizational theorists and psychologists. (Is it no more than a fragmented adhocracy? At least it is a fairly open society.) Whitley's contribution seems to me helpful and important. It could have been still more helpful had he not conceived it solely as a study of scientific fields as reputational work organizations. Although critical appraisal from another viewpoint may demonstrate (as it usually does) the need for some reconstruction, and even perhaps some demolition, there appear also to be good prospects of extension and integration. The analytical framework of this book already appears consensible; it should not be difficult to enhance its consensibility, which is a necessary stage on the way to more reliable knowledge.

4 Knowledge and organization: Marshall's theory of economic progress and coordination*

Style and purpose

'It's all in Marshall.' There is more truth in that once-familiar claim than there would be in a similar claim about any other economist; yet, as Samuelson (1967, p.25) rightly observed, what is in Marshall cannot be revealed by the reading of Marshall alone. What one sees is very largely a reflection of one's own viewpoint; often it is only after thinking about a specific issue that one realizes that Marshall had thought about it too, and had set down his ideas in his usual unemphatic way, as if they were already common property. His manner is very different from that of Hicks, who always explains what he is doing and why; neither in the *Principles of Economics* (1961) nor in *Industry and Trade* (1919) does Marshall attempt to distinguish his own contributions – though frequently acknowledging those of others – and his clear views on how economists should proceed are not allowed to mark out a distinctively Marshallian programme. Consequently, although he gained a great reputation, many of his ideas have had very little influence.

Marshall's method of presentation was adjusted to his primary objectives: to secure the position of economics as an academic discipline of the first rank, and to promote economic policy which should be securely based on economic knowledge. The first objective was achieved: he became the leader of the profession in Great Britain, and created both the Royal Economic Society and the Economics Tripos at Cambridge. One major purpose of the Tripos, it may be noted, was to provide a broad preparation for business (1961, II, pp.167–71). On economic policy he was less successful, partly because his own sense of the complexity of issues made him increasingly reluctant to commit himself to particular measures, apart from the preservation of free trade. The

*This chapter incorporates material from 'Whatever happened to Marshall's theory of value?', *Scottish Journal of Political Economy*, 1978, pp.1–12, reproduced by permission of the Scottish Economic Society, and from 'Marshall's economics of progress', *Journal of Economic Studies*, 1986, pp.16–26, reproduced by permission of MCB University Press Ltd. A shorter version was presented at the University of Florence in October 1987.

achievement of these objectives put a substantial premium on both consensus among the professionals and acceptance among the leaders of business and politics, and these desiderata meshed well with his own belief in the gradual improvement of knowledge and his personal aversion from controversy. In the footnotes to the *Principles*, his sharpest criticisms are reserved for those who, in his view, are unjustly critical of others.

Marshall's determination to build a consensus, like many carefully considered policies, had unintended consequences. One major sequel is examined in the following chapter; here the emphasis is rather on what did not happen – the analysis which dropped out of use. It seems to be generally agreed that the core of Marshall's *Principles* is contained in Book V: 'General Relations of Demand, Supply, and Value'. If one judges past economists by their contribution towards the development of modern microeconomic theory, which for many is the intellectual glory of our subject, then this is natural. But from such a perspective, Marshall's contribution must appear hesitant, fumbling, and sometimes even wilfully perverse. He fails to pursue the logic of his analysis, seems not to understand the formal requirements of perfect competition which are nowadays listed in elementary textbooks, wanders into imperfect competition without realizing it, and by his insistence on the prevalence of increasing returns exposes his whole theoretical scheme to destruction by Sraffa (1926). No wonder Samuelson (1967, p.24) believed that 'much of the work from 1920 to 1933 was merely the negative task of getting Marshall out of the way'. That task was very effectively done. It was only much later that Joan Robinson (1951, pp.vii–viii) realized that what had been 'got out of the way' included a richly detailed theory of economic development. As we shall see in Chapter 6, it was left for G.B. Richardson (1960) to demonstrate that Marshall also had at least the elements of a theory of the way in which equilibrium could be established – the missing half, as Hahn has so often reminded us, of general equilibrium theory.

Economic development
The analysis of this chapter is based on the proposition that much of what is in Marshall is far more clearly revealed if we approach him from Adam Smith rather than from modern microeconomics. For Marshall, like Smith, was primarily concerned with a topic alien to modern microeconomics, namely the nature and causes of the wealth of nations. The coordination problem – the prime issue of general equilibrium theory – is for both Smith and Marshall a secondary, though crucial, issue. It arises precisely because the increasing wealth of nations

is promoted by the division of labour; for, unless the resultant specialized activities can be effectively coordinated, the division of labour will lead not to prosperity but to chaos and misery. But the means of coordination should be chosen in such a way as to encourage, rather than frustrate, increasing productivity, and, as seems to be increasingly (albeit often dimly) recognized, a perfectly competitive general equilibrium does not obviously meet this requirement. Marshall's Book V is intended to do so; it must therefore appear unsatisfactory from Samuelson's perspective.

As we shall see towards the end of this chapter, Marshall's theory of value appears in a very different light when read in its proper sequence, after the relatively neglected Book IV of the *Principles*, which is entitled 'The Agents of Production. Land, Labour, Capital and Organization'. That Book too (supplemented by *Industry and Trade*) must be considered in the context of Marshall's motivation for studying economics – that characteristic Victorian desire to improve 'the condition of the people'. Marshall saw three means of improvement. I shall briefly consider the first two, before examining the third in some detail.

The first means of improvement was state and voluntary action. The idea that Marshall's economic theory was intended to demonstrate the impossibility of improving on the contemporary economic system is absurd. Although much influenced by Darwin, he was no uncritical admirer of the social consequences of Darwinian processes.

> We must call to mind the fact that the struggle for survival tends to make those methods of organisation prevail, which are best fitted to *thrive in* their environment; but not necessarily those best fitted to *benefit* their environment. (Marshall, 1961, pp.596–7)

In a competitive market, rewards go to those who offer direct and immediate service, and many businesses – especially cooperative associations, in which Marshall saw great potential for improving the lives of working people – do not survive long enough to generate their valuable but more distant benefits. Nor are inventors always adequately rewarded, for reasons which are now standard (1961, pp.597–8). 'There is no general economic principle which supports the notion that industry will necessarily flourish best, or that life will be the happiest and healthiest, when each man is allowed to manage his own concerns as he thinks best' (Marshall, 1919, p.736).

Adam Smith, as Marshall reminds us,

> . . . frequently stated or implied that it would be possible for an omniscient and omnipotent Government to direct the actions of merchants, and other

people, in a course more conducive to public well-being than that in which they would be led by their own interests. (1919, p.744)

But Adam Smith did not believe that governments could command either the knowledge or the moral integrity that would be necessary. Neither did Marshall:

> . . . the State is the most precious of human possessions; and no care can be too great to be spent on enabling it to do its special work in the best way: a chief condition to that end is that it should not be set to work, for which it is not specially qualified, under the conditions of time and place. (1919, pp.647–8)

Adam Smith acknowledged the limitations of those moral sentiments which he had examined at length before turning to the effects of self-interest. 'In civilised society [man] stands at all times in need of the cooperation and assistance of great multitudes, while his whole life is scarce sufficient to gain the friendship of a few persons.' That, as is often forgotten, is why 'it is not from the benevolence of the butcher, the brewer, or the baker, that we expect our dinner, but from their regard to their own interest' (Smith, 1976, I, pp.26–7). Self-interest, which is relatively abundant, must be substituted, according to the principle of comparative advantage, both for love and the beneficent power of the state, which are relatively scarce. Marshall agrees with Smith. Although we should take all regularly acting motives into account as far as possible (1961, p.vi), we must not forget 'the one fundamental principle: viz. that progress mainly depends on the extent to which the strongest, and not merely the highest, forces of human nature can be utilized for the increase of social good' (1919, p.664). Demonstration of market – or organizational – failure is no more than the statement of a problem: the suggested remedies may not only be imperfect but also have unwanted side-effects.

Marshall's second means of improvement was through the encourage-ment of higher-quality wants. Marshall's wish to encourage personal reform is reflected in the moralizing tone which pervades the *Principles*, and which most readers now find unattractive (as well as a violation of the rules of 'positive' economics); but he also placed much emphasis on the sociology of wants. Stigler and Becker's (1977, p.76) proposition that wants should be treated as uniform and unchangeable, whatever its attractions as a rule of model-building, would surely have been rejected by Marshall as stultifying his purpose.

Environment is important.

There is no better use for public and private money [*note that both state and voluntary action are invoked*] than in providing public parks and playgrounds in large cities, in contracting with railways to increase the number of workmen's trains run by them, and in helping those of the working classes who are willing to leave the large towns to do so, and take their industries with them. (Marshall, 1961, p.200)

But what is especially striking is Marshall's concern for the social consequences of the industrial system. He reverses the now-standard causation by claiming that 'each new step upwards is to be regarded as the development of new activities giving rise to new wants, rather than of new wants giving rise to new activities' (1961, p.89); thus, 'it is to changes in the forms of efforts and activities that we must turn when in search for the keynotes of the history of mankind' (1961, p.85).

As Parsons (1931), Whitaker (1977) and Chasse (1984) have emphasized, the influence of activities on wants is central to Marshall's view of human progress, and his concern with forms of economic organization is partly motivated by their supposed long-run effect on human character. In particular, schemes for encouraging the advancement of working men – which included the reform of English spelling, estimated by Marshall (1919, p.352) to set free at least one year of elementary schooling – were to be welcomed as much for their stimulus to greater care and forethought in consumption decisions as for the additional output which could be secured by redeeming otherwise wasted human ability. Marshall (1961, p.310) characteristically observes that the effects on consumption and character may be better if the rise of a family from the working classes is spread over two generations: he shared the Victorian gentleman's dislike for the *nouveaux riches*. Best of all, perhaps, was a worker's cooperative, where workers could learn to direct a business without being exposed to the temptations of unaccustomed wealth and power. The emphasis throughout, it may be noted, is on the working man; women are usually thought to be doing work of higher value in moulding the character of their children at home – perhaps a reflection of Marshall's own early experiences (Coase, 1984). Although Marshall was primarily responsible for extracting economics at Cambridge from the Moral Sciences Tripos, it remained, for him, a moral science.

The division of labour
We come now to the third means of improving the condition of the people, and the main theme of Book IV of the *Principles*. This means is not the promotion of an efficient allocation of given resources to given production sets through the creation of a competitive economy

(or its Siamese twin, the perfectly planned economy). Indeed, in the introductory chapter of the *Principles*, Marshall argues that competition – especially price competition – 'is only a secondary, and one might almost say, an accidental consequence from the fundamental character-istics of modern industrial life' (1961, p.5). These characteristics are listed in a marginal summary as 'self-reliance, independence, deliberate choice and forethought', and Marshall observes that they may tend in the direction either of competition or cooperation. What matters is the replacement of custom by enterprise.

The framework of progress, for Marshall as for Smith, is provided by the division of labour, continually extended by the growth of the market, to which its results contribute in turn. Marshall praises Smith for giving 'a new and larger significance to an old doctrine by the philosophic thoroughness with which he explained it, and the practical knowledge with which he illustrated it' (1961, p.240). As the author of *The History of Astronomy* (1980) (discussed in Chapter 1), Smith would surely have been gratified by the form of this compliment; he would also have appreciated the potential appeal of Marshall's characteristic invocation of biology in order to propound

> . . . a fundamental unity of action between the laws of nature in the physical and in the moral world. This central unity is set forth in the general rule, to which there are not very many exceptions, that the development of the organism, whether social or physical, involves an increasing subdivision of functions between its separate parts on the one hand, and on the other a more intimate connection between them. (Marshall, 1961, p.241)

The important distinction between social and physical organisms, which is very clear from Marshall's discussion but to which he does not draw explicit attention, is that social development is fostered by human initiative and creativity: it is for this reason that 'while the part which nature plays in production shows a tendency to diminishing return, the part which man plays shows a tendency to increasing return' (1961, p.318). Since the former has a physical and the second a social basis, it is dangerous to treat them both as technological data.

That increasing return has to be worked for, and cannot be selected from a previously defined production set, is implicit in Marshall's (1961, p.318) definition: 'The *law of increasing return* may be worded thus:– An increase of labour and capital leads generally to improved organiz-ation, which increases the efficiency of the work of labour and capital.' Nor is increasing return a return to scale, in the standard sense of a relationship between equi-proportional increases in all inputs and the resultant increase in output. It is indeed a relation between inputs and outputs; but the 'quantities cannot be taken out exactly, because changing methods of production call for machinery, and for unskilled and skilled labour of new kinds and in new proportions' (1961, p.319). Marshall excludes 'any economies that may result from substantive new inventions; but we include those which may be expected to arise naturally out of adaptations of existing ideas' (1961, p.460). He suggests, by way of example, that 'if the volume of production were greater, it would perhaps be profitable to substitute largely machine work for handwork and steam power for muscular force' (1961, p.344).

Thus, increasing returns result from the exploitation of possibilities of substitution which are opened up by production on a larger scale. This thoroughly confuses the distinction which we try to impress on our students between the law of variable proportions and returns to scale; but it happens to be the sensible thing to do. The falling unit costs that we habitually attribute to economies of scale do arise from the possibilities of changing proportions; and what we loosely call diseconomies of scale result from the inability to increase all inputs in the same proportion. The examples provided in textbooks typically rely on changing proportions despite their authors' intentions. Koutsoyiannis, after defining returns to scale in terms of equi-proportional increases in inputs (1979, p.77), states baldly (1979, p.81) that 'increasing returns to scale are due to *technical and/or managerial indivisibilities*'. Samuelson proceeds directly from equi-proportional change to examples which clearly imply factor substitution (Samuelson and Nordhaus, 1985, p.37). If we insist on our rigorous definition, then the only reasonable assumption to make about returns to scale is that they are constant.

Wealth through knowledge

The distinction between substantive new inventions and those naturally arising out of adaptations of existing ideas is clearly not precise, and Adam Smith's own discussion of the scope for the invention of machinery – one of the 'three different circumstances' which explain the increases in productivity which generally follow a greater division of labour (1976, I, pp.17–22) – suggests the rather different notion of a framework for continuing invention and discovery. Such indeed is Marshall's general theme in Book IV, and it is announced in the second paragraph of its opening chapter.

> Capital consists in a great part of knowledge and organization. . . . Knowledge is our most powerful engine of production; it enables us to subdue nature and force her to satisfy our wants. Organization aids knowledge; it

has many forms, e.g. that of a single business, that of various businesses in the same trade, that of various trades relatively to one another, and that of the State providing security for all and help for many. (1961, pp.138–9)

The twin themes of the Book are the effects of the growth of knowledge on organization and costs of production, and the effects of the organization of production on the growth of knowledge. These effects are not adequately represented within the structure–conduct–performance version of equilibrium analysis which, for many years, dominated economists' thinking – itself a striking example of the effects of the organization of economic theory production on the growth of economic knowledge. For Marshall, quite as much as for Schumpeter (1934, p.63), economic development was not a response to external stimuli but arose 'by its own initiative, from within'.

'The older economists took too little account of the fact that the human faculties are as important a means of production as any other kind of capital' (1961, p.229). We now have human capital theory to supply this deficiency, but it does not do all that Marshall would want, because human capital is not allowed to change the parameters of the system within which it is analysed.

> To be able to bear in mind many things at a time, to have everything ready when wanted, to act promptly and show resource when anything goes wrong, to accommodate oneself quickly to changes in detail of the work done, to be steady and trustworthy, to have always a reserve of force which will come out in emergency, these are the qualities which make a great industrial people. (1961, pp.206–7)

They are not obviously the qualities required in a system of general equilibrium, although they might be useful in a sequence economy. But this is not all:

> . . . the manufacturer who makes goods not to meet special orders but for the general market must, in his first rôle as merchant and organizer of production, have a thorough knowledge of *things* in his own trade. He must have the power of forecasting the broad movements of production and consumption, of seeing where there is an opportunity for supplying a new commodity that will meet a real want or improving the plan of producing an old commodity. . . .
> But secondly in this rôle of employer he must be a natural leader of *men*. He must have a power of first choosing his assistants rightly and then trusting them fully; of interesting them in the business and of getting them to trust him, so as to bring out whatever enterprise and power of origination there is in them. (1961, pp.297–8)

Now it is the manufacturer supplying the general market who is supposed to be represented by the perfectly competitive firm of later theory, and, in that theory, it is certainly no part of his business – still less the business of his senior managers – to be introducing either novel products or novel methods. But, for Marshall, that is precisely what he is expected to do. Marshallian competition is a Hayekian discovery process.

The role of the ordinary competitive manufacturer in contributing to the growth of knowledge, in production and in the market, pervades the analysis.

> At the beginning of his undertaking, and at every successive stage, the alert business man strives so to modify his arrangements as to obtain better results with a given expenditure, or equal results with a less expenditure. In other words, he ceaselessly applies the principle of substitution, with the purpose of increasing his profits; and, in so doing, he seldom fails to increase the total efficiency of work, the total power over nature which man derives from organization and knowledge. (1961, p.355)

The principle of substitution is not just a characteristic of a production function, defining a set of alternatives from which the businessman chooses according to the relative prices of inputs; it is a research programme which suggests how he might discover, or invent, one or more elements of better production functions, which are hitherto unknown.

Moreover, it is highly desirable that different manufacturers should try different experiments: for the 'tendency to variation is a chief cause of progress; and the abler are the undertakers in any trade the greater will this tendency be' (1961, p.355). The organization of various businesses in the same trade fosters the growth of knowledge because neither manufacturers nor the businesses which they control are homogeneous. 'Each man's actions are influenced by his special opportunities and resources, as well as by his temperament and his associations' (1961, pp.355–6). This differentiation, which is not easy to specify in a conventional model, rarely enters economists' discussion of the relative merits of concentration and dispersion of industrial research, where it may be crucial. Of particular importance are 'three closely allied conditions of vigour, namely, hopefulness, freedom, and change' (1961, p.197); 'and the advantages of economic freedom are never more strikingly manifest than when a business man endowed with genius is trying experiments, at his own risk, to see whether some new method, or combination of old methods, will be more efficient than the old' (1961, p.406).

These advantages could be substantially enhanced by improving the

education of the working classes. 'There is no extravagance more preju-
dicial to the growth of the national wealth than that wasteful negligence
which allows genius that happens to be born of lowly parentage to
expend itself in lowly work' (1961, p.212). Nor was inadequate
education the only obstacle. Greater insistence on social distinction in
the South of England than in the North had allowed fewer working
men into management, and thus hampered progress, which 'is most
rapid in those parts of the country in which the greatest proportion of
the leaders of industry are the sons of working men' (1961, p.212).

Marshall even indicates the circumstances which are likely to
encourage new ideas.

> By converse with others who come from different places, and have different
> customs, travellers learn to put on its trial many a habit of thought or action
> which otherwise they would always have acquiesced in as though it were a
> law of nature. Moreover, a shifting of places enables the more powerful and
> original minds to find full scope for their energies and to rise to important
> positions: whereas those who stay at home are often over much kept in their
> places. Few men are prophets in their own land. . . . It is doubtless chiefly
> for this reason that in almost every part of England a disproportionately
> large share of the best energy and enterprise is to be found among those
> who were born elsewhere. (1961, pp.197–8, note 2)

The outsider's advantages in perceiving, instituting or adopting new
ideas is not an unfamiliar theme in studies of the growth of knowledge
or the diffusion of innovations; neither is it irrelevant to Marshall's
account of the rise and fall of individual businesses, to which we shall
shortly turn.

Much of the capital of a business (defined either by the investment
of time and skill required or its ability to generate income) is to be
found in its internal organization, which both reflects the knowledge
which has been gained and provides the framework for the development
of further knowledge. Nelson and Winter's (1982) analysis of organizational routines is thoroughly Marshallian, not least in its recognition
of the importance of time and its irreversibility. Much is also to be
found in what Marshall calls its 'external organization' (1961, p.458)
or its trade connections (1961, p.377), which likewise both embody
knowledge and offer a basis for new experiments. Trade connections
are, of course, incompatible with perfect competition; their absence is
almost equally incompatible with progress, which perfect competition
cannot encompass. 'External organization' is perhaps the better term,
because it suggests the network of social, technical, and commercial
arrangements which link a business with its customers, suppliers (who

are usually of many kinds), and also its rivals, whose own experiments provide it with both incentive and information. Marshall draws attention to 'the length of time that is necessarily occupied by each individual business in extending its internal, and still more its external organization' (1961, p.500): it cannot choose its optimal position on ready-made demand and cost curves, but has to create them through the application of a well judged policy.

Marketing, in any sense that would be understood in a business school, is scarcely ever mentioned in economic analysis. It can clearly have no place in perfect competition; imperfect competition, in which there appears to be some scope for buying a demand curve, may allow for selling costs, including advertising, but these are rather simple concepts. Moreover, such costs are usually (but not quite always) considered to be wasteful, and sharply contrasted with production costs. Marshall's view is very different.

> Production and marketing are parts of the single process of adjustment of supply to demand. The division between them is on lines which are seldom sharply defined: the lines vary from one class of business to another, and each is liable to modification by any large change in the resources of production, transport, or the communication of intelligence. (1919, p.181)

This is a modern perspective, though one not widely shared by economists. If customers are to be induced to buy a new product, then that product must be designed and manufactured in a way which will make it acceptable, and the costs of doing so may very plausibly be assigned to marketing. Alternatively, if the object is to deliver satisfaction to the customer, then marketing, like transport and the services of retailing, may be considered as part of the process of producing that satisfaction. Marshall does not explicitly argue in these terms, for that would threaten the basis of his theory of value, which, like all subsequent theories, depends on a clear analytical separation of supply and demand; but he lays great emphasis on the importance and the expense of marketing, both of which help to explain the course of industrial development.

Internal and external economies
The businessman's development of his internal and external organization is the means by which he gains access to internal and external economies. From the point of view of the individual business, the internal economies which it may achieve are predominantly complements, while external economies often substitute for internal economies which might be within the reach of bigger competitors. It is by

exploiting external economies that small firms may be able to compete effectively with large, even in some industries in which large firms have important specific advantages. Both large and small firms, however, usually require to build up effective external as well as internal organizations – and that takes time.

Despite the apparent threat to a long-run equilibrium model of perfect competition (nowadays misleadingly abbreviated to 'a competitive economy'), Marshall himself never suggested that internal economies were relatively unimportant, or that they were likely to be exhausted at relatively low outputs. 'The chief advantages of production on a large scale are economy of skill, economy of machinery and economy of materials: but the last of these is rapidly losing importance relatively to the other two' (1961, p.278). The large-scale manufacturer can make more effective use of specialized machinery, and can afford to experiment in the design of improvements in methods of manufacture; he can also bear the costs and risks of undertaking 'a characteristic task of the modern manufacturer, that of showing people something which they had never thought of having before; but which they want to have as soon as the notion is suggested to them' (1961, p.280). (Enterprising firms may thus contribute directly to improving effective preferences.) Buying and selling on a large scale also generally produce economies; moreover a wider market provides more sources of information, and a wider product range allows a reputation to be more quickly created and more effectively used (1961, p.282). Thus the large firm may have advantages over the small, not only in its internal, but also in its external, organization. To secure them, however, will require time and effort: indeed, Marshall observes that the 'marketing reputation and connection of a business may be a larger property . . . than is the fixed plant' (1919, p.270). Once again, we must not think of predetermined demand curves and production functions.

Economies of skill parallel economies of machinery; but Marshall places particular emphasis on the large-scale employer's advantages in 'the selection of able and tried men, men whom he trusts and who trust him, to be his foremen and heads of departments' (1961, p.283). He is clearly thinking, to use modern terminology, primarily in terms of internal labour markets. These are the people on whom the reputation of the employer's business chiefly depends; and if he is confident that it is safe in their hands, he can concentrate his own attention on what would now be called the problems of organizational design and corporate strategy.

If the head of a large business is able to exploit the internal division of labour by freeing himself from detail, then the ability to attend to detail, when detail is crucial, and to avoid the problems of communication and control which so often plague large organizations, is the peculiar advantage of the owner of a small business (1961, p.284). Moreover, greater specialization between businesses, and greater subdivision of industries, may allow each process to be worked on a scale which permits 'the economic use of expensive machinery' (1961, p.271) so that a group of small firms may collectively enjoy the economies which are available to a large manufacturer.

Such increasing subdivision, according to Marshall's general rule quoted earlier, requires a more intimate connection. Marshall accordingly draws attention to two factors which facilitate such connection.

> Probably more than three-fourths of the whole benefit [England] has derived from the progress of manufactures during the nineteenth century has been through its indirect influences in lowering the cost of transport of men and goods, of water and light, of electricity and news: for the dominant economic fact of our own age is the development not of the manufacturing, but of the transport industries. (1961, pp.674–5)

The second factor is the concentration, not just of single industries, but often of clusters of industries, in particular localities – an important example of the organization of various trades relative to each other. Each locality develops a 'special industrial atmosphere' (1919, p.287), in which the inhabitants unconsciously absorb the aptitudes which its industries require. Moreover, within an industrial district, it is easier for each firm to create the network of personal contacts which will give it the confidence to integrate its activities with others – relying perhaps as much on moral sentiments as financial incentive. As Richardson (1972) was to remind us, personal contact is especially important when goods and services are not standardized (Marshall, 1919, p.285). This network also forms an invisible college, which fosters the development, appraisal, and application of new ideas.

> Good work is rightly appreciated, inventions and improvements in machinery, in processes and the general organization of the business have their merits promptly discussed: if one man starts a new idea, it is taken up by others and combined with suggestions of their own; and thus it becomes the source of further new ideas. (Marshall, 1961, p.271)

The industrial district is an appropriate environment for fostering and exploiting the tendency to variation on which Marshall, as we have seen, laid emphasis.

The anonymity of perfect competition is clearly incompatible with these activities, which are very helpful – perhaps indispensable – to the achievement of external economies. The attempt to reconcile falling long-run costs with perfect competition by attributing the fall in costs to external economies thus appears fundamentally misconceived: the presence of external economies is itself an indication that competition is not perfect. This is not, of course, a problem for Marshall, only for those who misinterpret him.

The rise and decline of firms

Marshall did not envisage any early exhaustion of the principle of increasing return; nor did he wish to, because it promised to make a major contribution to the improvement in standards of life which he wished to see. He did, however, envisage – and, indeed, had observed in his extensive study of British industries – a general tendency for the exhaustion of each individual firm's ability to achieve further internal economies. The problem lay not in the potential for further advance, but in the skill, incentive, and imagination needed to exploit that potential. As has been emphasized, the economies had to be worked for – indeed, they had to be created; and Marshall believed that there was a natural life-cycle of creativity which could be observed in very many, if not quite all, firms. The energy and flexibility of a newcomer gave him advantages which, when linked to a thorough knowledge of 'things in his own trade' (which might take some time to acquire), would allow his business to grow rapidly by the creation of internal, and the exploitation of external, economies and by the development of a pattern of internal and external organization which facilitated both.

The principal restraint on the firm's rate of growth, once it had reached a moderate size, might well lie in difficulties of marketing. These difficulties cannot be adequately represented by a falling long-run demand curve – which Marshall did not use – for they are the difficulties of building a market. For businesses, such as cotton spinners, which operate at several removes from the final consumer, building a market entails creating and maintaining a coalition. The problem is not best tackled by price alone; and the price reductions which are likely to form part of their marketing policy are intended not merely to attract customers who are already willing to buy at a lower price, but to build up a demand among those who had not previously considered the product but need to be encouraged to experiment. This use of pricing policy is a standard component of modern marketing; it was well understood by Victorian businessmen, and by Marshall, who had studied their policies and performance.

Thus, it takes time to build up a large business, and for each businessman time is short. His peculiar skills and abilities may dwindle, or become less applicable as circumstances change; or he may become less able, or less inclined, to make the effort needed. Enterprise may relapse into custom. Having created a large and profitable organization, he may therefore begin to lose ground to newer firms, just as, in the beginning, he had been able to expand at the expense of established businesses. He may choose to hand over to his son (rarely to his daughter) but, although sons of businessmen may have many advantages in business knowledge, they often fail to develop the special abilities or temperament necessary for success. They may not even be very interested, preferring a different kind of life. That, Marshall lamented, had hitherto been particularly likely if they were sent to university, where they would learn to despise their fathers' trades (1961, pp.298–300).

Decline might be averted by converting the business into a joint-stock company; and the family might be very willing to hand over management, or even ownership. But, although joint-stock companies provided access to people who had business skills but no capital (provided that they could convince others of those skills), they were unlikely to match the enterprise of the best private businesses. That joint-stock companies could prosper at all, Marshall thought, was a great tribute to the growth of business morality, which he regarded as a notable Victorian improvement (he clearly did not believe in the adequacy of capital market discipline); but, as with government, the bureaucratic methods which joint-stock companies were likely to adopt would discourage creative ideas and experiments (1961, pp.303–4). That view goes back to Adam Smith; Marshall's further concern that joint-stock companies would be tempted into excessive enlargements of the scope of their activities seems peculiarly apposite today (1919, pp.321–3).

Process and equilibrium: Marshall's theory of value

Marshall's law of increasing return was a summary of his own general and detailed observations of the course of industrial progress. It may also be derived from two basic Marshallian propositions: that people (especially, but not only, in business) strive to find better ways of doing things and better things to do, and that evolution tends to favour ever more complex patterns of differentiation and integration. Thus, efforts at improvement are particularly likely to be successful when they take the form of greater specialization; and that, as Adam Smith pointed out, is facilitated by an increase in the aggregate volume of business. Increasing return is therefore the form which improved productivity is especially likely to take, and any analysis of the working of a progressive economy must accord it a central place. But it is the outcome of a competitive process, and that too must somehow be handled.

Most economists would agree with Sraffa's (1926) charge that Marshall's insistence on increasing return destroyed his theory of value. I wish to suggest that Sraffa simultaneously claimed too much and too little. Sraffa established the standard doctrine that economies of scale which extend over more than a modest range of output are incompatible with perfect competition. But he was quite wrong to assume that perfect competition was the basis of Marshall's theory of value. On the other hand, Sraffa failed to notice that Marshall's conception of increasing return – unlike the modern concept of scale economies – included changes in factor proportions and depended on human effort and modest discovery: and these differences are even more difficult to reconcile with perfect competition.

We can go further – much further. Perfect competition requires an initial specification of preferences, resources, and technology which, for Marshall, were not only outputs of economic processes but outputs which could not conveniently be specified as dependent variables, since they derive from the knowledge which is generated within the processes themselves. Moreover, Marshall's description of the organization which aids knowledge is quite clearly the description of an imperfect market structure: indeed, it is a description of that most recalcitrant market structure – oligopoly. Thus, the conflict between Marshall's theory of economic progress and the requirements of perfectly competitive equilibrium is far deeper than Sraffa imagined or Samuelson has recognized. But for Marshall – unlike his successors – the problem was not that his theory of the growth of knowledge was incompatible with perfect competition, but that perfect competition was incompatible with the growth of knowledge. Book V of the *Principles* has to be accommodated to Book IV, rather than the reverse.

Marshall's attempt to provide an institutional structure which would provide a framework for progress has an important advantage for his theory of value. It allows him to suggest an answer to the problem which increasingly bothered Walras – the problem of adjustment. Walras (1874, pp.48–50) originally proposed a process of *tatonnement* as a theoretical formalization of the operation of organized markets. However, by the time of his last revision of the *Elements* (Walras, 1900, p.215), he was persuaded that the adjustment of production entailed both production and sale at non-equilibrium prices, which could invalidate the equilibria calculated from initial conditions, so he substituted a fictional *tatonnement* and implicitly withdrew his theory of adjustment (Walker, 1987). Nowadays we recognize (and usually ignore) the problem of path dependency and its associated difficulty that it is only in equilibrium that perfectly competitive analysis is logically valid. Perfect competition does not formally solve the coordination problem because it does not explain how coordination is to be achieved. The Marshallian organization of industry at least suggests how it might be done. Marshall's industries are information structures, which, unlike perfect competition, are capable of generating reliable expectations. Reliability is here used in the same sense as Ziman (1978); and it rests on an analogous process of discovery within an imperfectly specified structure (see Chapter 3).

Equilibrium models
As a mathematical scholar of distinction, and a major contributor to formal value theory, Marshall could hardly fail to be impressed and attracted by the power of equilibrium analysis; but he was aware of its limitations. Even in a static setting, it did not provide as complete an answer to the problem of coordination as at first appeared, and it had serious deficiencies as a method of analysing the generation of new knowledge.

Marshall's awareness of these deficiencies helps to explain his scepticism about the advantages of general equilibrium analysis.

> The element of time is a chief cause of those difficulties in economic investigations which make it necessary for man with his limited powers to go step by step; breaking up a complex question, studying one bit at a time, and at last combining his partial solutions into a more or less complete solution of the whole riddle. (1961, p.366)

The theoretical successes of general equilibrium have been achieved only by the exclusion of time as anything more than another kind of space; and this exclusion is one of the main reasons why the applicability of general equilibrium remains so problematic.

We know what Marshall thought of the non-rigorous general equilibrium model known as a stationary state. This produced a simple doctrine of value, but 'in the real world a simple doctrine of value is worse than none' (1961, p.368). Its defects result not from a lack of formal rigour, but from the inadequacy of the conception – the exclusion of endogenous change and of the processes which embody it. Partial equilibrium methods, however, enable us to look at particular processes on the provisional assumption that everything else is at rest (1961, p.369). 'This scientific device is a great deal older than science: it is the method by which, consciously or unconsciously, sensible men have dealt from time immemorial with every difficult problem of ordinary life' (1961, p.xiv). The principal limitation of a partial equilibrium model is not that it is partial, but that it is constrained by the method of equilibrium.

We should not therefore be surprised that Book V of Marshall's *Principles* is very far from a systematic demonstration of equilibrium modelling. The exposition does not qualify for the modern accolades of elegance and rigour; instead it is discursive and thoughtful. Equilibrium is treated as problematic throughout, and each particular model of equilibrium is supported by reasons why we might reasonably expect that equilibrium to be attained. Marshall's approach may be illustrated in the three contexts of temporary, short-run and long-run analysis.

Temporary equilibrium
Marshall begins with the temporary equilibrium of a market on a particular day (1961, pp.332–6); and he chooses for his example the corn-market in a country town. For this market he derives equilibrium price and output from demand and supply schedules of the type long since familiar. However, it should be noted first, that only in temporary equilibrium do Marshall's schedules purport to represent ordered pairs of price and quantity which can be simultaneously chosen, as is the standard interpretation of all such schedules in modern equilibrium theory and second, that even these schedules are influenced by the current expectations of buyers and sellers about the prospects for future prices.

Marshall immediately goes on to consider whether the price arrived at in the market will indeed approximate to the equilibrium price which he has calculated, and concludes that the process of 'higgling and bargaining' is likely to lead to this result, provided that the buyers and sellers are roughly equally matched and tolerably well-informed. Thus, we see that Marshall was well aware both of the need to explain how equilibrium is reached and of the crucial role of information in the explanation. His example was well suited to this purpose; for the corn-dealers in a country town are likely to be few enough to know each other fairly well, and to have been in business long enough to acquire a reliable fund of experience. They do not have to be infallible, for Marshall did not claim that the equilibrium price would always be attained. As in all Marshall's work, equilibrium rests firmly on expectations, and expectations derive from experience – which accumulates over time. Here too, organization aids knowledge: the organization of the market helps to produce the knowledge which is needed to achieve equilibrium.

Nowadays, of course, we have much better proofs of the existence of equilibrium, but we can say very little about its attainability. And this is no accident; for the very assumptions of perfect competition which strengthen the proof of its existence deny the possibility of the special local information which Marshall used to explain how it was reached. As G.B. Richardson has observed, 'the possibility of forming reliable expectations is not independent of the particular market conditions which define the model employed' (1960, p.29). Perfect competition, so convenient for demonstrating the existence of equilibrium, is a very poor basis for expectations.

The short run

Marshall's treatment of short-run costs is recognizably akin to that in modern texts. But his short-run supply curve is not at all the same. The fact that time has to be allowed for movement along it is of some importance, but of far more significance is the argument that, in times of bad trade, price will not follow the marginal cost curve down to the level of average variable cost. On the contrary, Marshall asserts that in times of bad trade:

> . . . the true marginal supply price for short periods . . . is nearly always above, and generally very much above the special or prime cost for raw materials, labour and wear-and-tear of plant, which is immediately and directly involved by getting a little further use out of appliances which are not fully employed. (1961, pp.374–5)

Prices are kept above marginal cost (as that is defined nowadays) first, by the individual producer's fear of spoiling his market, and, second, by his 'fear of incurring the resentment of other producers, should he sell needlessly at a price that spoils the common market for all' (1961, p.374). Both reasons are formally incompatible with perfect competition: the former because no individual producer can protect his future market by attempting to maintain his present price; the latter because the 'common market for all' is a public good, to the maintenance of which the individual producer in a perfectly competitive market has no incentive to contribute.

But, as we have seen, Marshall's world is one in which firms have regular customers and regular suppliers, and might thus expect to be able to transfer some business from a time of depressed prices to one in which they could cover rather more of their costs. Such trading relationships need not imply any possibility of obtaining a persistently higher price than one's competitors; this restraint operates only when demand is generally believed to be temporarily below its normal level, and when it is therefore not in the interests of a customer who is expecting a revival of demand to drive a hard bargain which may put his regular supplier out of business. The connections between buyer and seller, and connections between competitors, which facilitate the development and testing of new ideas, also make the public good of maintained prices rather more of a private good and reduce its private cost. Nor should we forget that, for Marshall, 'normal action is always to be viewed as the consequence of all motives, not the economic one alone' (Whitaker, 1977, p.196).

Like his very short-run theory, Marshall's short-run analysis is firmly based on an information network of a kind which is nowadays automatically dubbed oligopolistic. But it is precisely this 'oligopolistic' information network which makes possible a competitive solution – not the perfectly competitive solution, but not that of imperfect competition either. As Richardson (1960) has explained, the precise outcome for any particular market will depend upon the characteristics of that market, and in particular its information structure; the failure to deduce a general solution from the inadequate assumptions of orthodox theory does not imply that the outcome is indeterminate.

The long run
Long-run effects receive much the most detailed consideration in Marshall's Book V, not only because the long run is the natural home for a theory of economic development, but also because the problems of combining process and equilibrium are most pervasive in the long period. At one point in his exposition, Marshall observes that 'we are here verging on the high theme of economic progress' (1961, p.461) and immediately adds a warning that 'economic problems are imperfectly presented when they are treated as problems of statical equilibrium, and not of organic growth'. The limited applicability of his formal apparatus is a recurrent concern in these chapters. Marshall points out what Arrow and Debreu have since demonstrated, that the complete set of direct and indirect adjustments required for a theoretically perfect long period involves the assumption 'that the requirements of a future age can be anticipated an indefinite time beforehand' (1961, p.379). But no such assumption can be justified for industries which are discovering new combinations, especially those which give rise to increasing returns. Therefore the long-run equilibrium of the industry cannot be rigorously defined. For the firms within it there can be no long-run equilibrium at all.

Now, as has been argued, the pervasiveness of increasing returns was strictly essential to Marshall's view of the economic system, whereas static equilibrium was no more – though also no less – than an extremely convenient analogy. He attempted to preserve the analogy in three ways. First, as we have seen, he put substantial – but by no means exclusive – emphasis on the significance of external economies. Second, he pointed out that the generation of increasing returns through improvements in organization necessarily takes time; one of his marginal summaries affirms that 'the tendency to increasing return does not act quickly' (1961, p.455). His long-run supply diagrams are implicitly three-dimensional; when reduced to two dimensions the horizontal axis measures time as well as output. This practice, which has caused much confusion, symbolizes the impossibility of any adequate discussion of costs which neglects time; but Marshall acknowledged its weakness, and looked for 'a great advance if we could present the normal demand price and supply price as functions both of the amount normally produced and of the time at which that amount became normal' (1961, p.809). The third, and boldest, move was to base the equilibrium of the industry on the transience of its component firms.

Samuelson (1967, p.25) has argued that Marshall's emphasis on increasing returns, and his references to fears of spoiling the market, convict him of pretending 'to handle imperfect competition with tools only applicable to perfect competition'. This is a double error: Marshall neither relies on perfect competition, nor is he discussing imperfect competition as that term has come to be understood. Increasing returns necessarily belong in the long period; the individual businessman's fears of spoiling his market in the short: they never enter the same model.

> Every manufacturer, or other business man, has a plant, an organization, and a business connection, which put him in a position of advantage for his special work. He has no sort of permanent monopoly, because others can easily equip themselves in like manner. (Marshall, 1919, p.196)

The resemblance to conventional textbook models of imperfect competition is only superficial. Not only is quantity demanded a function of elapsed time as well as price; demand, even in this time-dependent form, is demand for a specialized product, not for the output of a particular producer. The ease with which many other firms can replicate his offering excludes any possibility of a falling demand curve for his own brand, as Andrews (1964, p.75) has pointed out. Thus, positions of advantage are not permanent: monopoly, in which they are, is treated quite separately. Firms remain open to competition, and, as they lose vigour, become less able to resist it. Industries survive, and may continue to expand; firms do not. 'Thus the history of the individual firm cannot be made into the history of an industry any more than the history of an individual man can be made into the history of mankind' (Marshall, 1961, p.459). No more can the long-run equilibrium of the industry be explained – or replaced, as happened in the theory of imperfect competition – by the equilibrium of the individual firm.

Nevertheless, an industry is composed of firms, 'and the aggregate production for a general market is the outcome of the motives which induce individual producers to expand or contract their production' (1961, p.459). Marshall sought to encapsulate these motives and their effects in his concept of the representative firm, which represents the reasonable expectations of those considering whether to enter the industry, and the standards of cost which competitors believe they have to meet. The price set by the representative firm covers both prime and supplementary costs, and the price at which it is just willing to undertake a discrete expansion is the long-run supply price of that industry.

Marshall's long-run supply schedule is then derived by examining the effects of different levels of demand on the costs of the representative firm. 'We expect a gradual increase in demand to increase gradually the size and efficiency of the representative firm; and to increase the economies both internal and external which are at its disposal' (1961, p.460). The increase in internal economies arises through the modification of the typical firm's life-cycle. An expansion of demand, by making its environment more favourable, tends both to prolong the period of growth and to increase the rate of growth during that period; and the longer the typical firm is able to grow before its inevitable decline sets in, the lower the level of costs it will achieve in its prime. This favourable shift in the lifetime pattern of costs is reflected in the costs attributed to that analytical fiction, the representative firm, and produces a fall in the industry's supply price. 'This then is the marginal cost on which we fix our eyes' (1961, p.460), not the modern timeless long-run marginal cost.

It is because the pace of growth and the period of growth for individual firms are both severely limited that a growing industry can yield the benefits of falling long-run costs without imposing the penalties of monopoly. In general, it is only when the whole industry is growing fast that the limits are significantly relaxed; and in these circumstances greater size need imply no increase in market share. That is Marshall's solution.

Method and vision
Marshall warns that

> . . . such notions must be taken broadly. The attempt to make them precise over-reaches our strength . . .

> The Statical theory of equilibrium is only an introduction to economic studies; and it is barely even an introduction to the study of the progress and development of industries which show a tendency to increasing return. (1961, pp. 460–1)

Nevertheless, economists were so impressed with the power of the equilibrium method that they began to enquire whether Marshall had made the best use of it. The currently received wisdom is that he did not, although it is not universally agreed whether the best policy is to enshrine perfect competition or to discard it. The initial response was to redefine Marshall's theory of value as a theory of perfect competition, add to it a long-run equilibrium model of the firm, and demonstrate that increasing returns were not compatible with this theory, thus stimulating the extension of monopoly theory into the theory of imperfect competition. (Chamberlin's analysis of monopolistic competition had somewhat different origins. Indeed it has been argued that Chamberlin's firms search for customers in a network of oligopolistic interdependence (Robinson, 1971, pp.33–4, 44–5) – a Marshallian analysis of competitive processes disguised as static equilibrium.)

Economists rediscovered Cournot, without rediscovering the difficulties which Marshall had found in his analysis. 'My confidence in Cournot as an *economist* was shaken when I found that his mathematics re I.R. led inevitably to things which do not exist and have no near relation to reality' (1961, II, p.521). Marshall had sought among businessmen the sources of Cournot's error; when Oxford economists talked to businessmen they likewise found something wrong with imperfect competition – although some Cambridge economists suggested that it was business practice that was wrong.

As was recognized from the outset, the shift to monopoly equilibria, which increasing returns was deemed to require, implied that the market system was not working well. Samuelson (1967, p.39) summarizes the accusation. 'Increasing returns is the enemy of perfect competition. And therefore it is the enemy of the optimality conditions that perfect competition can ensure.' If Marshall were to permit his spirit for once to engage in controversy, he might reply that perfect competition is the enemy of increasing returns (and also, as Chamberlin emphasized, of the product variety which consumers appear to want), and optimality is the enemy of economic progress. Perfect competition is like the perfect tense; it refers to action which is already complete. In Richardson's words, 'it might reasonably be regarded as a denial of Smith's central principle erected into a system of political economy' (1975, p.353). It is a denial of Marshall's central principle too. For a world of perfect competition is a world in which there is nothing further to hope for. As Marshall (1919, p.195) realized, it implies more than the end of economic progress. A 'perfect adjustment is inconceivable. Perhaps even it is undesirable. For after all man is the end of production; and perfectly stable business would be likely to produce men who were little better than machines.' Economics is part of the study of man; and that is why 'the central idea of economics, even when its Foundations alone are under discussion, must be that of living force and movement' (1961, p.xv).

5 Joan Robinson's 'wrong turning'*

In the introduction to the first volume of her *Collected Economic Papers* Joan Robinson declared that when she 'worked out *The Economics of Imperfect Competition* on static assumptions' she 'took the wrong turning'; the correct path would have entailed 'abandoning the static analysis and trying to come to terms with Marshall's theory of development' (1951, pp.vii–viii). This chapter is intended to suggest how she came to take what later appeared to be the wrong path, and to indicate some of the consequences of this error (if error it was). To do so it is necessary to examine the path for some little distance before the turning, and the features of the landscape and the guidebooks which made the wrong path appear so obviously right. We must therefore pay particular, if selective, attention to Marshall, Pigou, and Sraffa.

Marshall

As John Whitaker (1988) has emphasized, Joan Robinson's first book is a product of Cambridge economics; and Cambridge economics was dominated by Alfred Marshall, both directly and in reaction to his work. We therefore begin by considering the aspects of Marshall's thought which influenced the development which we are attempting to explain. Three aspects appear to have been of particular importance: his views of economics as a science, of the purposes of economic study, and of the dominant characteristics of the economic system which he was seeking to analyse.

Pigou (1925, p.86) observed of Marshall's *Principles* that on a first reading 'one is very apt to think that it is all perfectly obvious. The second time one has glimpses of the fact that one does not understand it at all.' Keynes (1972, p.212) made a similar judgement. 'It needs much study and independent thought on the reader's own part before he can know the half of what is contained in the concealed crevices of that rounded globe of knowledge.' This is not accidental; for the 'rounded globe' was deliberately constructed as a contribution to the establishment of economics as a science, which was a prime objective

*This chapter is also being published, with minor differences, in the *Eastern Economic Journal*. I would like to acknowledge helpful comments and suggestions from Geoff Harcourt, Denis O'Brien, and John Whitaker; none of them, however, has any responsibility for the parts of this chapter with which they do not agree.

of Marshall's career, and especially of his tenure of the Cambridge chair. The relabelling of the subject from political economy, and its extraction from the Moral Sciences Tripos, were also contributions to this objective.

Now science, in those days when Newtonian physics was believed to be definitive, appeared to be a body of well established knowledge, founded upon an agreed and systematically developed theoretical structure. There might be disagreement about the ways in which that structure should be extended for the analysis of problems currently unresolved, but its soundness and coherence was not in question. Marshall was therefore concerned to present his subject in a way which emphasized the solidity of its foundations, the continuity of its development, and the universality of its principles. This was especially important if economic ideas were to be widely used by non-experts, as Marshall desired. He appears to have had a personal aversion to controversy; he certainly had a professional aversion to controversy on fundamental issues, which seemed a threat to scientific status. As is well known, he was displeased by Jevons' attack on Ricardo, arguing that it was only by reason of carelessness or infelicity in expression that Ricardo may have inadvertently given the impression of not regarding demand as a major determinant of value. He likewise tended to play down inconsistencies and analytical difficulties in favour of an assured presentation of a complex body of knowledge.

It is not easy to convict Marshall of error (and, as we have already seen in Chapter 4, Sraffa did not in fact do so); but his very careful presentation was sometimes so skilful that it concealed the need for care by those who wished to make use of his ideas. There were indeed a number of very explicit warnings, especially of the dangers of following the logic of static equilibrium analysis too far, but the dangers were not explored and explained: and so, although Joan Robinson's wrong turning was quite clearly signposted by Marshall as a 'no through road', it was as if the sign had been written in invisible ink.

The problem of presentation was made particularly acute by Marshall's motivation for the study of economics – his desire to foster an improvement in the condition of the people. The improvements which he wished for could not be secured merely by a redistribution of income, although his (characteristically cautious) use of the concepts of cardinal utility and consumers' surplus were, in part, intended to facilitate an analytical consideration of redistribution. As with many other reformers of the time, Marshall was much concerned with the ways in which some of the poorer people spent their money, and wished to see improvements in the quality of their demands. This was partly a matter of education and advocacy (the moralizing passages in the *Principles* no doubt reflect Marshall's evangelical background and early clerical ambitions). It was also partly a matter of environment, at work and at home – thus he believed that small firms, by offering more opportunities for working men to exercise their talents, would also tend to improve their preferences, and that suburban living, which could be promoted by the railway companies through an appropriate fares policy, was better than city-centre living. Although demand curves at any one time reflect given preferences, consumers' wants change over time – and these changes are not independent of the economic system. This denial of the exogeneity of demand was to become a characteristic – though not especially Marshallian – theme in Joan Robinson's work.

The influence of activities on wants provided one reason for Marshall's (1961, p.85) agreement with Ricardo that supply required more elaborate attention than demand, as is evidenced by the relative lengths of Books III and IV of the *Principles*, as well as by the bulk of *Industry and Trade* (1919). But that was not the only reason: he believed that there were great possibilities of increasing the productivity of the economy, not so much by efficient allocation (although that was not to be neglected) as by the discovery of better ways of doing things, as well as better things to do, under the stimulus of competition. It was important to Marshall that firms should not be identical, although they might be similar; for it was the continuing experimentation in both product and process which led to steady improvement in the range, quality, and affordability of goods and services. These fairly small differences between firms played a role equivalent to that of genetic variation in Darwinian theory (which was a great influence during Marshall's formative years as an economist).

Progress was likely to be most rapid in those industries in which demand was expanding, and Marshall (1961, p.318) defined his law of increasing returns in terms of the improvements in organization which normally follow upon an increase in demand and thereby lead to more efficient use of both capital and labour. Such increasing returns differ from modern concepts in two ways: they are not strictly returns to scale, and they have to be worked for. Marshall's generalization that 'while the part which nature plays in production shows a tendency to diminishing return, the part which man plays shows a tendency to increasing return' (1961, p.318) embodied a theory of development in which man continually strives to find new ways of loosening or evading natural constraints: in terms of theoretical structures it implied a clear distinction between a static analysis in which costs rise with output and a historical view in which costs fall over time, as a consequence of human efforts and human ingenuity, which are stimulated by an expansion of the market and the threats and opportunities of competition. This insistence on development, and on competition as an agent of progress – as fundamental as with Schumpeter, but very differently handled – is the third aspect of his thought to be noticed; it was the importance of this aspect which Joan Robinson belatedly recognized.

Marshallian increasing returns do not imply a schedule of falling costs in long-run static equilibrium: the costs fall through real time. But Marshall's concern to present his economic world as a rounded globe, and in a way which carried conviction, led him to incorporate increasing returns in a long-period analysis which also made cautious use of the methods of static equilibrium. Although the long period in economic analysis makes no reference to calendar time, but is simply a code-phrase for full adjustment, nevertheless the non-expert reader, whom Marshall was keen to reach, would naturally tend to think in terms of calendar time; and indeed it is a natural question to ask of any long-run adjustment theory how long the process of adjustment may be expected to take. Although Marshall (1961, p.460) distinguished between the cost–quantity relationships appropriate to a formal static analysis and the effects on costs of new methods which were likely to be worked out under the influence of expanding markets, he clearly expected the latter to be important in most examples of sustained growth; since the static long-run analysis by itself would therefore be an inadequate guide to the consequences of increased demand, he did not wish to present it on its own. That would not be true knowledge. A strictly coherent static model might be adequate for the short run (although Marshall did not care to produce what would now be termed a strictly coherent model – he did not assume anonymous competition), but it clearly would not be adequate for the long run, and therefore was not offered. However, although he gave warnings of the danger of pushing static analysis too far, he never gave a precise explanation of what he was doing and why. Much of the argument was inserted into concealed crevices. He thereby laid up a great deal of trouble.

Marshall came to economics because he was anxious to do good; indeed J.M. Keynes (1972, p.200) thought that he was too anxious, and therefore gave insufficient attention to the refinement of analysis in ways which had no apparent practical application. As has been seen, he was primarily concerned to foster improvements within the system by voluntary action, but he also had a vision of an increasing role for government, which was expressed in a remarkable fashion in 'The social possibilities of economic chivalry' by reconstruing *laissez-faire* as 'let the state be up and doing' (Marshall, 1907, p.19). Yet, in his concern to promote the scientific status of economics, he became increasingly conscious of the limitations of economic analysis (limitations which were to be much more tightly drawn by the development of the logic of welfare economics in the 1930s) and correspondingly cautious of specific pronouncements on policy. He thus established an activist tradition in Cambridge which was almost bound to create greater expectations than he was himself prepared to fulfil.

Pigou

That, in Cambridge, the subject-matter of economics was accepted to be economic welfare is clear from the testimony of Sir Dennis Robertson (1952, p.14); and the study of economic welfare included the study of what has come to be called 'market failure' and of the (apparently) corresponding scope for government intervention. This was the major concern of Marshall's successor, A.C. Pigou, whose *Wealth and Welfare* (later developed into *The Economics of Welfare*) appeared in 1912. But with Pigou came an important shift of emphasis; historical development and the working of the competitive process faded into the background and formal analysis became more prominent. Pigou's most influential contribution was the distinction between private and social costs, which was clearly capable of being used to produce a wide-ranging indictment of capitalism – although Pigou himself was usually reluctant to claim that obviously superior arrangements were always readily attainable.

Among the divergencies between private and social costs to which Pigou drew attention, we should particularly note those which arose from the absence of constant returns. He argued that industries subject to diminishing returns would become larger than was socially desirable, while those subject to increasing returns would remain too small: government intervention by taxation and subsidy (or even government operation) would therefore be capable, in principle, of improving on private enterprise. If, like Clapham (1922), one believes that constant returns must always remain a mathematical point, at which the balance of forces changes, then this critique of capitalist efficiency is all-embracing, as J.A. Hobson (1914, p.174) was quick to notice. It is true that Pigou's arguments (which were developed from Marshallian origins) were effectively criticized by Young (1913), Robertson (1924) and Knight (1924) and had to be drastically amended, but the amendments did not appear at all quickly in a revised version of *The Economics of Welfare*, and were never as extensive as they should have been (Ellis and Fellner, 1943).

Marshall's own objections, recorded in his copy of *Wealth and*

Welfare, are of particular significance. He correctly observed that the apparent inefficiency of diminishing returns industries resulted from Pigou's confusion of real costs and transfer payments within static equilibrium, but it was Pigou's strict adherence to static analysis in his treatment of increasing returns industries which attracted particular criticism: 'I think he overrates the possibilities of the statical method.' A more general unease with Pigou's method is reflected in Marshall's comment: 'When he translates W and W into realism, then I may perhaps raise a question' (Bharadwaj, 1972, p.53).

It was Pigou's concern for improving the formal rigour of economic argument which exposed the contradictions between long-run falling costs and perfect competition, which Marshall well understood; and it was Pigou, who was assumed – not quite correctly, as we have just seen – to be the authorized interpreter of Marshall's thought, who translated Marshall's long-period analysis into the language of static perfect competition. He did so with much less qualification than F.H. Knight (1921), who, in his own formalization of perfectly competitive static equilibrium, drew attention to its limitations for the analysis of growth and change. In the process, Pigou (1928, p.239) redefined Marshall's representative firm as an equilibrium firm – although it remained an analytical device with no necessary real-world counterpart – and the equilibrium as perfectly competitive. He then identified the position of equilibrium with the minimum point on the equilibrium firm's U-shaped cost curve, thus throwing the whole burden of increasing returns onto external economies.

If any single action led to the overthrow of the Marshallian system, it was Pigou's establishment of the equilibrium firm as the central instrument of analysis; for it was now a simple step (though not one taken by Pigou) to define an industry in equilibrium as a collection of equilibrium firms (Moss, 1984, p.66); and this exaltation of the equilibrium firm was the work, not of a critic, but of a 'loyal but faithless Marshallian'. The phrase is D.H. Robertson's (1952, p.73); but it has to be admitted that Robertson was also faithless. In his criticism of Pigou's analysis of the welfare gains supposedly attainable by subsidizing industries which were subject to increasing returns, he had insisted that these returns were the results of time and the progress of organization; yet in the symposium which followed the publication of Sraffa's (1926) article, he accepted Pigou's definition of perfect competition as a correct (if uncomfortable) interpretation of Marshall's competition (Robertson, 1930). Mrs Robinson would therefore have been entitled to claim that, if she took the wrong turning, the diversion signs were erected by Marshallians.

Sraffa

Although clearly intended as a criticism of Marshall, and so regarded by supporters and opponents alike, Sraffa's famous article, 'The laws of return under competitive conditions' (1926), had nothing to say about economic development; it was an exercise in the logic of long-run static equilibrium and was therefore not applicable to Marshall's system. If read now, without reference to its context, it appears to be a somewhat schizophrenic exercise reflecting its origin as an amalgamation of two papers, for its criticism of contemporary value theory is directed primarily at the use of a partial equilibrium framework, while its principal proposals are clearly conceived within that very framework.

Sraffa argued that the use of partial equilibrium methods was premised on the negligibility of interactions between the part of the economy (typically a single industry) under consideration and the remainder; interdependency of costs was therefore not acceptable. Yet, only if diminishing returns were attributable to a factor employed solely in the sector being analysed would the consequent increase in costs fail to be experienced simultaneously by other sectors. Any increasing returns which resulted from external economies were similarly inadmissable if they conferred any benefits outside that sector. Economies internal to a single firm were clearly incompatible with perfect competition; so for perfectly competitive partial equilibrium, one was left only with economies which are external to a single firm but internal to the industry. The conclusion to this part of Sraffa's argument is that 'the cost of production of commodities produced competitively . . . must be regarded as constant in respect of small variations in the quantity produced' (1926, pp.540–1). But, instead of developing a competitive analysis based on constant costs – which might appear the natural sequel – Sraffa took a very different line: his response was 'to abandon the path of free competition and turn . . . towards monopoly' (1926, p.542).

Now, there are two odd features of this proposal. The first is the apparent assumption that only perfect competition can be free. The second is that it follows a paragraph in which the illegitimacy of partial equilibrium analysis is restated. It would appear therefore that Sraffa's recommendations apply only to industries in which any scarce factor is peculiar to that industry, and that the sources of decreasing costs are also severely restricted. Analysis of single-industry monopoly has no obvious advantages in handling, or evading, problems of interdependence between industries.

Moreover, despite Sraffa's claim, the path of monopoly does not allow one to make any simple use of a 'well-defined theory' when each industry is populated by a number of rival producers. Sraffa's proposals for the modification of the familiar monopoly demand curve simply ignored the problems of interdependence between firms, in a manner not entirely dissimilar from the ways in which he claimed that interdependence was ignored in partial equilibrium models when costs are not constant. These problems were carried over into the economics of imperfect competition, where they were no better handled.

Joan Robinson's research programme

As the great-granddaughter of the Christian socialist F.D. Maurice, and the daughter of a general who sacrificed his military career for what he thought was his duty to bear witness to the truth, Joan Robinson comfortably assimilated the Cambridge objective of improving the condition of the people, and in particular Pigou's programme of identifying deficiencies in the existing system which might be amenable to governmental remedies. As we have seen, Pigou's treatment of increasing and diminishing returns appeared to reveal such deficiencies in almost every industry, and, although that analysis had to be modified, Sraffa's criticism seemed to reinforce the conclusion that increasing returns would be associated with prices which were too high and outputs which were too low in comparison with the welfare ideal. In this sense what Joan Robinson offered, as O'Brien (1984b) and Whitaker (1988) have pointed out, was a substantial supplement to Pigou's *The Economics of Welfare*. (By contrast, Chamberlin's *Theory of Monopolistic Competition* (1933), as O'Brien has also pointed out and as Chamberlin himself (1961, p.519) made clear, was not intended – although it was often misused – as a contribution to welfare economics.) The debt to Pigou is both general (the theme of market failure) and particular (the explanation of industry equilibrium through the specification of the conditions of equilibrium for the individual firm).

Joan Robinson also followed Pigou in choosing to develop formal models. Indeed, as is often the way with eager and forceful newcomers, she went well beyond him. She was very explicit about her research programme: indeed, the contrast with Marshall is as striking in the clarity of her methodological manifesto as in her method of analysis. Where Marshall had sought to make his analysis its own justification, and to make that justification the provision of useful knowledge for those who were not specialist economists, Joan Robinson began with a clear warning. In words which embody a stronger statement of Keynes's editorial introduction to the Cambridge Economic Handbooks, she presented her book as 'a box of tools . . . [which] can make only an indirect contribution to our knowledge of the actual world' (1933, p.1). Moreover, it was presented to the analytical economist; there was nothing in it for the practical man. 'It is natural enough for the practical man to complain that he asks for bread and the economist gives him a stone. . . . The practical man must be asked to have patience', and may have to wait a long time; meanwhile the economist has a duty to make clear that the questions which can be answered are not the questions which the practical man would like to ask (1933, p.2). It is a remarkably austere vision, especially for someone committed to the view that the task of economic analysis is to improve human welfare.

Later in the book (1933, p.91) the research programme was outlined. The first stage was to analyse the industry supply curve as 'the most abstract problem, in which there is neither time nor market imperfection'. It is not clear whether she accepted Sraffa's argument that such a supply curve must be horizontal. The second stage, represented by her book, was to allow market imperfection but to insist on the full equilibrium of every firm; whether the failure to derive a uniquely determinate supply curve under her assumptions was to be regarded (in 1933) as unfinished business is not clear, but later, when the rest of the research programme had been abandoned – or perhaps transferred elsewhere – the failure was used as a proof of its non-existence. Time was to be introduced at the next stage, and lastly 'factors connected with ignorance, inertia and the "human element" generally would have to be fitted into the scheme'. All this reads nowadays rather like an adumbration of the general equilibrium research programme; and indeed it can hardly be denied that Joan Robinson's first book gave a powerful impulse towards the development of formalism which has been so characteristic of the last fifty years, and which she came to regard with such dismay. That is not to say that any other course of action by her would have stopped or diverted that development; Kaldor (1934), then at the London School of Economics (LSE), who later also became a sceptic, was at that time no less committed to the development of formal and restricted models of equilibrium. Indeed, the eclipse of economic growth by the theory of value may have been an inevitable consequence of the rise of neoclassical economics. It was certainly not by Marshall's desire or design.

Monopoly and competition

Joan Robinson's analysis of monopoly was conventional; it differed from Marshall's, as she noted (1933, p.54), only in its use of marginal conditions in place of the (formally equivalent) maximization of the area which represents profit. It was, however, developed much further, notably by applying the theory to factor markets in order to undermine the marginal productivity theory of wages – which, according to the

Preface to the second edition (1969, p.xii), was for her the main point, as it appears to have been in the capital-switching controversy. (Partial equilibrium analysis is, of course, not a satisfactory basis for a general treatment of income distribution.) Indeed, as Whitaker (1988) emphasizes, this elaboration of monopoly theory, including a comparison with perfect competition, and a general concern, as with Pigou, for welfare implications occupies most of the book. Sraffa had released the analysis of monopoly from its uncomfortable pen, and it had immediately swallowed up the analysis of competition (Robinson, 1933, p.4): what Joan Robinson had done was to exploit the Sraffian emancipation of monopoly to extend the Pigovian programme of welfare economics (disregarding, along the way, Sraffa's objections to partial equilibrium analysis).

One thing is missing from this view of Joan Robinson's book; and that is precisely the analysis which is nowadays known as the theory of imperfect competition – in a phrase, the tangency solution. Here, with the help of Kahn, she took the ideas of group equilibrium which were somewhat insecurely developed in the last part of Sraffa's article, and removed Sraffa's simplifying assumption that the number of firms (and, by implication, the set of products) was fixed. By so doing, she produced an analysis which was apparently more rigorous than Sraffa's, but was actually even less secure.

The problem lies in the demand curve. Marshall considered a statutory monopoly, in which a single firm was granted control over an industry; the demand curve for the industry therefore became the demand curve facing the monopolist. Sraffa's monopolists, however, clearly have no such privileged access to an industry demand curve: as he observed (1926, p.547), one firm's price rise will cause some of its customers to switch to the products of another industry, but some to rival producers within the same industry. Not surprisingly, his treatment of the demand curve facing the individual firm was less than satisfactory.

Joan Robinson (1933, p.21) stated the difficulty very clearly – and defined it away, as Triffin (1940) observed:

> The demand curve for the individual firm may be conceived to show the full effect upon the sales of that firm which results from any change in the price which it charges, whether it causes a change in the prices charged by the others or not. It is not to our purpose to consider this question in detail.

She recognized that this procedure entailed discounting the consequential patterns of future revenues – a 'distressingly vague' conception – but the difficulties must be ignored so that the analysis may proceed

(1933, p.23). The stratagem of dealing with the problems of interdependency by assuming them to have been solved is still a favourite ploy. Indeed, it appears to be an essential element in any 'solution' of the oligopoly problem; and one of the paradoxical consequences of the search for formal rigour which was being pursued by Pigou and Sraffa in their various ways (as well as many others, some of them much better equipped with the mathematical expertise which came to be necessary) is that, far from unifying theory, as Joan Robinson claimed, it caused its disintegration. The pursuit of clarity and rigour led to confusion. How the leading economists of the inter-war years brought about the collapse of the Great Theory, most of them with no such intention, is the theme of Shackle's (1967) masterly survey of this period, which was examined in Chapter 1.

Sraffa's assumption of a fixed set of firms, buttressed by some references to barriers to entry (1926, p.549), gave at least some cover to his use of demand curves appropriate to protected monopoly, and he realized well enough that the less elastic the demand for each of the firms the more plausible was his equilibrium story. However, unlike Sraffa, Joan Robinson had learnt economics at Cambridge, and, in Cambridge, long-run equilibrium had to accommodate changes in the number of firms. This indeed is how she achieved the most striking welfare proposition in the book: that the absence of monopoly profits does not signify the attainment of the desirable equality of marginal cost and price. Looking back in 1969, Joan Robinson selected as the first strong point of her analysis its effective undermining of 'the complex of ideas erected on the slogan of "price equals marginal cost"' (1969, p.xi). In 1933 it provided a new argument to extend Pigou's proposition – based on the shapes of cost curves alone – that competition in a capitalist economy would quite generally fail to achieve the maximization of welfare (in later language, that it would normally be Pareto-inefficient). With falling long-run costs, no firm could secure normal profits without setting price above marginal cost, whatever the demand conditions it faced; if, as Joan Robinson claimed, competition was generally imperfect, then the discrepancy, and the welfare loss, was so much the greater.

It may just be worth speculating (one cannot do more) about Marshall's influence on Joan Robinson's treatment of imperfect competition. Marshall's distinction between the general market and the firm's special market, and the need in some instances to couple the firm's supply curve with its own demand curve, which might be very steep (1961, pp.458–9), are perhaps sufficiently familiar to need no elaboration and were presumably known, even if their significance was not always understood, in the 1920s. (Marshall's discussion contains no hint of a long-run equilibrium of the firm.) What is less familiar – and nowadays quite unacceptable – is that, as was observed earlier, Marshall treated human wants as malleable to education and advocacy, and to the economic process itself. The malleability of wants is clearly an assumption which Joan Robinson found congenial, although she was inclined to redirect the emphasis towards deliberate attempts by firms to mould preferences for their own benefit. Such activity does not appear incompatible with Marshall's treatment which made no claims of optimality. It is perhaps possible that this Marshallian approach may help to account for the absence of any explicit consideration of the determinants of demand (apart from the demand for factors) and, in particular, for the unanalysed assumption that demand curves would both shift and change shape between short-run and long-run equilibrium. But Marshall himself would surely have wished for some explicit treatment of product differentiation, which received no mention in *The Economics of Imperfect Competition*.

The formal analysis of demand in this book consisted of nothing more than a definition of each producer as a monopolist of his own output (1933, p.5), facing a demand curve which was determined by the availability of substitutes; this demand curve was normally falling, but as a special case might be perfectly elastic (1933, pp.50–1). Joan Robinson clearly had in mind a situation in which preferences are defined over producers; but she neither considered what preferences are consistent with an economy of optimizing agents – the 'assumption which makes the analysis of value possible' (p.6), nor recognized (as Chamberlin did from the first) that such preferences undermined the strong welfare implications of her analysis.

The analysis itself was weakened, rather than strengthened, by her insistence on developing a long-run equilibrium. For she gave no sufficient reason why any single firm should be able to sell a product, however differentiated – and remember that product differentiation was not explicitly considered in her book – at a price higher than that acceptable to any other firm; and all firms were assumed to have access to the same technology and the same costs. This conclusion is not invalidated by increasing returns – which we had better call economies of scale, since Marshallian increasing returns are the result of a historical process. If these extend over a sufficient range of output, there may indeed be only one firm, but that firm will only be making normal profits, since those are the only terms on which it can obtain the business. In modern phraseology, even if economies of scale exclude competition in the market, there will still be competition for the market.

With fully rational producers and consumers, it is impossible for any monopoly advantage to be permanently exploited. Exploitation is incompatible with equilibrium. That conclusion was reached by Andrews (1964) and by Schumpeter (1943).

This argument does not demonstrate that welfare losses through imperfections of competition are no problem (although both Andrews and Schumpeter, for their different reasons, thought that they did not call for much action); what it does demonstrate is that the first two stages of Joan Robinson's research programme are not adequate to establish the case. Only by examining processes can one hope to demonstrate that the sloping demand curves for individual firms will be preserved. But, of course, by examining processes one also brings in many more considerations, not least the changes in technique and costs which are produced by continuing competition and enquiring minds; one therefore loses the simplicity which is attainable by abstract models. It was to obtain this simplicity that the Marshallian programme was gradually (and not always consciously) abandoned.

Analysis and policy
The change in style between Marshall and Joan Robinson could hardly be more marked. The sociological and psychological arguments disappeared (in contrast to Keynes's work) and we are left with an abstract presentation which clearly points the way to the axiomatic method. As we have seen, Joan Robinson emphasized that her analysis leaves us some way from any clear policy conclusions, although, since she appears to have been somewhat disappointed by the apparent policy ineffectiveness of Marshall's more direct approach, she maintained (at that time) her faith in the superiority of roundabout methods of theory development for generating policy prescriptions. Her warnings were repeated at the end of the book, and most – but not all – of her suggestions were fairly cautious: in effect she argued that her analysis allows one to identify the elements about which more information is required, those which require further analysis, and those which depend on political or social judgement.

The programme is clearly indicated, but it was not followed. There was not even any attempt to examine the evidence on demand and competition, absolute reliance being placed on the 'well-known fact' that firms would be only too happy to increase sales at their present prices, if such sales were to be available. That Marshall had offered a rather different explanation for such phenomena, in terms of growth and change, seemed to demonstrate that Marshall's explanation was inadequate. Such evidence as did appear, notably from the Oxford

Economists Research Group (Hall and Hitch, 1939), was met (primarily by Joan Robinson's allies) with the argument that it was inconsistent not just with the particular analysis of imperfect competition, but with the notion of rational behaviour which was fundamental to all economic theory. That it might suggest the need to proceed to a later stage in the research programme outlined in 1933 seems never to have been considered. Of course, it should not be forgotten that by the time the results of the Oxford inquiries became known Joan Robinson, along with other economists, had switched her principal attention to Keynes's theory of unemployment, and, although she commented occasionally on imperfect competition, she never attempted any significant further development or revision of the theory.

In those later comments she did not always heed her own warnings. Her methodological prescription of 1933 appears to have been seen increasingly as a serious impediment to her desire to build a better society; it was unreasonable to ask the practical man to have patience for the length of time which might be necessary. Having, in her own phrase, given a stone when asked for bread, she was inclined to invoke a miracle, and command that the stone be made bread, basing policy prescription directly on the abstract theory. But it was not Joan Robinson who offered the most detailed blueprint; that distinction goes to James Meade (1936) who, in a volume of confident proposals over a wide range of economic issues, explained how easy it would be to restructure industry in a way which, even allowing for some unfavourable incentive effects, could not fail to produce substantial improvements in economic welfare.

As we have seen more recently in other contexts – notably in monetary and macroeconomics – the rhetoric of the formal model is extremely powerful; other models no further from the beginning of their research programmes than Joan Robinson's imperfect competition have had greater influence on policy than hers. The desire to do good does not always have beneficial results. The Marshallian balance was lost. Yet Marshall is perhaps not without responsibility: despite his great respect for many businessmen, he had concluded his inaugural lecture with his hopes of increasing 'the numbers of those, whom Cambridge, the great mother of strong men, sends out into the world with cool heads but warm hearts' to change that world for the better (Pigou, 1925, p.174). That governments advised by Cambridge economists could substantially improve economic welfare is a belief which Joan Robinson shared with Keynes; it is a belief which seems to be part of the Marshallian tradition. It is not extinct in Cambridge today –

although there seems to be some disagreement about which Cambridge economists can be trusted to give the advice.

Conclusion

Marshall's desire to present economics as a body of established and agreed knowledge led him to be cautious in his claims; his desire to make his work generally accessible led him to banish mathematics from his text and to allow no more than geometry in his footnotes. Although he took proper note of unresolved issues, he did not place them firmly on the research agenda in the manner of Hicks: in building a coalition one normally gives little attention to those differences between the parties which cannot easily be accommodated. What made this attitude particularly important was his third objective, which was to present the subject-matter of economics as a study of the forces which cause change and movement. By 1890, the analytical methods of economics were developing in a way which was making this more difficult. Marshall valued these methods highly and had made his own contribution to them. But there was simply no way in which equilibrium analysis and economic development (which implied changes in the data from which equilibria could be derived) could be combined in a single consistent body of theory. Nevertheless, in order to promote his first two objectives he wished to present it as a single body, which was not obviously inconsistent: hence what Richardson (1960, p.23) called his 'characteristically . . . careful imprecision', and what Joan Robinson called fudge.

His motto 'the many in the one, the one in the many' – an old favourite by the time it was inscribed in *Industry and Trade* – was intended simultaneously to warn of the need for care in the application of economic doctrine to problems which are necessarily complex and to insist nevertheless on the fundamental unity of the discipline. Yet his very success in presenting his 'rounded globe of knowledge', with its crevices so deftly concealed, was a source of danger. It is an interesting question whether Marshall would have contributed more effectively to the development of economics if his caution in drawing conclusions had been matched by candour in explaining the formidable obstacles to the development of economic analysis. If Joan Robinson took a wrong turning, it was at least partly because Marshall had striven so hard to convince everyone that there was a single broad highway.

6 The working of a competitive economy: G.B. Richardson's post-Marshallian analysis*

The coordination of economic activity is, for most economists, the central issue in our subject. Most attempts to demonstrate either the potential for, or the obstacles to effective coordination have focused on the logical possibilities of equilibrium, and the implications for equilibrium of alternative economic (especially market) structures. Few economists have enquired how equilibrium might be achieved. As we have seen in Chapter 4, Marshall was one of the few; but his treatment was characteristically diffident and soon disregarded. Forty years after the last edition of the *Principles* to be published in Marshall's lifetime, there appeared what might be called an extensive post-Marshallian analysis of the relationships between structure, knowledge and coordination. G.B. Richardson's *Information and Investment*, published in 1960, was also disregarded, but is now being rediscovered. This chapter is intended to promote further discovery.

Richardson's primary concern is economic policy. Now, the standard theoretical approach to economic policy has been based on the concept of Pareto efficiency, and, hardly less fundamentally, on the proposition that 'Every competitive equilibrium is a Pareto optimum; and every Pareto optimum is a competitive equilibrium' (Dorfman, Samuelson, and Solow, 1958, p.410, quoted by Richardson, 1960, p.43). This equivalence between perfectly competitive equilibria and Pareto-efficient allocations might seem automatically to demonstrate the supreme virtue of a perfectly competitive market structure – subject, of course, to the usual reservations about distribution, externalities and public goods, none of which are at issue in this chapter. But we need to show that this structure is capable first of generating and then of maintaining such an equilibrium; and that entails some explanation of causes and

*This chapter is a revised version of 'Competition and imperfect knowledge: the contribution of G B Richardson', *Scottish Journal of Political Economy*, vol. 33, pp.145–58, and is reproduced by permission of the Scottish Economic Society. An earlier version was presented at the annual conference of the History of Economics Society, at George Mason University, Virginia, in May 1985.

consequences, which, as Hahn (1984) keeps reminding us, no investigation of equilibrium conditions can in themselves provide.

Expectations and equilibrium

Formal microeconomic theory is founded on the logic of rational choice; but that theory is quite regularly used to predict the outcomes of a set of choices. Now choices depend upon beliefs, but outcomes depend on the facts of a situation. Here are two distinct analytical problems: only by confining ourselves to equilibrium situations can we collapse them into one. There are a number of circumstances in which choices may produce the outcomes expected, and for which equilibrium solutions derived from models of choice may therefore be valid predictors; the most obvious, and at first glance the simplest, are those circumstances in which beliefs correspond to facts. Indeed, the assumption that beliefs are correct is, under the title of perfect – sometimes probabilistically perfect – knowledge or of rational expectations, routine in many equilibrium models. The need for such an assumption has been strongly reinforced by the direction which theory has taken. As long as one is content with an equilibrium of the industry, it may be permissible to have erroneous decisions, provided that the errors cancel out; but once theorists chose to insist on the equilibrium of every single transactor (including all potential transactors) in the economy, the requirements became much more stringent (Richardson, 1960, pp.4–5). Just how stringent has not been properly recognized.

The significance of beliefs is not confined to questions of movement towards equilibrium; even if equilibrium has been achieved, an appropriate set of beliefs is essential to its preservation. Richardson notes (1960, p.8) that 'equilibrium is not secured merely by the existence of a particular set of economic activities in themselves, but by their coexistence with a particular set of beliefs'. But the standard type of analysis offers no reasons why economic agents should come to hold the special set of beliefs required to sustain equilibrium. Proofs of existence do not demonstrate the feasibility of realization.

As Hayek observed:

> The statement that, if people know everything, they are in equilibrium is true simply because that is how we define equilibrium. The assumption of a perfect market in this sense is just another way of saying that equilibrium exists, but does not get us any nearer an explanation of when and how such a state will come about. (1937, p.45)

Rational expectations equilibria are likewise defined, but not explained. Hahn's (1973; 1984, p.59) redefinition of equilibrium as a state in which the economy 'generates messages which do not cause agents to change the theories which they hold or the policies which they pursue' does get us somewhat nearer an explanation by identifying the elements which require analysis, but Hahn (1973; 1984, p.61) seeks to dissuade us from investigating the processes by which agents might acquire theories or policies which would meet his conditions. Can a perfectly competitive market structure generate a set of beliefs which will enable the economy to achieve and maintain a perfectly competitive equilibrium? This is the question which Richardson poses.

Producers require two types of information. First, they need to know the production possibilities open to them. Richardson (1960, pp. 29–30) calls such knowledge *technical information*; it may be regarded (for the present) as objective and available, and producers have an obvious incentive to acquire it. But if there are costs of obtaining such information, some will not be sought, and thus beliefs about the available technology may be erroneous. This practical difficulty – potentially of great importance for appraisals of both allocative and X-efficiency – Richardson does no more than mention, for he wishes to concentrate on the theoretical difficulties inherent in the second kind of information, which he calls *market information*. He admits that this term is being used in an unusually wide sense, to include knowledge not only of market demands but also of potential market supply – that is, the intentions of those in a position to supply competitive and complementary products. Now it turns out that much of the necessary information cannot be supplied by a perfect market.

The problem can be seen most clearly by postulating an out-of-equilibrium situation (Richardson, 1960, pp.17–20). Suppose that there is an excess demand for a particular commodity which is produced under perfectly competitive conditions. We ignore the well known difficulties of reconciling the standard conditions of perfect competition with excess demand or supply, and follow the standard practice of imposing a demand shock on a perfectly competitive equilibrium. Then the price of this commodity (however it is set) must exceed the average costs of production, including normal profits. Let us suppose, further, that all producers and potential entrants believe that present demand conditions will persist indefinitely, an assumption for which there is no warrant in formal theory, although it is made automatically in standard comparative equilibrium analysis. There is thus a need to increase capacity in order to achieve a new long-run equilibrium; and the excess of short-run price over long-run costs signals an opportunity for profiting by additional investment. It is normally taken for granted that the profit opportunity will ensure the necessary investment. At this point Richardson invites us to pause and consider a simple question: how does each producer, and potential producer, know how much plant to order?

The question is simple; the answer is not. If he is to maximize his profit, each producer needs to know what the total increase in capacity will be in order to decide how much plant he should install (Richardson, 1960, p.33). Even if the optimum size of plants is known to be unaffected by the change in demand – and Marshall, at least, made no such assumption – each potential entrant needs to know whether the entry of others will leave profitable room for him. But there is no mechanism whereby such information about investment intentions can be made available, given the initial assumptions about the nature of the market. As practical economists, we may argue that producers grope their way towards equilibrium by some process of trial and error; but the imaginary groping which might be organized by a fictitious (and monopolistic) auctioneer is the only process obviously compatible with the model which is supposed to guide policy choice.

Richardson (1960, p.34) uses the analogy of a peculiar lottery in which all are free to subscribe as much as they wish: if total subscriptions fall short of £1 million, each subscriber receives a proportionate share of a prize; if the total exceeds £1 million, then each subscriber loses a part of his subscription, the proportion being dependent on the total amount of the excess. Investment in the conditions of a perfect market appears to be just such a lottery. Nor is this simply a problem of information transfer: there is a logical dilemma. Each individual can make a fully informed decision only if every other decision-maker has made a firm commitment; and this situation applies to them all. As Coddington (1975b, p.154) has observed, perfect information for all decision-makers is logically impossible; there can be, at most, one omniscient being and there is no particular reason why there should even be one.

Richardson (1960, p.35) points out that the theoretical difficulty is precisely that which makes oligopoly outcomes indeterminate in standard theory; although the assumption of perfect competition avoids overt interdependence between any two or more specified competitors, it does not avoid interdependency between any one competitor and all the rest. Now oligopoly is the one market structure in which the need to explain equilibrium as the result of interaction between agents has long been recognized; yet no general rigorous theory of the process has been discovered. We can thus hardly expect to find a ready-made solution anywhere within the analysis of perfectly competitive markets. Indeed, given the supporting assumptions about freedom of entry, the information requirements for fully informed optimal decisions in perfect competition appear even more formidable than in oligopoly. 'A general profit opportunity, which is both known to everyone, and equally capable of being exploited by everyone, is, in an important sense, a profit opportunity for no-one in particular' (Richardson, 1960, p.57).

Interdependency persists when equilibrium is reached (if ever); and the consequential problems remain. The knowledge that the present price yields precisely normal profits is not adequate for a decision to replace plant which has come to the end of its useful life: that decision requires information about the price to be expected when any new plant is in production, and, even if producers are assured (and how is this assurance to be provided?) that demand conditions are fixed for ever, the future price will still be affected by investment (and disinvestment) decisions by competitors. A perfectly competitive market structure can provide no information about such decisions.

Essential imperfections

If the perfectly competitive model leads us into this theoretical impasse, how then is the necessary information made available to producers in a competitive industry? Richardson's (1960, pp.49–71) answer to that is, quite simply, that the provision of adequate information depends on what are usually regarded as the imperfections of competition. Imperfections are rather like friction – a complication to abstract theory, but essential to the working of the world as we know it. The imperfections are what makes competition possible.

Richardson (1960, pp.53–7) discusses two kinds of imperfection. One is implicit collusion, by which all producers act in what is recognized to be the general interest of them all. We may here, of course, be faced with a public goods problem, in that the direct pecuniary interest of one producer may very well conflict with the general benefit of the group; but this problem may be circumvented in part by allowing a wider definition of producer preferences than is normally permitted. For, if a producer obtains satisfaction from cooperative behaviour and suffers, either in social contacts or in his conscience, as a result of pursuing his own narrow interest (and the connotations of such words as 'blackleg' and 'antisocial' suggest that these may be rather strong preferences), then we may well expect such implicit collusion. Marshall (1961, pp.374–5) certainly expected it, and he was a good theoretician who knew what went on in the world.

Richardson relies on implicit collusion for stability rather than for balanced response, although if there is collusion over, for instance, market share, then responses may be tolerably well coordinated also.

The weight of the argument is placed upon a series of constraints on independent action – usually regarded as imperfections – which limit the response of competitors and therefore provide some reassurance that there is room for each of them to expand a little in response to market opportunity. Thus, restraints on free choice are the condition for any intelligent choice at all (Richardson, 1960, p.56).

Richardson presents the first of these constraints as a paradox (1960, p.57). If perfect information is logically impossible, may not highly imperfect information serve? An opportunity may be the more readily seized if it is not widely known. 'Ignorance, by checking the response of some, may be a necessary condition for any response by others.' This idea accords well with Shackle's (1972, pp.409–21) concept of profit arising from differential valuation: the imagination, or privileged knowledge, of a few leads them to anticipate a higher value for a collection of assets (perhaps by their transformation into new products) than the generally agreed valuation which is reflected in their current price.

Kirzner's (1973) explanation of equilibration through the actions of entrepreneurs who are more alert than their fellows similarly rests on an explicit rejection of perfect knowledge as an adequate explanation of the working of markets, and of a perfectly competitive market struc-ture as a policy ideal. Casson's (1982) more elaborate treatment of entrepreneurship and the market economy also places considerable emphasis on the competitive threat to the entrepreneur, leading to the implicit paradox that a perfectly competitive market structure is a fatal obstacle to the attainment of perfectly competitive equilibrium.

Both Kirzner and Casson assume that the entrepreneur is likely to be 'right, while everyone else is wrong' (Casson, 1982, p.14); but there is no need for us to ignore the possibility either that his ideas are mistaken or that he is himself ignorant of impending actions by other entrepreneurs which will invalidate his own estimates. Richardson does not ignore such possibilities, which would be a serious embarrassment to a theory which sought to demonstrate the inevitability of equilibrium. But, if Richardson is aiming at an explanation of the working of a competitive economy, there is no reason for him to provide mechanisms which are guaranteed to work well; mechanisms which are clearly fallible have more appeal. Indeed, there must be something seriously wrong with any general model of perfect coordination.

The second constraint to be considered is the set of limitations on the rate of expansion. Richardson's firms, like Marshall's, operate in time. Therefore a capacity for infinite expansion over many years creates no particular difficulty for him; all that is necessary is that each firm should be confident that its competitors cannot do very much before the fruition of its own, similarly limited, expansion plans. Richardson (1960, pp.59–60) points to financial and managerial limitations on the rate of growth of a firm – limitations now familiar from the work of Marris (1964) and Mrs Penrose (1959) – noting that these limitations appear as imperfections in standard theory. He further explains how barriers to entry, imposed by the need to acquire particular skills, may severely restrict the influx of newcomers within the time-span that is crucial to the making of present commitments. It is relevant to note that both natural and artificial barriers are similarly invoked by Schumpeter (1934) to provide the temporary protection needed by entrepreneurs in their beneficial activities.

The third constraint exemplifies most clearly of all the way in which Richardson turns to those elements which have regularly been used to demonstrate the inefficiency of markets in order to explain how competitive markets can operate at all; for this third factor is the imperfection of the product market. Expansion of competitors will be checked by the prospective difficulty of achieving more than a limited increase in sales (1960, pp.64–5), because of the marketing problems noted by Marshall (1961, pp.286–7, 457–8), while the firm's own market connections, which Richardson discusses in some detail (1960, pp.62–71), afford some protection to prudent expansion. The protection afforded by goodwill, as Andrews (1964, p.77) also observes, takes the form of stable custom, rather than higher prices. This dual function of a supposedly obnoxious feature of a market economy was an essential element in Marshall's theory of economic evolution (which has been examined in Chapter 4), and was not, as is usually assumed, a careless aberration from a rudimentary theory of perfect competition. In fact, the theory of perfect competition is a careless aberration from Marshall's account of the working of a competitive economy (O'Brien, 1984a, pp.26–31). Andrews' (1949; 1951) endeavours to preserve and develop Marshallian analysis were not well received outside Oxford but, within Oxford, they appear to have influenced Richardson.

Market connections may also be important for another reason: the achievement and maintenance of equilibrium is likely to require the coordination not only of competitive but also of complementary activities (Richardson, 1960, pp.72–87). Such coordination is fostered by the firm's 'external organization', on which Marshall (1961, p.458) placed characteristically discreet emphasis; but this part of his analysis was firmly lodged in the 'concealed crevices of that rounded globe of knowledge' (Keynes, 1972, p.212). Even if the information problems of competitive equilibrium had been appreciated, it is unlikely that any difficulties would have been recognized with complementarities, since the perfectly competitive firm which supplanted the firm of Marshall's analysis is characterized as a purchaser of primary inputs and supplier of final outputs – inter-firm transactions being netted out in the interests of a simple model. Few organizations resemble this model; the characteristic transaction in the market economy involves the purchase or sale of an intermediate good or service, as Andrews repeatedly emphasized. Thus, the establishment of equilibrium requires the simultaneous adjustment of a variety of related activities which are undertaken by different organizations.

When inter-firm trade is in standard goods and services – the homogeneous commodities of the perfectly competitive models – the information problems and the means of coping with them are similar to those of competitive interdependencies; but, as Richardson has explained in some detail in a later article (1972), many inter-firm transactions involve goods or services which are designed to meet the specific needs of the purchaser. It is clear that such 'closely-complementary activities', as Richardson (1972, p.891) calls them, cannot be reconciled with a world of perfectly competitive markets; but although the relationships often exhibit the features which, according to Williamson (1975), lead to the coordination of activities within a vertically integrated business, the need for collaboration does not always lead to the replacement of market by hierarchy, or to the exclusion of substantial elements of competition. Indeed, one may be struck by the variety of arrangements to be found (Richardson, 1972, p.896).

The assortment of production

The argument so far has been conducted within the usual specification of the economic problem: the allocation of economic activities in relation to a notionally complete listing of goods, preferences, resources, and technology. Richardson contends that a perfectly competitive market structure, although it may be formally compatible with a perfectly competitive allocation, is incapable of allowing agents to acquire the information which they would need to arrive at such an equilibrium; only market imperfections can permit that – although they certainly do not guarantee the attainment of equilibrium, even within this specification of the problem. Kirzner's (1973) critique of the perfectly competitive market, though differently directed, operates within the same rules.

The criticism of standard equilibrium models is obviously strengthened when one admits that some of the data which are notionally provided at the outset are in fact generated by the economic process

itself. Technical information is not, after all, objective and available.
If the initial lists are open to extension by the exercise of entrepreneurial
imagination (Richardson, 1960, p.105), then neither general equilibrium
nor Pareto optimality can have any precise meaning, and the conditions
necessary to secure a perfectly competitive market structure are incompatible with economic progress. Here Richardson is to be compared
with Schumpeter (1934) instead of Kirzner. This is not to deny that
equilibrium models, used with modesty and discretion, may be useful
aids to both prediction and evaluation. Indeed, Richardson's emphasis
(1960, pp.103–4) on the ability of a changing assortment of goods
to satisfy, in various ways, a relatively stable structure of consumer
preferences foreshadows Lancaster's (1966) respecification of consumer
theory in terms of characteristics – although Richardson might refer
interested enquirers to Marshall's (1961, pp.86–91) treatment. But such
models can hardly provide rigorous solutions to the problems of real
economies.

Theory and policy
Economics attempts to deduce behaviour from a specification of structure, but economists (unlike students of organizational behaviour) have
not often considered the effects of structure on information. Richardson
alone has thought to investigate the logic of information flow within a
market system, and the structural requirements for adequate information. He concludes that, in perfecting the model of perfectly competitive equilibrium, economists have refined away the essential mechanism. As Samuelson (1955, pp.1769–70) once acknowledged, 'it may
be precisely the ignored variables that keep the real world stable'.

The implications may not be very serious for some simple uses of
comparative equilibrium analysis – although economists who are not
content with instrumentalism might wish for better theories. For welfare
economics, however, they are of fundamental importance. The features
to which Richardson has called attention are all incompatible with the
achievement of Pareto-optimality, as usually defined, and indeed with
any simple rules of policy for mergers, monopolies, and restrictive
practices. Richardson discusses these policy issues at length, and time
and again reaches the conclusion that particular attitudes and patterns
of behaviour may be harmful or beneficial, according to degree and to
circumstances.

Let us take just one example. Short-run price stability in the face of
fluctuating demand may be highly beneficial; as E.A.G. Robinson
(1931, p.96) pointed out in a similar context, it is not usually the most
productive beasts that survive a famine. But stability in the face of

long-run trends is much less likely to be desirable. It is not easy to find an arrangement which will achieve the former while avoiding the latter (Richardson, 1960, pp.130–3); it apparently becomes no easier when governments take a hand. For demand changes do not usually carry a label which identifies them as short-term or long-term (still less a money-back guarantee).

Much of Richardson's discussion of industrial policy turns on the need to provide some assurance to decision-makers. This assurance is normally supposed to be contained in the assumption of perfect knowledge, apparently so convenient but, as Richardson has shown, logically untenable. (Schumpeter (1934) paradoxically, but unjustifiably, relies on the values of what appears to be a perfectly competitive general equilibrium to provide the basis for those rational calculations which, he claims, entrepreneurs must be able to make if they are to destroy that equilibrium.) One dangerous consequence of this assumption is that it has led microeconomists seriously to underrate the importance of stability of expectations. Against a background assumption of perfect knowledge it is easy to call for adjustment of prices, and of government policy, to each new situation – even though such adjustments would not be necessary if earlier knowledge had indeed been even probabilistically perfect. But the effect of such frequent adjustments is to produce a well-founded distrust in the durability of whatever may be the present price or policy. At best, this destroys the effectiveness of such changes; at worst, it may destroy the confidence needed to make any positive decisions at all.

The weighting of opinions
As we have seen, Richardson begins by examining the effects of structure on the dissemination of information – a theme which Leijonhufvud (1981) has pursued in other contexts; the argument is then extended to embrace the problems which arise when the list of data cannot be completed. As Richardson observes (1960, p.202), 'it seems highly inappropriate to graft on to these circumstances the assumption of perfect knowledge, however interpreted'. Towards the end of his book, he turns to a more substantial discussion of what might be called the Shackle problem: that the basic data simply do not exist, and cannot exist, no matter what information system is devised. There is no certain knowledge about the future, not even certain knowledge of probability distributions. There are expectations (or guesses) formulated with greater or less care; and unfortunately those formulated with the greatest care are by no means always the most accurate. The New York State legislature has deliberated on these difficulties, and enacted in

Section 899 of the Code of Criminal Procedure that persons 'Pretending to Forecast the Future' shall be considered disorderly under Subdivision 3, Section 901 of the Code and liable to a fine of $250 and/or six months in prison. Many businesses implicitly share this view, and have abandoned conventional forecasts in favour of a range of plausible scenarios.

Thus, it is necessary to decide whose view of the future to accept, or what weight to give to differing views. As Richardson (1960, p.201) emphasizes, this decision cannot be avoided (although it may be taken by default): 'the need to choose between different opinions, and therefore the need to specify the mandate to be given to particular decentralized agencies, will impose itself on any economic system, however organised.' In an administrative system, the mandate may depend on hierarchical status, skill in advocacy or in intrigue, or political clout. In a market system, mandates are allotted through the capital market – more precisely, through imperfections in the capital market.

If the future is known for certain, or with assured probabilities, then any restriction on a producer's access to funds prevents the achievement of optimum patterns of investment; but if we do not know whether the producer's estimates of profitability will turn out to be well-founded, then we do not know whether it will be optimal to give him access to unlimited funds at the market rate of interest. 'In view of this consideration, it is misleading to regard the differences between firms, with respect to borrowing power, as evidence of "imperfections in the capital market"; they are merely evidence of the particular weighting system which the competitive economy employs in distributing the authority to allocate resources' (Richardson, 1960, p.201). The need to decide how much trust to place in the producer's forecasts introduces another reason for distinguishing between borrower's and lender's risk: the risk that the lender takes on the borrower's judgement. It is surprising that Keynes, who, as Richardson (1960, pp.100, 144) notes, was well aware of the uncertain foundations of investment decisions, makes no mention of this factor in his brief discussion of the two types of risk in the *General Theory* (1973a, pp.144–5).

Given the need to decide on the mandate for each producer, and given the argument that this mandate should depend on some judgement by others of his credibility, then differential access to funds would appear to be one (but not the only) reasonable basis for such decisions. Large and well established companies are favoured; but, in a competitive economy, a company is unlikely to become large and well established except through success in anticipating profitable opportunities. It is perhaps just as reasonable to put ever-increasing trust in a firm whose credibility has been steadily reinforced by the success of its ventures as it is to put increasing reliance on a scientific hypothesis that has been repeatedly tested without refutation. Indeed, the fundamental process is the same in the two cases. Similar reliance on past success is also likely to be the principal criterion for extending the mandate of a manager or a government planner – or for awarding research grants to academics. Experience from the past provides the only evidence from which we can attempt to anticipate the future.

The scientific analogy reminds us that the method of allotting mandates is far from infallible. The next venture may destroy a firm's credibility just as the next test may destroy a hypothesis; and any failure means that, in hindsight, resources have been misallocated. More serious is the possibility that the quality of a firm's judgement may be highly dependent on a certain range of activity or a certain range of conditions and that success within this range may tempt it outside (maybe unwittingly) and may tempt investors to provide it with ample funds for doing so. If investors follow success, without understanding the conditions of success, the capital market is likely to make a good many mistakes. So too are economic theorists.

The counterpart to this problem is the poor credit status of the newcomer with a brilliant idea. The deficiency of the capital market as a provider of venture capital has long given rise to complaints, and it presents difficulties for Kirzner's analysis of entrepreneurship. But although the deficiency is serious, we should be clear as to its basis, which is the problem of estimating the credibility of an untried person with an untried idea. Almost all brilliant ideas are failures; if much money is put into them, they may become very expensive failures. Even within a company, great difficulties are experienced in sorting out the few winners (which is why research and development is mostly development, and why most development leads to rejection); nor do governments seem to find it easy. It is fairly clear that the capital market does not do a particularly good job here; but its performance looks rather less dismal when compared with that of the alternatives.

What are called capital market imperfections limit the mandate of any producer; but producers rarely use their mandate to the full (Richardson, 1960, pp.150–66). For they are unlikely to have absolute confidence in their forecasts, and will therefore wish to retain some reserves against adverse contingencies and some spare capacity to respond to unforeseeable opportunities. This is one important consequence of a rational expectation of unpredictable shocks. They wish, that is, either to retain cash or to leave some potential credit untapped, lest some unforeseen demands on their resources bring them to ruin, or (more hopefully) offer a brighter prospect than any which is presently avail-able. This desire for liquidity causes part of the mandate to remain unused, and part to be employed in securing Ansoff's (1965) flexibility objectives. Here is a further source of inefficiency, when judged on the assumption of perfect knowledge; it is also a further example of the propensity of that assumption to produce misleading judgements. There are macroeconomic implications too. Unwillingness to use the mandate is (in very nearly these words) the beginning of Marshall's explanation of trade depression: 'though men have the power to purchase they may not choose to use it' (1961, p.710); on the other hand, reserve capacity may permit increased economic activity without higher prices.

Search and competition
The implications of ignorance for the allocation of resources reinforce Richardson's argument that failure to achieve some artificially specified Pareto-optimality is insufficient reason for condemning a market (or any other) system. For now, as Demsetz (1969) has also argued, we have not only to judge one economic system in relation to another, rather than to some unattainable ideal; if the fundamental data cannot exist, except by mere assertion, then no appropriate Pareto-optima can be computed. We are not simply choosing between solution programmes for very complex, but precisely stated, problems; we are interested in the search for data, and even for the problems themselves, and in a search programme that, like science, must work by trial and error (as explained in Chapter 2). As Popper has repeatedly emphas-ized, certainty is not attainable. The best we can do is to seek to ensure that the trials are well thought out and carefully conducted, and that any errors are not too disastrous and are swiftly recognized.

A market system may be readily characterized as a means of organ-izing these processes, and it is Richardson's central theme that familiar elements which are usually disparaged as imperfections are essential parts of the search mechanism. The replacement of markets by a tightly coordinated planning system does not obviously resolve the problems. Although it may formalize communications, it does not necessarily improve them, for reasons well known to organization theorists. More-over, it is likely to reduce the area of search and to concentrate the mandate for decision to a dangerous extent.

An economy, like a scientific community, should be open to criticism and to novel conjectures. The lack of coherence between the planning assumptions of different firms is a means of avoiding that close-coupling which can be disastrous in the event of error (Richardson, 1960, p.87), as has been demonstrated in more than one electrical distribution system, and in planning systems too. 'While every man will admit to his fallibility, few of them, as Mill observed, think it necessary to take precautions against it' (Richardson, 1960, p.219). The precautions must therefore be built into the system. This, of course, is Popper's (1966) argument for the open society. It is very different from the conventional argument for perfect competition.

Conclusion

Richardson was unfortunate in his timing, for his analysis raised unwelcome questions about the value of the general equilibrium research programme which Debreu (1959) had recently anchored in seemingly impregnable axiomatic foundations, and might have inhibited the exploitation of the magnificent theoretical opportunities embodied in that research programme. Richardson's arguments directed attention towards the study of processes and institutional arrangements, a prospect hardly to be compared with the alternative attractions of rigour, elegance, and generality so persuasively counterpointed by the irrelevance of empirical study – especially the empirical study of institutions. Herbert Simon's work, which in some respects is complementary to Richardson's, has encountered similar obstacles over the same period. Indeed, the clear preference for rigorous abstraction over institutional inquiry – even for problems of economic policy – had been clearly registered thirty years earlier (O'Brien, 1984a, pp.36–9).

In the past twenty-five years the power of the general equilibrium research programme to generate theorems about an ever-increasing range of carefully constructed puzzles by means of ingenious redefinitions of preference, production, and information sets has been abundantly demonstrated. Yet the opportunity costs to the science of economics of this revealed preference of its most eminent theorists are beginning to be recognized: the concentration (with some distinguished exceptions) on equilibrium states at the expense of adjustment processes and the assumed irrelevance of institutions have simply excluded a whole range of questions. As Shackle (1972, p.10) has pointed out, each Gordian knot which is cut with such superb professional skill has been 'carefully tied up in advance . . . by the very man who is going to cut it'; and not every issue can be tied up in a fashion which yields even to expert swordsmen.

Indeed, to some of the most expert the possible limitations of their technique are becoming more obvious. Hahn, contemplating with dismay the illegitimate uses made by rational expectations theorists of the theory of general competitive equilibrium to pronounce on issues which that theory is incapable of handling, has summarized the achieve-

ments of the research programme in terms which were hardly anticipated by its practitioners twenty-five years ago. 'This theory at the end
of the twentieth century can at best be regarded as scaffolding and not
as the building' (Hahn, 1982, p.106).

Despite Debreu's (1984, p.268) assertion that 'one of the aims of the
mathematical theory that Walras founded in 1874–77 is to explain the
price-vector and the actions of the various agents observed in an
economy in terms of an equilibrium resulting from the interaction of
those agents through markets for commodities', we still, as Hahn (1984,
p.11) observes, have no Walrasian model of the process by which such
interactions lead to equilibrium. The standard stability analysis does
not confront the real problems of adjustment through time, even with
respect to a single equilibrium; and when one tries to handle continuing
change, the difficulties increase. The comparative equilibrium method,
by the principles of its own construction, cannot provide a formally
rigorous analysis of change: the actions which might move an economy
from one equilibrium to another are not modelled.

Moreover, to say that changes are unpredictable does not justify
using a model in which agents anticipate a future without change of
any kind. An economy known to be subject to exogenous shocks is an
economy for which the list of future states, and therefore the list of
contingent commodities, cannot be completed. We need to consider
with some care the role of expectations in achieving and maintaining
the equilibria which theorists discuss, and the relationships between
expectations and the structure and institutions of the economy. These
are the issues which Richardson addresses.

They are not novel issues. Richardson (1960, pp.14–23) draws attention to Marshall's treatment of them, regretting Marshall's failure to
make clear whether he believed that imperfections (in the modern
sense) were essential to the working of free competition, and discussing
(1960, pp.38–45) the reasons for the adoption and persistence of the
perfectly competitive model. But perhaps economists are more sensible
of the critical importance of the assumptions made about the quality
and availability of knowledge than they were thirty years ago. If so,
they may wish to take note of the increasing attention which has been
given, over this period, to the importance of frameworks – impediments
to perfect competition – in theories of the growth of knowledge, which
were considered in Chapters 2 and 3. Richardson's analysis may turn
out to be part of a research programme somewhat broader than that
of general equilibrium.

7 Managerial theories of the firm: advance or diversion?*

Modern textbooks on theories of the firm include a section devoted to what are called managerial theories, in which price and output are derived from the optimization of an objective function other than pure profit. The relative size of this section indicates that these theories are considered to be much less significant than profit-maximizing theories; and this assessment seems to be justified by the current allocation of research effort in this area of economics. Perhaps the time has come to consider whether a section on managerial theories still merits a place in textbooks of contemporary economics. Do they offer the prospect of any worthwhile improvements in our ability to analyse phenomena of interest, or should they now be recognized as an unsuccessful, and perhaps unnecessary, diversion?

Orthodox theorizing about the firm was for long dominated by the structure–conduct–performance framework, a kind of controlled thought-experiment in which the firm's costs and objectives are held constant while it is exposed to a variety of market structures. The systematic relationship thus derived between structure and outcome (which has been called situational determinism) may then be used either for prediction or for evaluation of the relative desirability of the alternative market forms. Managerial theories are generated by a simple mutation of this research strategy: instead of exposing an invariant firm to a range of environments, theorists hold the environment constant and vary the firm's criterion of choice. What does this change of research strategy achieve, and can it be justified? In attempting to answer these questions, I shall pay particular attention to Baumol's sales revenue maximization hypothesis. This was the first of the managerial models and has a prior claim for that reason; moreover, as I shall argue, both Williamson's hypothesis of managerial utility maximization and Marris's theory of growth maximization may be regarded as variants of Baumol's theory, both in their analytical method and in the justification which is offered by their authors.

*This chapter is a revised version of a paper presented at the University of Pisa in October 1987

Sales revenue maximization: the formal model
I propose to begin, like the textbooks, with a summary of Baumol's (1959, 1967) formal model. Baumol replaces the standard objective of profit maximization by the maximization of sales revenue; but profit is not banished, simply demoted to a constraint. This profit constraint is not imposed by shareholders, or the possibility of takeover, but results from the need to finance the expansion which is implied by considering revenue maximization in a dynamic setting. Profits are essential to such finance in one or both of two ways: they provide internally generated funds or the evidence on which potential investors decide to commit more capital to existing businesses (1967, pp.49–50). Shareholders matter, it seems, not because they may be provoked into action by inadequate performance, but because inadequate performance may deter them from subscribing to new issues.

Now, if the only opportunity cost to managers of sacrificing present profit for present sales is the future sales revenue which those profits would have directly or indirectly financed, we would appear to have an intertemporal optimization problem. Baumol, however, does not formally recognize that his profit constraint is logically a proxy for future revenue forgone, and (in Part I) conforms to standard practice in offering a single-period analysis. He might perhaps justify this apparent sub-optimization on the part of his decision-makers by invoking the arguments for simple rules in complex situations, which we will consider later.

Since Baumol insists that it is sales revenue, and not sales volume, which is to be maximized, price-inelasticity of demand may make the profit constraint ineffective; and so he ensures that the constraint is always binding by including the possibility of advertising, with the assumption (which he recognizes might occasionally not be justified) that the marginal revenue product of advertising is always positive (1967, p.58). The completed model, Baumol claims, offers determinate solutions for any given demand, cost, and advertising functions and profit constraint; and these solutions are significantly different from those produced by profit-maximizing theory (1967, pp.71–5). Compared with profit maximization, sales revenue maximization yields a greater output, lower price, and more advertising; and the first two of these imply a closer approximation to a welfare optimum. Furthermore, the raising of price in response to an increase in fixed costs or to the imposition of a lump-sum tax now appears as rational behaviour. But most important of all is Baumol's claim that he has produced a determinate solution to the oligopoly problem, where determinacy has proved so elusive.

The claims examined

Unfortunately, these claims are not well-founded. The introduction of advertising suffices to make any simple comparison of profit and sales revenue maximization impossible. The sales revenue maximizer will indeed either advertise more or set lower prices than the profit maximizer; he may do both, but we cannot depend upon it, as Hawkins (1970) demonstrated. For, while advertising and price reductions are alternative ways of seeking greater revenue, the effect of advertising on price-elasticity of demand has an impact on pricing policy. If advertising can significantly reduce price-elasticity, then the maximization of sales revenue may require a higher price and lower output than under profit maximization. Moreover, the introduction of advertising, unless it is purely informative, undermines the conventional basis of welfare comparisons (which Baumol does not question) by converting preferences into dependent variables.

We must now enquire into the precise nature of this profit-maximizing model with which the consequences of sales revenue maximization are being compared. What we have been implicitly using is a monopoly model, and this is not accidental. But Baumol claims to be offering an oligopoly model, and his own assertion – which would be widely accepted – that there is no single acceptable profit-maximizing model of oligopoly means that there is no obvious basis of comparison. What precisely is the profit-maximizing price and output in oligopoly? Will it change if fixed costs change? We still do not know and, from the defining characteristics of oligopoly, it seems as certain as most things in economics that we never will. So the claim that price and output configuration differ between profit and sales revenue maximization is of dubious validity. Baumol's achievement is not the production of an alternative result, but the provision of a determinate general solution to a previously intractable problem. Unfortunately, however, his solution will not do.

Baumol offers two keys to the solution of the oligopoly problem. The first is the shift of objectives from profit to sales revenue; the second is the decision to take no account of interdependence. Now the first key, on examination, is quickly seen to be irrelevant; it is the assumption that interdependence is ignored in making decisions which – as Baumol (1967, p.28) apparently recognizes – does the trick. (As we shall see shortly, in fact it does not: the determinacy is false.) There is thus no need to give up profit maximization.

Baumol tries to use the shift of objectives to make his solution strategy more plausible, but his arguments are logically flawed. He suggests that sales revenue maximization will be regarded by competitors as less provocative than profit maximization; but is it really less provocative to increase sales, especially if this is done by cutting prices, than to restrict sales in order to achieve higher levels of profit? (High profits, we should note, are not used to fuel takeovers in the world of this model.) Moreover, Baumol (1967, p.31) lays considerable stress on the importance which many managers attach to market share; and the search for market share, unlike the search for profit, is strictly a zero-sum game. Indeed, in the dynamic model of Part II, which is described (1967, p.ix) as 'only slightly related', active competition for market share, in the full recognition of interdependency, provides the 'contagion in company expansion' which promotes growth (1967, p.101).

Baumol's second argument in support of the proposition that decision-makers in oligopolistic firms ignore interdependency is a little better founded, but it is much more dangerous. This is the argument that the complexity of the firm's internal organization leads to a reliance on 'simple, orderly routines . . . which do not make provision for a variety of contingencies' (1967, p.30). There are dangers on both flanks: either large oligopolistic firms stray far from optimization and suffer in competition with smaller, more tightly managed enterprises; or these routines should be taken seriously by the analyst and not hastily bundled up into an objective called sales revenue maximization. But Baumol invokes the practical problems of management strictly for the purpose of excluding interdependency from his specification: these problems are not allowed to have any impact on the formulation of objectives or the precision with which managerial decisions are represented in the formal model.

The justifications which Baumol offers for sales revenue maximization as an objective, though all professedly realist, are of rather different kinds and point in various directions. The first justification is that sales revenue is an operational variable which can serve either as a means to achieving ultimate objectives or as an indicator of success in achieving them. If, as he suggests (1967, p.35), larger firms tend to earn larger profits because, in addition to taking any opportunities also open to small firms, they have access to opportunities from which small firms are excluded, then 'even to the profit maximizing firm the scale of its operation can become an important proximate objective' (1967, p.33). A decline in sales not only threatens market power and negotiating strength, but also indicates that there is something wrong either with the firm's present strategy or its execution. This justification points in the direction of the management of complexity, which Baumol is determined to avoid.

The second justification is the personal self-interest of managers, in an environment where salaries and promotion 'appear to be far more closely correlated with the scale of operations of the firm than with its profitability' (1967, p.46). But Baumol neither pauses to consider what this correlation might tell us about the problems of incentive and control in large organizations, nor whether sales revenue maximization, as it is worked out in his formal model, adequately represents the kind of managerial decisions which are likely to result from this desire for higher salaries.

First, although the purpose of sales revenue maximization, from this point of view, is to generate extra salaries and extra staff, nevertheless within the model salaries and staff are kept down to the minimum necessary to generate those additional sales. Thus, benefits are derived from the necessary costs of additional sales, but not from any unnecessary costs of sales. This seems a roundabout way of obtaining managerial objectives; its virtue is that it keeps Baumol's objective function simple. As we shall see, Williamson's (1964) concept of expense preference may be regarded as an obvious improvement on Baumol's formulation. Second, sales volume may be a more relevant objective than sales revenue for some managers, particularly those in production departments. Third, in a multi-product firm – as one might expect most of these firms to be – managers may disagree about the relative desirability of promoting alternative product lines. Baumol's (1967, p.57) formula for determining the optimum composition of output by equating the marginal revenue yield of a dollar of profit sacrificed across all products is not obviously one to which all managers will agree. But he has no suggestion to offer for surmounting the problem of deriving a group preference function from the preferences of individual managers; indeed, there is no suggestion that it is recognized to be a relevant problem.

The third justification for his use of sales revenue maximization – that 'people's objectives are whatever they are' and that, for many, the evidence is that 'sales have become an end in and of themselves' (1967, pp.46–7) – also entails the construction of a group preference function. Moreover, Baumol's presentation of the evidence calls into question the basis of his model, for he suggests that the attraction of sales volume in particular markets is so strong that the profit constraint does not operate effectively at that level: 'A program that explicitly proposes any cut in sales volume, whatever the profit considerations, is likely to meet a cold reception' (1967, p.47) even though the avoidance of such unprofitable sales allows an increase in total sales volume and is accordingly predicted by his formal analysis (1967, p.58). We may agree with Baumol that there is nothing necessarily irrational in wishing to maximize total sales revenue but, on Baumol's own definition (1967, p.47), it must be irrational for managers who wish to maximize sales revenue to refuse to take actions which would enable them to do so. Managers may have good reasons for such behaviour – it is not difficult to think of some – but they are not reasons which Baumol wishes to use.

Even if all these objections were to be waived, the analysis is still flawed. Baumol repeatedly talks of managerial decisions, but his models have the appearance of static equilibrium models – despite his strange reluctance to use the word equilibrium. Since the comparative static exercises take the usual form of response to fresh data, it is presumably to be understood either that there is no trial and error, or that whatever trial and error turns out to be necessary is quickly accomplished, with no more than local disturbance. Decisions, we are presumably to suppose, achieve roughly what they were intended to achieve. This is a standard – indeed rarely questioned – assumption in conventional theory, but it is peculiarly awkward here. It begins to look as though sales revenue maximizing managers have something akin to perfect knowledge after all: certainly, the diagrams and algebra all embody perfect knowledge and, if they do, what is the justification for ignoring interdependency in decision-making?

But even if we can accept this curious notion of well-informed decisions which ignore interdependency, we have not escaped the difficulty. That oligopolists neither calculate the likely reactions of rivals nor respond to rivals' actions does not ensure that the outcomes of their isolated decisions are determinate. In an oligopoly, one firm's actions will influence the outcomes of another firm's actions, whether or not they are intended to. Nothing that Baumol has done can prevent interdependency in an oligopolistic equilibrium. Equilibrium requires prereconciled choice; oligopoly equilibrium requires prereconciled interdependent choice. Baumol has not solved the oligopoly problem.

Baumol's purpose and presentation
However, solving the oligopoly problem was not Baumol's fundamental objective. That judgement may appear to conflict with the simple statement (1967, p.ix) in his original preface that the first part of the book is 'a study of static oligopoly theory' – an emphasis apparently supported by the use of the phrase 'oligopolistic interdependence' in the titles of Chapters 3 and 4, and the straightforward description of the formal analysis, in Chapters 7 and 8, as an oligopoly model. But in the preface to the second edition (1967, p.vii) the underlying purpose is made very clear, together with an assurance that this always was so. 'Though the

very reappearance of the book indicates that there has been no basic change in my position, I should like to affirm this explicitly . . . I do not believe that all firms need have the same objectives, and I think I have succeeded in demonstrating that objectives other than profit maximization are also amenable to rigorous analysis.' This position is restated in the section, 'Afterthoughts on sales maximization', added to Chapter 6 where Baumol (1967, pp.50–2) is careful not to claim any exclusive theoretical privileges for sales revenue maximization compared with other business objectives, though arguing that the evidence seems to support its practical significance.

Why, then, does he place so much emphasis – and in the first edition, apparently primary emphasis – on the market structure rather than the objectives of firms within it? One reason, presumably, is that the separation of ownership from control, introducing the possibility of managerial objectives, is always associated with large firms which are naturally thought of as oligopolists. Baumol might have criticized the standard (and thoughtless) association of owner-management with profit objectives: after all, if 'people's objectives are whatever they are', why should not owner-managers – who do not have shareholders to worry about, and (unless they become insolvent) cannot have their firms taken over against their will – be allowed by economists to pursue sales, growth, civic honours, or a quiet life? It would appear that some of them do. But Baumol was probably wise not to involve himself in this argument and to direct his analysis towards the well-recognized problem of the implications of management control, especially as he wished to use the complexities of management as one of his arguments for ignoring interdependency in the formulation of managerial decisions.

The emphasis on oligopoly was also tactically wise if Baumol wished to persuade other economists to consider alternatives to profit maximization. To achieve that it was not enough – though it was certainly necessary – to demonstrate that other objectives were analytically tractable; it was also necessary to show that they allowed one to do what profit maximization could not. Baumol (1967, p.5) does devote two short paragraphs to distinguishing his position from Friedman's 'apparent denial of the importance of assumptions': even if sales revenue maximization does yield similar conclusions to profit maximization, he seems to be saying, sales revenue maximization is to be preferred if it more closely represents the objectives in the minds of decision-makers. But the main burden of his case is that the conclusions are not similar, and the intendedly clinching argument is that sales revenue maximization allows one to reach conclusions in one very important case where profit maximization does not. That, I believe, is why he places such emphasis on oligopoly, and on the inability of standard analysis to handle it.

The introduction to Part I opens with the following sentence. 'Perhaps the most remarkable failure of modern value theory is its inability to explain the pricing, output, and other related decisions of the large, not quite monopolistic firms that account for so high a proportion of our economy's activity' (1967, p.13). (It is surely no coincidence that Simon has also drawn attention to the 'scandal' of oligopoly theory in his attempts to persuade economists to turn towards his own preferred alternative.) Thus, in Baumol's strategy, oligopoly and sales revenue maximization stand in a paradoxical means–end hierarchy: the switch to sales revenue maximization is presented as the key to the solution of the oligopoly problem, while the solution to the oligopoly problem is the primary evidence for the benefits to be gained by adopting sales revenue maximization.

The paradox may be extended. As has been pointed out, the switch of objectives actually contributes nothing to the solution of the oligopoly problem, although it does affect the particular price and output configuration: what apparently makes the problem determinate is the exclusion of interdependency. Through its association, in Baumol's presentation, with managerial complexity, sales revenue maximization becomes part of the complicated and not entirely consistent story which purports to justify the disregard of interdependence; but fundamentally, it is the rejection of interdependence from the analysis that produces the determinate answer which Baumol needs in order to demonstrate the analytical advantages of switching objectives.

Consciously or not, Baumol was also extremely shrewd in limiting the novelty in his model to the change in objective. Dispensing with interdependence might even be regarded as the removal of an unwelcome novelty which had been encountered in the attempt to apply standard theory to oligopoly. In all other respects he presents a conventional neoclassical partial equilibrium model, arriving at price and output configurations through the application of a criterion function to an attainable set, all fully specified. In case readers have not fully recognized the orthodoxy of the analytical method, Baumol draws our attention to it. He includes a section (1967, pp.63–6) on full cost pricing, in which he claims to have captured whatever is of interest in that approach while avoiding its inadequate analytical basis by employing 'the marginalist calculations implicit in sales maximization (or in the maximization or minimization of any other variable, for that matter)'.

Earlier (1967, pp.32–3) he explicitly rejects 'Simon's suggestion . . .

that the firm does not maximize anything'. Acknowledging that business practices lend some support for this view, he rejects it as producing 'no theory that is tractable analytically' by which he seems to mean – like so many economists – 'no theory which relies on optimization'. But, perhaps because of his earlier advocacy of the quest for plausibility in assumptions, he also asserts that satisficing 'does not seem to capture the very real striving for preeminence that characterizes so much of business behaviour'. Now this comment reveals a failure to understand the satisficing approach: managers may set themselves, and each other, challenging targets rather than easy targets, and the process of target-setting (formal and informal) is necessary both in business and in the analysis of business by Simon's methods. Nor does the complaint come well from an author who has appealed to the use of non-maximizing procedures (1967, p.30) and even the desire for a quiet life (1967, p.31) in the course of his somewhat miscellaneous arguments for removing interdependency from oligopolistic price and output decisions: indeed, 'the striving for preeminence' suggests precisely the consciousness of rivalry which he is determined to ignore.

The essential flaw in Baumol's objection to satisficing is that this is precisely what Baumol's managers are doing when they accept, as a 'good enough' basis for their decision, a model which is a less than accurate representation of their situation. (Recall that the outcome of one oligopolist's decision will be affected by the decisions of his rivals, whether they seek to affect it or not.) Calculation of an 'optimal choice' on the basis of a model which is known to simplify – and probably distort – the true situation is a very common means of satisficing in business. It is also precisely what is done by any economist who ever uses the technique of optimization – not least Baumol himself. That is not an objection to the use of optimization, only to naive ideas that optimization is, by definition, always best. Baumol (1967, p.14) acknowledges that sales revenue maximization 'is at best only an approximation to a set of complex and variegated facts', but that does not lead him to doubt the superiority of optimization as a means of handling these complex and variegated facts. In this, he was no doubt in tune with those whom he was trying to persuade.

Another feature of Baumol's presentation which probably improved its reception but is open to question is its ambiguity about the range of choice being modelled. At its simplest, are we being presented with a short-run or a long-run model? For much of the time, the impression is of short-period analysis. Very early on, Baumol (1967, p.13) argues that 'in practice, management is often not deeply concerned with . . . elements of interdependence in its day-to-day decision-making', and the discussions of complexity and rules of thumb (1967, pp.29–30) are set in a context of day-to-day management. Moreover, in the 'after-thoughts' of 1967 (p.52) he declares that he is 'really somewhat sceptical about the very concept of the long-run goal', asking 'must we not simply file suggestions for *long-run* objectives under the heading 'not relevant', or at least 'not settled'? This implies that long-run analysis is itself dispensable. But Baumol's distinction between short-run and long-run analysis is not the conventional distinction of neoclassical price theory; the long-run is reserved for strategy, presumably relating to product range, while his model is presented as appropriate to 'the ordinary problems of value theory, the routine pricing and advertising decisions' (1967, p.32).

Nevertheless, Baumol does implicitly recognize that whether a problem is short-run or long-run is determined not by the objective situation but by the decision-maker. 'The oligopolist has a fiercely tender regard for his share of the market and, if ever he finds himself losing out, energetic steps may be expected' (1967, p.31). These ener-getic steps may even derive from fancy rather than fact. 'A small reversal in an upwards sales trend that can quite reasonably be dismissed as a random movement sometimes leads to a major review of the concern's selling and production methods, its product lines, and even its internal organizational structure' (1967, p.45). He does not suggest how such decisions should be treated by economists, nor – more seriously – how economists are to decide, on the basis of their external observations, when his model may be safely applied. The most serious implication of all is that outcomes may depend upon unpredictable perceptions, or even mistakes – possibilities which economists have found it essential to exclude from theories of rational choice. Baumol's book is littered with reservations and caveats but, since these are never collected and evaluated, one is left with the impression that the formal analysis presented in the most clearly theoretical chapters is intended to be of wide validity.

Many of the features of Baumol's model – and still more of his discussion – which on close inspection appear most dubious may also be regarded as elements in an intelligent marketing strategy for promoting that model. In summary, he claims a significant advantage for an innovation which is fully compatible with the fundamental notion of a rational choice equilibrium. The strategy was moderately successful. Sales revenue maximization came to be recognized as a respectable method of analysis to apply to large, complex firms – although they were usually treated as monopolists rather than oligopo-lists. It was accepted by many industrial economists as an extension of the neoclassical research programme of constrained optimization and situational determinism, allowing for managerial objectives without requiring the analyst to have any contact with managers.

Baumol helped to open up the academic market for the managerial models of Williamson (1964) and Marris (1964), which are close analytical relatives. Williamson's managerial preference function seems to offer both realism and a closer parallel with consumer theory, while Marris's hypothesis of growth maximization, subject to both an internal financial constraint and the threat of takeover, may be regarded (even though it was not conceived) as a direct descendant of Baumol's formulation.

Managerial preferences

Baumol, it will be recalled, presented his theory as a solution to two problems in contemporary economics: oligopoly and the separation of ownership from control. Williamson is concerned only with the second. He makes no attempt to relate his theory to the classification of market structures used in conventional economics, and his discussion of the environment of his firms is brief and imprecise. This has no doubt reduced the attraction of his theory. He simply takes it for granted, as a well known fact, that there are firms whose managers enjoy considerable discretion in the choices which they make and take advantage of that discretion in an orderly way. His formal model is in the perfect knowledge tradition: the firm's objective function is clearly specified, the conditions in which it operates are clearly specified: managers know precisely what will be the result of their actions and choose accordingly. Not only is there no danger of reaction by other firms which might cause expectations to be disappointed; there is not even any possibility that expectations will be disappointed through the independent actions of other firms. No outside decisions impinge upon the firm; all outside influences are incorporated in demand and cost conditions. Logically, Williamson's model must be of monopoly equilibrium, although he is reluctant to admit this.

The principal interest of Williamson's model lies in his treatment (1964, pp.28–37) of managerial preferences, and the implications of that treatment. He claims that, in a large firm which is sheltered from competition, there will be a number of people – possibly quite a large number – in a position to influence the way in which the situation is exploited; although, in principle, any supplier of inputs might benefit, he argues that managers, especially senior managers, are much the best placed, and that therefore it is the interests of these people alone which should be incorporated into a formal model.

He then goes on to consider what these managers will try to achieve. The first suggested objective is extra salaries. These additions to salary might be regarded as managerial rents, except that they do not strictly conform to the standard economic conception in which rent results from a degree of inelasticity in supply and is received by intramarginal suppliers; in Williamson's model, marginal inputs too are paid more than their supply price. Williamson chooses to amalgamate such additions to salary with the category of unnecessary staff. Such staff are assumed to be a source of satisfaction to their superiors in their own right but, in so far as managerial salaries depend on the number of a manager's subordinates, unnecessary staff also lead to higher salaries, and it is this connection which provides Williamson's justification for amalgamating the two. The third category, which remains separate, is that of slack absorbed as cost: in this are included unnecessary costs – what one usually considers as managers' perquisites – which are incurred because they are a source of utility to those who make the decision to incur them.

The final category is that of retained profit for discretionary investment. In Baumol's theory, the long-period growth plan, which was kept quite outside his static model, imposed an investment requirement which in turn determined the amount of profit which a firm had to earn. Williamson's managers might also have such a target and such a constraint. In the model, they certainly do have a number of investment projects which would bring them personal satisfaction. These may include a splendid research department, or an imposing head office building; or they might enjoy a reputation for being in the forefront of technology, and buy new equipment earlier than could be justified on grounds of profit maximization. Since they are not designed primarily to generate income, any of these possibilities will need to be financed by surplus profits; so, unlike Baumol's managers, Williamson's managers are prepared to operate at a level of profit which is higher than the minimum. Profit is restored from a constraint to a choice variable – but not, as in conventional models of the firm, the only choice variable.

Williamson makes use of the concept of the firm as an organization to generate this set of objectives, but ignores the problems of combining them into a single function. Somehow all the managers agree on a set of preferences. Of course, there is no reason to suppose that there will be a single view on the relative attractions of the three arguments in the objective function, or that there will be no differences of opinion about the merits of alternative components within each: a splendid new research laboratory, which is not, remember, primarily intended to discover new profitable products, will not do much to satisfy either the sales director or the head of production engineering. Like Baumol, Williamson uses the interior of the firm solely to justify his model; he makes no attempt to incorporate it into his analysis. He recognizes (1964, pp.145–62) the threat posed by Arrow's impossibility theorem to social choice in the business firm, and relies on 'institutional uniformities' to produce consensus but, though referring to Simon and also to Cyert and March, is content with what is in effect an inadequately specified rational expectations equilibrium.

What Williamson does is to bring consumer preference theory into the analysis of the firm. Having constructed – we cannot tell how – his managerial preference function, he can put it to work (1964, pp.38–60) by comparing equilibrium positions. Thus, he concludes that an increase in demand, which increases the scope for discretion, will lead to an increase in staff, in slack, and in retained profit. For this result it is sufficient to assume that each of these is a normal good; increased income therefore leads to greater consumption of all three. A rise in fixed costs, outside management's control, has the effect of reducing discretionary income, and therefore leads to a reduction in all three. The novelty in Williamson's analysis arises with a postulated change in the rate of profits tax. Since retained profits have to bear this tax, while costs do not, this increase is equivalent to an increase in the price of retained profits, while the price of the other two goods remains unchanged. This increase in the price of profits has, like all price increases, an income effect and a substitution effect (1964, p.45). Both effects will tend to depress retained profit but, for the other two managerial goods, they will work in opposite directions. The scope for discretion will be reduced but, within this reduced scope, the cost items, staff and slack become more attractive. So, on the general analytical level, it is not possible to predict the direction of change: an increased rate of profits tax may lead firms either to increase or to cut into 'unnecessary' costs. By most economists' criteria of useful theory this inconclusive result is a serious defect.

Let us observe what Williamson has done to the conventional structure of theory. In that structure, production and consumption have been kept separate. The only reason why anyone, including owner-managers and salaried managers, engages in production activity has been to acquire income; that income has been taken home and spent according to the individual's preference function. Baumol claimed that, for managers who were not owners, the way to maximize their income was through the maximisation of sales revenue, but he did also suggest that there might be some direct utility from larger size. Williamson boldly argues that some satisfactions are derived directly from the firm: extra subordinates, bigger offices, newer equipment, larger research programmes are valued for their own sake. That satisfactions, and not just the income with which satisfactions may later be purchased, are obtainable within the firm, is a novel idea for modern economists; it is not a novel idea for industrial psychologists or organizational sociologists.

Perhaps unconsciously, Williamson introduced an innovation more radical than Baumol's – and less welcome, since it breached the very convenient line of demarcation between theories of production and consumption. It has an implication which some have found even more disturbing. The satisfactions which Williamson discusses are gained by allowing costs to rise. It is not just, as with Baumol, that extra costs are incurred to produce extra saleable output; since the objective in Baumol's model is to obtain as much extra output as possible, these extra costs are kept to the minimum. In Williamson's model, however, some extra costs are incurred for their own sake: costs become an object of preference. The reason, of course, is that some costs are now transfer payments, and therefore not costs to the managerial system.

An alternative way of expressing the difference is to note that, whereas for a conventional profit-maximizing firm the only benefits to be set against costs are the additional revenues which they make possible, for the managerial utility maximizer there are additional benefits in the form of managerial satisfaction. Since the total benefits are therefore larger, optimization now entails a higher level of costs. There are externalities to be taken into account. Consequently, the level of the cost curve depends on managerial preferences. In all the conventional profit-maximization models, and with sales revenue maximization too, the cost function has been part of the data – a consequence of the standard assumption of given resources and given technology. But, in a managerial preference model, the cost function is not an input into the model, but one of the outputs.

If the interdependence of decisions in oligopoly does not allow us to draw a simple demand curve and managerial preferences do not allow us to draw a cost curve, we may well wonder what is happening to economic theory. There has certainly been no rush to follow Williamson's path, and even Williamson himself has backed away from managerial discretion, as we shall see. However, the opportunity has been taken by one economist, Harvey Leibenstein (1966; 1976), who has focused attention on the difference between the level of costs attainable with best practice technology and at the current market prices of inputs – in other words, the level of costs assumed in conventional theory – and the level which is actually attained in an organization, and has called the difference *X-inefficiency*. In everyday managerial language, this is just inefficiency; but since economists have long associated the concept of efficiency with the allocation of resources according to preferences and technology, a new name was needed. (And, of course, a new name also helps to advertise a new idea.) Leibenstein set out to develop a theory of the determination of X-inefficiency. He has found no followers, and has attracted a determined critic in Stigler (1976) who well appreciates the issues at stake. A simple adjustment to neoclassical theory, Stigler asserts, will incorporate all that is useful in Leibenstein's ideas; the remainder is bad theory. On Stigler's definition of bad theory, he is right; but his definition prohibits many questions.

Growth maximization

Baumol and Williamson both offer single-period models; however, as has been noted, Baumol also sketched out a theory of growth. Marris (1964) made growth the focus of his analysis. Although he provides a substantial discussion of consumer behaviour and marketing strategy, rather little of this is reflected in his formal model which is quite simple. His treatment of managerial preferences is very close to Baumol's: he argues (1964, pp.101–6) that growth facilitates the achievement of whatever objectives managers may reasonably be expected to have, and that growth is therefore sufficient for the purposes of analysis. Consumption is thus kept separate from production, and costs remain parameters, not objects, of choice. As with sales revenue maximization, the direction and content of growth is assumed either to have no effect on the distribution of managerial benefits or to be agreed without difficulty.

Marris's treatment of profit differs from that of both Baumol and Williamson. Although present profits provide funds for future growth, they do not, as with Williamson, appear directly in the objective function. Before profits have been reduced to a level which threatens to frustrate managerial plans for growth, they will have reached a level which threatens managerial security. Even if current shareholders are not roused to demand higher profits (perhaps because their stakes are small), the firm's market valuation, which is based on the income stream associated with present policies, will fall short of the valuation appropriate to the income stream which would be generated by profit maximization; and this shortfall offers capital gains to anyone who buys out the present shareholders and installs a profit-maximizing management (Marris, 1964, pp.29–40). However, instead of a simple valuation constraint, at the level which would trigger takeover, Marris postulates an increasing probability of takeover as valuation declines. The managerial choice set is thus composed of various combinations of growth rates and takeover probabilities, and equilibrium is derived by the application to this choice set of managerial preferences – essentially risk preferences (1964, pp.254–65).

Although nominally incorporating the effects of time, this is effectively (as with Baumol and Williamson) a simple equilibrium model: a single growth rate over all future periods, together with its associated constant probability of takeover, is chosen. It also resembles its predecessors in assuming that decision-makers are extremely well-informed (though some of their information now appears as probability distributions), and also in insulating both managerial decisions and their consequences from the decisions, either concurrent or subsequent, of any other firm – even though a firm's ability to grow, and especially to grow indefinitely at a constant rate, might be thought to be somewhat dependent on other firms' activities.

The principal attraction of Marris's model to industrial economists has been its apparent relevance to the study of takeovers, and it has been frequently cited in studies of merger activity. No attempt will be made here to assess its suitability for that purpose. The principal obstacle to its general acceptability has been its incompatibility with the rapidly developing structure of modern finance theory, resting on the twin pillars of efficient markets and the capital asset pricing model. Within such a framework, which is itself closely integrated with the corpus of standard microeconomics, it is difficult to see how managers could have enough discretion to be worth modelling – especially in long-run equilibrium.

The managerial diversion
On closer examination, all these models are extremely vulnerable to a neoclassical counterattack. All are constructed as equilibrium models of fully-informed rational choice, and yet all embody unexploited opportunities in the profits which their managers decline to take. Even if shareholders and takeover bidders do not tighten the constraints, it is open to other professional managers to improve their own position by offering shareholders a better deal. Williamson's more recent work on organizational design (1975; 1985; 1986) might be regarded as a refutation of his earlier theory: the M-form firm is claimed to be a highly effective device for eliminating managerial discretion by placing control in the hands of head office management who are closely associated with the overriding incentive of profit.

The full force of the counterattack has been developed by Fama (1980), who argues that efficient capital markets and efficient managerial markets will combine to ensure that firms maximize profits, and perfect commodity markets will ensure that profit maximization yields a Pareto optimum. The separation of ownership from control is not a problem but an efficient solution, because management and risk-bearing are naturally distinct functions that are best kept separate. Shareholders optimize by holding diverse portfolios, and eschewing managerial responsibilities; since share prices embody all publicly available information, efficient procedures for monitoring management will be in place. Managers competing for promotion and seeking to maximize the value of their investment in human capital have a powerful incentive not only to perform effectively as profit-generators, but also to expose the failures of others. The ownership of a firm is not a sensible idea anyway, since only specific inputs to the firm can be owned; the firm is simply a label for a particular network of contracts. Thus, managerial theories of the firm offer nothing but false solutions to non-existent problems; they are a diversion from the most important tasks of economic theory.

The previous sentence expresses my own view. Managerial theories are indeed a diversion from the most important tasks of economic theory: these are to study the problems of decision-making, including especially the problems of coordination within an interdependent system where knowledge is incomplete and often precarious, and where rationality is always bounded.

These three managerial models are remarkably similar in what they avoid. None of them even hints at a general theoretical challenge to profit maximization (although their authors might claim that the importance of the kind of firms at which their analyses are directed constitutes a substantial practical challenge). Despite their reliance on the concept of firms as organizations run by managers in order to justify their objective functions, they make no attempt to consider the firm as a system. They invoke group preference functions without enquiring how these might be formulated or why they might actually be relevant to decisions; they invoke complexity without considering how that might affect the definition of problems, the options considered, or the choices made. They are managerial models without management.

The fundamental reason for questioning profit maximization as a basis of analysis, in both large and small organizations, has nothing to do with any differences between managers and owners. It is the result of complexity, partial ignorance, and bounded rationality. As Ansoff (1965) and Drucker (1955) among others have emphasized, any profit

function which can be precisely formulated will be so incomplete and
replete with potential error as to be a misleading single criterion for
decision. Baumol comes very close to this position in querying the
concept of a long-run goal, but does not face up to the implications.
Organizations need a set of objectives. But the factors which dictate this
requirement for effective management – even for an owner-manager –
also call into question the possibility of collecting these objectives into
a well-defined preference function. The challenge to profit maximization is a challenge to both terms: neither profit nor maximization, but
multiple partial objectives and satisficing. One should add, also, not
equilibrium but process.

8 Frank Hahn's 'struggle of escape'

This chapter is an attempt to present, and comment on, the view of economics which appears to underlie the collection of Frank Hahn's essays published as *Equilibrium and Macroeconomics* (1984). The treatment is selective: no reference will be made to Hahn's discussion of international monetary economics and of the neo-Ricardians – not because of doubts about the importance of the issues or the quality of Hahn's treatment, but in order to concentrate attention on what appears to be the undeclared theme of the book: the uses, abuses, limitations and continuing potential of general equilibrium theory.

One of the clearest impressions from this collection is that Hahn's views have been changing. In earlier essays, although the incompleteness of currently available theory is recognized, the emphasis is on its uses and potential; but his determination to counter what he regards as serious abuses has led him to place ever-increasing stress on its limitations in a way which brings the whole approach into question. As he warns us several times, at least one half of the story is missing; and he does not suggest how the general equilibrium method might supply it. Considered in chronological sequence, these essays give the impression, to borrow Keynes's description, of 'a long struggle of escape . . . from habitual modes of thought and expression . . . which ramify, for those brought up as most of us have been, into every corner of our minds' (1973a, p.viii). The struggle appears to be largely unconscious, and it is certainly not resolved. Some suggestions towards a resolution will be made later.

Theory
On one point Hahn will find few supporters. He remarks (1984, p.1) that he has sometimes had to translate mathematics into English, at which he is 'not outstandingly good': for the next 380 pages he then demonstrates that he is among the very finest practitioners of this art. In the same paragraph he notes that 'Marshall advised economists to follow this course on all occasions. I am not convinced that this is sound advice.' It is worth reflecting, as Hahn does not, on the reasons for it. Mathematics is a splendid instrument of precise argument, but, as economists ought to be the first to recognize, its use carries an opportunity cost. In Bertrand Russell's (1963, pp.59–60) words, quoted in

Chapter 3, 'mathematics may be defined as the subject in which we never know what we are talking about'; or to put it another way, mathematical arguments are metaphorical, and the applicability of the metaphor cannot be established by the arguments themselves. That was why Marshall advised translation – to test for applicability; and it is clear that he had doubts about the range of application of the equilibrium method which has been so richly extended since his day. Indeed, he backed away from extensions which were clearly within his power and it is far from obvious that his only reason for preferring partial equilibrium to general equilibrium analysis was its greater tractability at the time. The price, which must still be paid, of accepting, for example, a complete initial listing of endowments, preferences and technology, would, I suspect, still seem too high.

Hahn's claim (1984, pp.5–7) for the value of a general theoretical structure, to which special theories can be referred, and by which the significance and possible applicability of their special assumptions can be judged, is well-founded; and he is right to insist that failure to establish a unique conclusion does not mean that anything is possible. Some readers will no doubt construe his arguments into the language of 'research programmes', but Hahn has more than once expressed his reluctance to enter into formal methodological arguments, although he frequently discusses methodological issues. But although general equilibrium theory is certainly more general than the new classical macroeconomics, from some other viewpoints, as we shall see, it appears very special indeed.

Themes
Hahn (1984, pp.1–2) helpfully sets out three basic themes which guide his thinking

(1) I am a reductionist in that I attempt to locate explanations in the actions of individual agents.
(2) In theorising about the agent I look for some axioms of rationality.
(3) I hold that some notion of equilibrium is required and that the study of equilibrium states is useful.

These themes do not define a unique research programme. Reductionism is a very common principle, especially if one allows for external influences on the perceptions and preferences of the individual. Some notion of rationality is also indispensable for many kinds of analysis of human behaviour. Hahn, however, takes a very limited view, which is not entirely explained by his desire for axiomatization. A complete pre-ordering of alternatives is required only for an axiom of unbounded rationality, and, as Hahn observes, some restriction on the set of alternatives is necessary for theoretical fruitfulness in particular cases. He does not, however, recognize that some alternatives are excluded even in his most general definition of the choice set. But one can invoke 'the superior "advantage" of an action to serve as its explanation' (1984, p.3) without being committed to an unlimited axiom: indeed, Hahn's brief discussion of the problem appears to point directly towards a recognition of the theoretical – and not just the practical – significance of bounded rationality. Such a concept is always, if unconsciously, present in general equilibrium theories. Moreover, it applies to the analyst as well as the agent: the analyst imposes non-rational restrictions on economic agents (they are forbidden, for example, to consider the possibility of devising new products or new processes) and accepts non-rational restrictions on his own choice of problem and of analytical method. The theoretical method is not exempt from normal human limitations.

The third theme may also be interpreted very modestly, since equilibrium and equilibrium states can play a helpful, if sometimes minor, role in many research programmes. But although Hahn now (1984, p.4) wishes to advertise the danger of considering nothing but equilibrium, he has not in the past (1973; 1984, p.67) been averse to equating the limits of equilibrium theorizing with the limits of economics. Much of his more recent unease seems to be associated with a feeling that equilibrium models leave too much not merely unexplained but even apparently inexplicable within their own framework; and yet he is apparently not yet quite ready to trust himself to any alternative.

Axioms

'Axioms . . . mark the stage beyond which one does not seek to explain' (1984, p.6). These limits to enquiry can hardly be set by an optimizing procedure – the standard theory of choice cannot be used to select the limits within which it will be employed – but they are intended, Hahn claims, to encapsulate a set of empirical phenomena. Indeed, the desire to make the conclusions of theory directly applicable to the real world is, we are told (1984, p.7), 'precisely why good theorists devote much care and attention to the formulation of these axioms'. This statement is very hard to accept. The proposition that 'the axioms have summed up what one regards as pretty secure empirical knowledge' is frankly incredible. Empirical reference may act as a constraint, but 'precisely why' theorists formulate axioms with care is surely to establish a tractable analytical system.

There is nothing to be ashamed of in this: why should one wish to substitute an artificial analytical system for the real world unless the artificial system is more manageable? But since any such system (and certainly not just in economics) is necessarily not a replica of the phenomena which it is to be used to study, its applicability cannot be ensured by the way in which it is formulated. The formulation may, however, make applicability more likely; and although the 'observation that preferences themselves are the result of complex social and biographical processes has of course nothing to do with the issue' of how preferences should be defined by theorists (Hahn, 1984, p.58), a claim that preferences are modified by the very economic processes which are to be analysed would enjoin great caution in the use, if not the formulation, of conventional preference axioms. Such a claim, as is not always realized, was made by Marshall, and helps to explain his insistence on translating mathematical precision into English which was, for many, disappointingly vague.

The basic axiom (1984, p.10) 'to the effect that at any moment agents do what they prefer to do' has to be applied, as Hahn makes clear, to some specification of what agents can do. A specification which allows for continuous market clearing is not at all to Hahn's taste. But one has to ask where the limitations on agents' possible actions come from. Hahn's suggestions (1984, p.10) that 'an unemployed worker cannot accept a lower wage without union agreement or without social action, and . . . an employer cannot lower the offered wage without courting a costly strike' seem to be commonsense possibilities. Yet it is a proclaimed virtue of high-class theory that it does not accept common-sense propositions without rigorous analysis: can it be consistent with the standard axioms for an economy of self-seeking individuals to get itself into a situation in which some – perhaps many – of them are unable to do what they prefer to do? (Of course, one might say that without a theory of processes there is no telling what situations such an economy might get itself into.) Can this be an equilibrium? It may be if rationality is appropriately bounded; but the bounds need to be properly defined. Hahn's own concept of equilibrium offers a basis for definition, as we shall see towards the end of this chapter.

Equilibrium
Hahn has generally produced a twofold argument for the study of equilibria: first, it allows us to derive general, though often not unique, conclusions from first principles, which the study of disequilibria and adjustment do not; and second, it allows us to say something about the only kinds of states which can persist. However, he has become increasingly concerned with the dangers in the second kind of argument,

particularly when it is coupled with the pre-emptive definition of equilibrium as a unique and stable Walrasian competitive equilibrium. He has become increasingly unhappy with the adequacy of Walrasian models; yet the amendments required do not seem easy to accommodate within the analytical scheme which he has done so much to develop. Moreover they call into question the relevance of conclusions so far reached. No-one would doubt the intellectual achievement of the Walrasian system, especially as embodied in Arrow–Debreu; but what precisely does it tell us? In two famous papers of 1973, Hahn claims that modern general equilibrium theory, 'by making precise an economic tradition which is two hundred years old and deeply ingrained in the thinking of many (including non-economists), has also greatly contributed to practical argument' (1984, p.137); in particular, Arrow and Debreu 'provide the most potent avenue of falsification of the claims . . . that a myriad of selfseeking agents left to themselves will lead to a coherent and efficient disposition of economic resources' (1984, p.136). The demonstration that an economy is not in Arrow–Debreu equilibrium apparently refutes the case for the invisible hand (1984, p.52). Yet in later articles Hahn himself argues that the invisible hand often works better than any alternative which seems to be available, and does so in a style which Arrow and Debreu had apparently discredited.

Now, there are certain limitations to the Arrow–Debreu system, as Hahn is quick to point out. '*The assumption that all intertemporal and contingent markets exist has the effect of collapsing the future into the present*' (1984, p.81); the economy works once only, through a single *tatonnement* – and this 'is a far cry from Adam Smith' (1984, p.92). How, then, can it serve to refute Smith's propositions? Moreover, although the system can accommodate growth through the intertemporal allocation of resources, it cannot handle innovation (1984, pp.130–1) – that is, the development of goods and technologies which are not on the initial list from which equilibria are to be computed. Although Hahn does not say so, this too is a far cry from Adam Smith, for whom the need for coordination arose from the superior effectiveness of the division of labour, not least in generating improvements.

The need, in Smith's vision, to incorporate into economic analysis the elements that emerge in the course of its working accentuates the central internal deficiency of microtheory which Hahn (1984, p.175) recognizes very clearly. 'This is quite simply that general equilibrium theorists have been unable to deliver one half at least of the required story: how does general equilibrium come to be established?' The not uncommon theoretical incidence of multiple equilibria urgently requires that half of the story (1984, p.4). What one most needs to ask is not 'whether it is possible to have a decentralised economy in which agents have adapted themselves to their economic environment' (1984, p.61), for by then all the action is over. As Hahn put it in 1970, 'the most intellectually exciting question of our subject remains: is it true that the pursuit of private interest produces not chaos but coherence, and if so, how is it done?' (1984, p.102). General equilibrium theorists cannot tell us. Although 'we seem to live in an economy which on the whole is orderly . . . if indeed there is order we do not now understand how it is brought about' (1984, p.11). We do not then, after all, have any satisfactory technique for analysing the claim that 'is as old as Adam Smith' (1984, p.136). It is clearly Hahn's present view that, for tackling this 'most intellectually exciting question', formulations in terms of equilibrium are inadequate. One needs theories of adjustment; but he does not explicitly state that one needs to study processes.

Processes
Processes cannot be studied with the standard set of general equilibrium assumptions. In particular, we need to consider knowledge and institutions. Hahn notes the central importance of 'the question of what signals are perceived and transmitted in a decentralized economy and how' (1984, p.175) and recognizes that Keynesian economists make some attempt to deal with it.

The inadequacy of general equilibrium formulations to handle such questions can be seen in two ways. First, it is well known that the Pareto-optimality of competitive equilibrium establishes the isomorphism of ideal markets and optimum planning and is therefore of limited use in resolving the choice between systems. Indeed, it actually seems to point in what Hahn, like most economists, regards as the wrong direction. 'Paraphrased, it states that anything the ideal economy can do the state can also do, but not vice versa since there may be externalities and public goods' (1984, p.347). Hahn is in no hurry to draw the obvious conclusion of recommending full state control (even under a planning commission of expert general equilibrium theorists), and to avoid that conclusion he turns, significantly, to Hayek. Now, Hayek has consistently argued that the general equilibrium formulation has simply assumed the problems of information and incentive to have been solved, and that it is only this assumption which leads to the apparent equivalence of planning and markets, or even the superiority of the former. In other words, the second half of the required story invalidates one of the most important conclusions of the first half.

Other important conclusions may be overthrown if we consider the second inadequacy. As a substitute for the missing half of the story, economists regularly invoke the law of supply and demand (1984, p.125). But unless one is very cautious, and summons an auctioneer to cope with excess demands before any trading takes place, one is in deep trouble. Trading at non-equilibrium prices is a threat to the calculated equilibrium (1984, p.92), and so, of course, is any payment for the auctioneer's services. But the absence of the auctioneer is a threat to the whole theoretical method. On the one hand, 'when one insists on retaining the perfect competition hypothesis . . . there is no one agent who can actually be taken to do the price changing' (1984, pp.125–6); on the other, any agent who can change a price has market power, and market power is incompatible with the Arrow–Debreu system (1984, p.79).

Hahn seems to attach some importance to the fact that market power generally leads to Pareto-inefficiency; but he does not explicitly state that, in general, any plausible adjustment theory will be Pareto-inefficient – or, to put it bluntly, that only 'inefficient' economies can actually work. Presumably he still hopes that the concept of Pareto-efficiency might have some practical use. But 'economics without the auctioneer requires non-perfect competition economics' (1984, p.189). This has long been recognized by the Austrians, among whom Kirzner (1973) has given most attention to the market processes which lead to adjustment; Richardson (1960), in a more Marshallian fashion, has paid particular attention to the institutional setting within which decisions are made. The failure, with a few exceptions, to take adjustment processes seriously is perhaps the most important general reason why the interaction between economics and the study of management has been so slight. This failure, it must be said, is by no means confined to general equilibrium theorists.

One area in which economists might seek help from management theorists is in the study of information and incentives. As Hahn remarks in several places (1984, pp.16, 118, 320), outside perfect competition (which itself can exist only in equilibrium, where no actions, and therefore no signals, are required) price signals are not enough, although he is wrong (1984, p.320) to ascribe a Marshallian foundation to Keynes's reliance on prices: Marshall's businessmen used other signals as well, as was demonstrated in Chapter 4. He is also rather quick to label the non-Walrasian equilibria which he believes can represent Keynes's theory as inefficient and to conclude (1984, p.187) 'that there is something for government to do', without considering what the government might be able to do or be interested in doing. Of course, not only 'Keynesian dynamics is ill served by a perfect competition postulate'

(1984, p.190); adjustment – indeed, the central question of the coordination of economic activities – requires the displacement of perfect competition, and with it conventional criteria of Pareto-efficiency.

Market failure

Hahn is still prepared to praise the Arrow–Debreu structure not simply as an intellectual achievement but as 'a benchmark. By this I mean that it serves a function similar to that which an ideal and perfectly healthy body might serve a clinical diagnostician when he looks at an actual body' (1984, p.308). But what is the relevance of an ideal and healthy body which is incapable of movement, and which even has no capacity (and fortunately no need) to learn? It is not a particularly good aid to the diagnosis of situations in which the invisible hand 'trembles or fails' (1984, p.111) to rely on an ideal scheme in which the hand never moves at all. We need to acknowledge Richardson's (1960) argument (examined in Chapter 6) that what are usually called 'market imperfections' – signs of market failure – are actually parts of the necessary mechanism for market success although, just like money, they are not always and everywhere conducive to success. Thus Pareto-inefficiency, as defined by Arrow–Debreu, may actually be superior to Pareto-efficiency.

It does not follow directly from the establishment of a misfit between the theory and the world that 'one can describe some form of collective or co-operative action which would improve the lot of everyone' (1984, p.124). If such action were available, why does an economy of rational and self-seeking agents not take it? If they do not, then precisely who is available to organize such action? The same questions apply to Hahn's (1984, p.13) assertion that 'Keynesian economics is about co-ordination failure which leads to outcomes which can be Pareto improved'. To show coordination failure, against new classical macroeconomists, is relatively easy: to devise effective policies is much harder.

If we have a government (an institution for which general equilibrium analysis has neither theory nor explanation), on what grounds can we argue that 'it would be rather foolish of it to decide on some allocation which is not Pareto efficient' (1984, p.115): it is not always through inadvertence that governments repeatedly take actions which make some people worse off. Why should we assume an ideal democracy – or indeed any kind of democracy? Moreover, although government can, under rather special circumstances, decentralize a Pareto-efficient allocation, there is no obvious reason why it should: with the information that it needs to secure efficient decentralization, it is simpler –

and no doubt more satisfying – just to give orders. The economy must be one in which no agent has any effective discretion anyway.

The real argument for delegation, as Hahn notes elsewhere (1984, p.128), is that the government does not have the information needed to make good decisions. We find repeated calls in planned economies for more delegation for this reason. But, if an economy is to work well, it needs rather more than an arrangement which will make use of existing information to compute an equilibrium. All general equilibrium formulations require the set of alternatives to be closed (1984, p.63), and that seems a rather odd assumption to apply to the economic history of the last five years, to take no longer interval, or the possibilities for the next five.

Hahn recognizes (1984, p.120) that the results of 'market failure' should be compared with those of possible 'government failure' but, apart from some qualified endorsement (1984, pp.128–9) of Hayek's arguments on the availability of information (which does not seem to be reflected in any of the models discussed in these essays), he has nothing to offer to the analysis of government. He does note that, if we incorporate government into our model of the economy, then expectations about government policy must themselves become part of the model (1984, p.123). This, of course, is just an application of the general rule that agents must have expectations about the actions of significant other agents – a rule which, as Richardson (1960) has shown, applies even to an atomistic economy. The recognition that 'in evaluating the policy we must not model the actions of agents as if they were independent of the government's policy' is credited to modern monetarists (1984, p.287). However, the principle has been known for some time, and it was being applied over twenty years ago to the evaluation of management control systems. Nevertheless, its obvious relevance for government policy escaped the attention of those few economists who were interested in problems of management control.

Expectations

To assume that agents know, before the adjustment takes place, the equilibrium prices to which they should adjust, is to assume too much; but, as Richardson (1960) has demonstrated, it is also to assume too little. One has to take explicit account of what they might know, or surmise, about other agents' plans. As Hahn has suggested, agents' theories and policies are crucial concepts, but an analysis of the conditions in which such theories and policies would not change is chiefly of service in helping us to understand what may prevent adjustment. That may be an extremely valuable service. Work on conjectural equilibria, as reported by Hahn (1984, pp.186–7), appears to come very close to this point in demonstrating the coherence of sets of beliefs which inhibit the kinds of adjustments which are required for continuous market clearing. Marshallian short-run quantity adjustment could no doubt be expressed in similar terms. But if the economy is ever to move from its original (supposed) equilibrium, expectations must change (1984, p.36).

Unfortunately, as Hahn (1984, p.81) is the first to point out, we have no theory of expectations. 'We know next to nothing about expectations, and that is why we take the step of demanding that they be rational' (1984, p.313). This step is not one which entirely commends itself to Hahn, although he does point out that it is not itself sufficient to ensure either Walrasian equilibrium or optimality. As he observes, those who invoke rational expectations have not offered any adequate explanation of the processes by which they are arrived at (1984, p.82). New classical macroeconomists seem to believe that all economically significant events in the world are drawn from their own stationary stochastic distributions, that these distributions may be discovered by simple inductive reasoning, and that it is in agents' interests to undertake such reasoning. This, of course, is nonsense. But the failure to produce a good theory of the establishment of rational expectations simply mirrors the failure of general equilibrium theorists to produce a good theory of the establishment of equilibrium. If general equilibrium theories may be used nevertheless, why should not the assumption of rational expectations?

Although he never says so, it appears that this question has been increasingly troubling Hahn. In some of his earlier pieces he draws strong conclusions from equilibrium results in a fashion which seems remarkably similar to that used by new classical macroeconomists but, more recently, he has used the absence of any theory of the approach to equilibrium as an argument for refuting new classical macroeconomists' claims (1984, p.315). He is much too intelligent not to appreciate that his own earlier claims for the applicability of the well established theoretical results need to be reconsidered; and indeed one has the impression that he now recognizes how seriously the missing half of the story threatens the usefulness of the first half.

Hahn is no longer prepared to accept any simple proposition that in an economy of rational agents there could be no unexploited gains from trade. As he points out, 'opportunities for mutually advantageous trade must be recognised and hence signalled' (1984, p.127). If this observation suggests the possibility of a limited alliance with neo-Austrians, his comment, a few sentences later, that 'the manner in which potential traders can communicate is of basic significance' suggests the need for a systematic treatment of institutions. It is rather disappointing that, at least in the article from which these observations are quoted, he seems to be content with the conclusion that the price mechanism does have considerable success in the necessary task of utilizing private information, whereas 'it is not at all clear in what fashion it could be performed without the price system altogether' (1984, p.128). Unfortunately, it is not at all clear from general equilibrium models how it is performed by using the price system. Nowhere in this collection does he give any attention to attempts to develop theoretical structures for handling these questions.

Sequence economies

What seems to be the preferred general equilibrium strategy for dealing with movements of an economy through time is to have recourse to models of sequence economies (1984, p.82), although Hahn is clearly conscious of some of their limitations. They do not successfully evade the problem of incorporating expectations into the story. 'Taking expectations seriously causes us to recognise that the short period depends on an unalterable past and a conjectured future' (1984, p.186). That sounds remarkably like Shackle, who is mentioned only in the earliest article in this collection (originally published in 1952). One would not expect Shackle's treatment of expectations as the product of imagination to have much appeal to Hahn, but if one wishes to provide some basis for expectations which is neither imagination nor the currently fashionable complete rationality, then one surely needs to consider institutions.

The study of sequence economies is an attempt to provide the illusion of an economy in motion. Hahn emphasizes the need 'to recognise explicitly the essentially sequential structure of the economies which we study' (1984, p.68), and to develop a model which is 'sequential in an *essential* way' (1984, p.53). In a paper of 1970, he retains the Pareto-optimality of a Debreu economy as the criterion of efficiency, which immediately poses the problem of the conditions in which a sequence economy could generate Debreu prices (1984, p.93). One obvious requirement is that the expectations of agents should not differ; why this requirement should be satisfied is much less obvious. It is also necessary that no production or consumption should take place in the process of establishing these prices: here it is not only Pareto-optimality which is at risk, but the analytical method (1984, p.94).

In later papers, further difficulties are noted. If we allow sufficient uncertainty to generate a stochastic equilibrium, then there is a need for agents to forecast adjustment processes, 'and I cannot see how that is to be done' (1984, p.322). In perfect competition, as Richardson (1960) showed, it cannot be done. Nor is it clear what a firm should maximize, once we allow for the possibility of divergent expectations among its decision-makers, with no markets on which they can trade (1984, pp.82–3, 180). There is then 'no meaning to the assumption that profits are maximized' (1984, p.334) – a proposition that Drucker (1955) was arguing thirty years ago, but which is still almost universally ignored by economists.

Hahn is much exercised by the incompleteness of markets. He notes that a full set of markets is essential for some of the standard claims for market efficiency (1984, p.113) but does not raise the question of who is supposed to make markets (a problem which is central to Casson's (1982) analysis of the entrepreneur) and what happens to the definition of optimality when the costs of market-making are allowed for. The lack of contingent markets is a source of uncertainty (1984, p.123); but uncertainty is not recognized as a reason for the lack of markets. Contingent markets provide complete insurance (1984, p.113); but how could they if the future is in some respects unknowable?

The theorist's response to the incompleteness of markets is to enquire whether a satisfactory equivalent story can be told which does not depend on them (1984, p.121). Others may prefer careful attention to such questions as: what are the incentives to create markets, and what are the costs of creating them?; what are the alternatives to markets, especially future markets, and what are the implications of these alternatives? Such questions lead towards the study of liquidity, and of other ways of providing oneself with the means to take action in an uncertain future – which, as noted by Hicks (1976), are problems of the economy in time – and also to the study of the firm as an organization. We might even wonder whether there are any respects in which the absence of markets actually contributes to the working of an economy.

Inventory and prices
In the absence of futures markets, some assets must be held to provide for future exchange (1984, p.176). Consumers hold money, producers hold money and inventory. These stocks allow agents to respond to fresh circumstances by quantity adjustment, without changing prices, and generally without any need for rationing. Stock adjustment, rather than rationing, Hahn reasonably suggests (1984, p.189), is the appropriate conception for Keynesian economics. (Quantity-constrained equilibria are considered in Chapter 11.) But why should agents adjust stocks and not prices? It is a rational response if they have a strong

sense of 'normal prices', so that any adjustment is expected to be reversed fairly quickly. Hahn gives the credit for this argument to Kaldor (1939) but, of course, it should go primarily to Marshall (1961), perhaps also with some acknowledgement to Hall and Hitch (1939). Andrews's (1949) elaboration of firms' pricing and inventory policies met with incomprehension from theorists whose vision was bounded by a market-clearing equilibrium of optimizing agents. Casson (1982) explicitly recognizes that the expectation of stable prices is a great encouragement to hold stocks of both goods and money, and thus helps entrepreneurs to make and maintain markets.

Keynes emphasized the interaction of normal price expectations and stock adjustment in the market for loans (Hahn, 1984, p.189); he seems to have assumed continuous market clearing (with what look like rational expectations) in the market for consumer goods. Keynes produced a model of short-period equilibrium which rested upon a particular set of long-run expectations; these expectations, however, were not explained – and, according to some interpretations, were inherently incapable of being explained as the product of a fully rational model. Each shift of long-run expectations caused a discontinuous shift to a new short-period equilibrium.

This strategy may be thought appropriate for Keynes's immediate purposes; but the two-way association between stock adjustment and expectations of normal prices seems peculiarly well-fitted to explain why an economy may be able very comfortably to accommodate modest changes, but be tipped into recession or an inflationary boom by larger and more persistent shifts, as Leijonhufvud (1973) has suggested. If stocks are exhausted, agents' theories about normal prices may be deemed, in Hahn's (1973; 1984, p.59) phraseology, 'sufficiently and systematically falsified'. If cash is exhausted, agents are bankrupt and, as Hahn observes, 'the possibility of bankruptcy is . . . also a possibility for the occurrence of some rather sharp discontinuities' (1984, p.156). Moreover, an economy in which agents have been accustomed to adjust quantities may have lost the art of adjusting prices; if one is committed to a particular theory and policy in the belief that they are true, it may not be easy to find adequate replacements. As Hahn (1984, p.40) remarks, 'short run instability does not necessarily imply long-run instability'; but in a slightly wider context, it is also true that short-run stability does not necessarily imply long-run stability – a short-lived fall in demand, for example, may cause no serious problem, but its prolongation may precipitate a crisis.

Money

Adjustment and uncertainty in incomplete markets seems to be the appropriate framework for the consideration of money, as Hicks (1982, p.7) has argued. It has certainly proved impossible to find any essential role for money in a theoretical world of complete markets. That is not to say, as Hahn (1984, p.182) properly points out, that it is only by the introduction of money that one can devise a theoretical structure which generates Keynesian results. Barter economies with any non-reproducible asset will suffice (1984, p.183). But we do not have to agree with him that 'money in all of this has been a disaster from beginning to end' (1984, p.192). Though crediting Keynes with the realization that the choice among alternative stores of value was an essential part of the story (1984, p.183), Hahn seems reluctant to recognize the double insight which provides the basis of the Cambridge monetary tradition: money provides the transaction technology which makes plausible an analysis of the economy formally cast in terms of direct exchange of commodities; but money necessarily introduces a new possible source of disorder. Hahn's claim 'that Keynes was the first economist to notice the tension . . . between the paradigm of the inessential economy and monetary phenomena' (1984, pp.162–3) does not, contrary to his view, seem hard to dispute; the perception goes back through Robertson to Marshall's (1961) Appendix on Barter.

The absence of any general equilibrium model of the economy which can account for the existence of money and allow it to have real effects (1984, pp.162, 261) might be thought to raise some questions about the direction taken by 'highbrow theory' (to use a Robertsonian phrase) in the last fifty years. Nor are these doubts confined to positive economics. 'The necessary conditions for Pareto efficiency in a world of uncertainty with intertemporal choice will in general be fulfilled in a market economy only if money plays no role' (1984, p.270). But, if 'a monetary economy needs to have certain special features such as transaction costs and/or missing markets – features which do not appear in the classical theorems of welfare economics' (1984, p.14), what precisely is the significance of those theorems? Again and again, when we demonstrate that a particular outcome is not Pareto-efficient by established standards, what one is bringing to judgement is not the particular outcome but the definition of Pareto-efficiency. Hahn is surely right in claiming (1984, p.173) that the incorporation of essential money into our general models 'will make a fundamental difference to the way in which we view a decentralised economy'. It will make a greater difference than he is always ready to admit.

Money, like any other institution, needs an explanation if it is to perform an essential function (1984, p.12). It is perhaps the most serious general limitation of the Arrow–Debreu world that it provides scope for no institutions whatever. Even the celebrated auctioneer has no role to play in proving the existence of an equilibrium. What he does accomplish is to encourage what Hahn calls 'the central confusion between the sentence starting "there exists" and one starting with "it is the case"' (1984, p.315). Unfortunately, this confusion is not, as Hahn may appear to imply, peculiar to monetarists; it is embodied in every judgement which relies purely on existence proofs, either positive or negative. In his most recent essays, it is notable how much less reliance Hahn places on formal analysis – except to expose the formal deficiencies of other formal analyses – and how much more he depends on what Nelson and Winter (1982) have labelled 'appreciative theory'. His limited approval of the working of the invisible hand owes nothing whatever to formal argument: his conclusion (1984, p.133) that 'the wishy-washy, step by step, case by case approach seems to me the only reasonable one in economic policy' is a damning indictment of the achievements of the research programme to which he has given so much.

New classical macroeconomics

Hahn (1984, p.177) is surely right in declaring that Walrasian short-period equilibrium, which appeared for some time to be the appropriate neoclassical framework for exploring Keynes's analysis, is not the right model. The monetarist analysis which relies on this framework not only leads to the conclusion that Keynesian remedies are ineffective, it also appears to demonstrate that the problems at which they are to be directed are logically inconceivable. 'In a sense, then, not only is monetary policy ineffective, but happily there is no Keynesian need for it' (1984, p.287). Now as Hahn himself acknowledges (1984, p.65), the Arrow–Debreu model, with its complete set of markets for all dates and all contingent commodities, does indeed define a world in which there can be no Keynesian problems. It is also, of course, Pareto-optimal (if the characteristics of the economy are appropriately specified), and so there are no alternative arguments for government intervention. What new classical macroeconomists apparently want is the set of policy implications in Arrow–Debreu without using the Arrow–Debreu model.

The obvious difficulty is that, if we did live in an Arrow–Debreu world, all the necessary decisions would have been optimally made long ago and there could therefore be no current economic problems of any kind. Thus, to provide anything worth arguing about, one must at least switch to a sequence economy with incomplete markets. As Hahn repeatedly emphasizes, this switch calls into question many of the results of Arrow–Debreu; the role of rational expectations is to provide a substitute for the missing markets – a substitute which is believed to be good enough to reinstate those results. Hahn (1984, pp.285–6) points out that, to achieve the theoretical goal of a unique rational expectations equilibrium, further assumptions are necessary: for example, creditors and debtors must be sufficiently alike to eliminate any effects of redistribution, agents must be able to calculate correctly the future tax burden of government debt (of which each must expect to bear an appropriate share), the real tax system must not be progressive, and the money supply must not be systematically dependent on the state of nature.

There are two ways of defending such a set of assumptions (together, of course, with the assumptions that are required for any kind of Walrasian model), and both have been used by new classical macroeconomists. One may take Friedman's (1953, p.14) position that *of course* the model is 'wildly inaccurate' as a description of the world, and the only valid test is its predictive success. However, we often seem to be faced with the problem not of using evidence to discriminate between theories, but of using theories to interpret evidence – notably to explain the historical record of the numbers described as 'unemployed'. In such a situation, Friedman's argument is not relevant. It probably never was very appealing to theorists, who are more likely to agree with Hahn: 'If a monetarist model is logically flawed then I for one do not give a fig for its predictive power' (1984, p.312).

The alternative defence is an appeal to theoretical coherence. Hahn, as usual, poses the issue clearly. 'In the first instance the question is a theoretical one: can one describe an economy in non-Walrasian equilibrium without violating the fundamental rationality postulate of economic theory?' (1984, p.292). His answer, however, is disappointing: 'Up to the degree of rigour employed by monetarists the answer is pretty clearly that one can.' Since he draws attention repeatedly to the inadequacy of monetarist rigour, we might look for something better. But if one insists on equilibrium and rationality in an institution-free economy, it is not easy to provide a formally rigorous rebuttal of 'perfect adjustment' models. Is it logically acceptable to define a full equilibrium of an economy of intelligent self-seeking agents in which there are unexploited gains from trade or from knowledge? Lucas and Sargent surely believe that they are realizing the potential of the general equilibrium method; theoretical superiority counts for even more than policy conclusions.

Hahn (1984, p.292) recognizes that non-Walrasian models require imperfect competition – which 'causes me very little concern'. But what can be the rational basis of imperfect competition in the kind of theoretical world which he inhabits? Joan Robinson (1933) provided no such basis; nor, for all his explicit consideration of product differentiation, did Chamberlin (1933), as Andrews (1964) has demonstrated. Chamberlin did, however, provide a good basis for a process story of imperfect competition; and we know that process stories require non-perfect competition. Hahn realizes that the absence of any process story leaves general equilibrium analysis dangerously incomplete; does he agree that the incompleteness, and the danger, are especially evident in the analysis of Keynesian problems?

The limits of general equilibrium
Hahn (1984, p.77) claims that 'there exists at present no alternative theory which explains what general equilibrium theory seeks to explain', which presumably is the working of an economy of independent and self-seeking agents, its successes and its failures. That claim invites a double response: that there are alternatives, and that general equilibrium theory is not very successful in its own explanation. When Hahn (1984, p.132) claims that 'it is a great virtue of the theory that it suggests ways in which institutions and policies might be devised, which harness self-interest and render it socially acceptable', are we to assume that only general equilibrium theory does this and to forget that it appears to offer somewhat greater support for the replacement of self-interest by central planning? The implication that acceptable institutions must leave no agent with market power would be fatal to any adjustment process, and of course eliminate any possibility of economic progress through either Marshallian incremental change or Schumpeterian creative destruction.

Hahn is well aware of many of the problems within the general equilibrium theoretical method. In these essays, he pays particular attention to those problems which impinge on macroeconomic analysis: 'the Walrasian model does not capture any of the market failures macroeconomists have been concerned with for forty-five years' (1984, p.290). He wishes to encourage work on non-Walrasian models, arguing (1984, p.293) that, although the Walrasian model is 'theoretically more securely based . . . the non-Walrasian construction is sufficiently coherent to warrant the belief that it can in due course be as polished and as tightly knit as its Walrasian competitor'. In choosing between theories, the first requirement is actual or potential rigour and coherence; the opportunity costs of coherence and rigour are considered, if at all, only in choosing between those theories which survive the first stage.

The assumptions of serious theory make 'explicit what the man of faith and the man of affairs must reasonably be taken to be implicitly supposing' in order to justify their conclusions (1984, p.329). This may be a negative function – to demonstrate the implausibility of the conclusion. But the method is not entirely reliable. It was used, rigorously and honestly, to demonstrate the impossibility of continental drift. It has similarly been used to demonstrate the prevalence of market failures. The rejection of continental drift was based on the wrong model; but 'geologists . . . rejected first-rate evidence from fossils, rocks and landscapes because they thought it was in conflict with quantitative mathematical reasoning which few of them really understood' (Ziman, 1978, p.94). Similarly, and despite Hahn's (1984, p.136) claims, the general equilibrium method does not provide the only scientific approach to the study of competitive markets.

If 'one of the reasons why an equilibrium notion is useful is that it serves to make precise the limits of economic analysis' (1984, p.56), we must conclude that the study of market processes – or of any other kind of process, certainly including the ways in which agents may change their theories and policies – are to be placed beyond those limits. Perhaps Hahn has never really believed what he then wrote (during his career he has given considerable attention to adjustment problems) and he certainly seems to believe it no longer. He now (1984, p.4) draws attention to the dangers of considering 'nothing but equilibrium. . . . What is plain is that by narrowing our viewpoint in this manner we shall remove a great deal of interest and importance from scrutiny.'

What has prompted this warning is clearly the practice of Lucas and his followers, whose pronouncements on the state of the economy and on economic policy rely on the use of a particular – but widely accepted – kind of equilibrium model, and on the assumption that the existence of an equilibrium is equivalent to its speedy realization. Hahn has striven to demonstrate that there are other general equilibrium formulations which do not always yield the favoured results. But the framework of fully rational equilibrium is against him: as he once observed, 'it is the models that lead people to view the economic system as they do' (1984, p.88).

The study of equilibrium is surely motivated by rather more than 'a very weak causal proposition . . . that no plausible sequence of economic states will terminate if it does so at all, in a state which is not an equilibrium' (1984, p.47). The motivation extends to a belief that equilibrium will be reached fairly quickly, and with no serious accidents along the way. The new classical economists have taken just a little further the principles regularly used to appraise a competitive economy. Hahn may find flaws in their technical logic; but their methodological logic is a more rigorous version of what used to be his own. The obvious questions to direct at new classical macroeconomists – what can agents be expected to know? How can they find out? By what processes may people make the adjustments needed to bring them into equilibrium? – are precisely the questions to be directed at the kinds of equilibrium model which Hahn himself has favoured.

Agents' theories and policies

Hahn has suggested a way of coming closer to such questions. Indeed, for those who are not committed to equilibrium models, his respecification (1973; 1984, pp.54–9) of equilibrium in terms of the theories and policies of economic agents is ample justification of his claim that the notion of equilibrium is valuable. He was anticipated by Hayek (1937), but his formulation is potentially more fruitful. It focuses attention more clearly on the agent's situation, and the problems which the agent may have in making sense of it, thereby allowing equilibria to be boundedly rational. It offers genuine escape from the assumptions of perfect knowledge, which the concept of contingent markets does not, and suggests helpful ways of thinking about stability and adjustment. It allows us to separate the stability of agents' theories and policies from the stability of prices, production and sales, or indeed from the stability of rates of growth of these variables. In his original exposition, Hahn dissociated an equilibrium of theories and policies from market-clearing, but appeared to underestimate the potential divergence; now that the definition of equilibria in which some markets are far from cleared is much more important to him, he might wish to reconsider.

But, although the behaviour of such agents may be describable by structurally stable equations (1973; 1984, p.56) and may therefore be termed routine (1984, p.9), it does not, as Hahn (1984, p.25) apparently thought in 1952, require a systematic set of experiences on which such a routine could be based. Hahn appeared there to come close to formulating a concept of rational expectations, as indeed did Hayek in 1937; but, although rational expectations would support one kind of Hahn equilibrium, that is by no means the only kind. As with Hayek's (1937, p.51) exposition, not only is equilibrium defined in relation to the knowledge which an agent is bound to acquire in attempting to carry out his policy, ignoring the knowledge which would cause him to revise his theory or his policy if he were to acquire it by accident; the revision of theory and policy need be no simple function of the data.

Indeed it is one of the virtues of Hahn's broad definition that it can encompass the kinds of routine described by Nelson and Winter (1982), which may be highly resistant to messages from the economy. As economists should surely recognize, a theory in apparent trouble is not easily superseded; it is rarely obvious whether it should be replaced rather than amended, and suitable replacements may be hard to devise. There is, of course, no need to follow Hahn's own method (1973; 1984, p.59) of defining the conditions which would lead to a change of routine in the language of statistical decision theory. Procedural rationality does not require – although it does not exclude – such a formulation. Hahn's (1984, p.27) suggestion, in 1952, that 'it may be sensible to imagine producers as changing routine behaviour at discrete time intervals rather than as continuously taking new decisions' may actually be closer to some modern ideas than his later proposals. Certainly his warning that non-equilibrium dynamic models cannot legitimately assume unchanging routine is well taken.

Hahn's intellectual future
The later papers in this book enjoin caution in the application of general equilibrium models. Indeed, 'serious theory . . . provides quite clearly the documentation of its own inadequacies and incompleteness' (1984, p.333). It nevertheless appears to define the scope of economics. 'A function of axiomatic theory is to provide the logical framework deduced from agreed general first principles in which contingent knowledge can be shown to have its particular consequences' (1984, p.330). Hahn is particularly concerned to emphasize that this framework permits a range of possibilities: to put it in language which he does not use, he is critical of situational determinism. But does he still believe that the general equilibrium method, as it has been applied, for example, by Radner and Stiglitz as well as himself, provides the only framework? When he writes (1984, p.341) that 'the set of possible outcomes is a good deal larger than the set arrived at by economic theory', does he mean simply that the theorists have not yet completed their work, or that there are possible outcomes which the theory is unable to encompass? When he warns us (1984, pp.331–2), very properly, that 'one must be sure that the simplification was not essential to the insight one claims to have gained', does he have in mind the simplifications which are axiomatized in all general equilibrium models, or, as seems more likely, 'those macroeconomists who are filling the journals with three or four log-linear equations' (1984, pp.313–14)?

While defending the simplifying coherence of general equilibrium models against Kornai's demand for adequate complexity, Hahn (1984, p.139) observes that general equilibrium models are frequently criticized for being too complicated in comparison with the Marshallian tradition. Whatever may be thought of the Marshallian tradition, Marshall's own theoretical structure, as we have seen in Chapter 4, was very far from simple: his models may have been partial rather than general, but they incorporated, for example, non-atomistic competition (in respect both of rivalry between suppliers and of supplier–customer relationships), the rise and decline of firms, the introduction of new products (including those which customers had never thought of), and the gradual improvement of productive methods. Indeed, much of the theoretical development since Marshall has taken the form of drastic simplification for the purpose of enhanced tractability.

In his introduction to this collection Hahn (1984, p.7) declares that 'the most strongly held of my views . . . is that neither is there a single best way for understanding in economics nor is it possible to hold any conclusions, other than purely logical deductions, with certainty'. Does that mean that he is prepared himself to try alternative approaches to that of general equilibrium? Of course there are 'difficulties . . . in transcending a well developed and articulate tradition' (1984, p.177); but the concepts employed in Hahn's own definition of equilibrium offer a means of escape.

Let him consider, for example, the implications for agents' own theories and policies of his own two statements just quoted. Suppose that agents themselves do not believe that there is a single best way for understanding, and that their conclusions are always subject to uncertainty (in Shackle's sense); suppose also that there are difficulties in transcending a well developed tradition – difficulties easily found in British industry, politics, and academia. What might these assumptions imply, for example, about the relationship 'between the perceived environment and the environment' (1984, p.58), about the demand for various kinds of liquidity and reserves, about the intellectual and psychological problems of revising theories and policies, about the difficulties of matching unemployed resources with unsatisfied wants? It would certainly be something different from the new classical macroeconomics. The strongest single impression left by this collection is Hahn's progressive disenchantment with the accomplishments of general equilibrium theory, as, despite the best efforts of most of the best theorists, it is applied in ways which he clearly finds morally as well as intellectually reprehensible. The most fascinating question which the collection raises is whether he is yet prepared to try another approach.

9 Herbert Simon's human rationality*

The sixty papers included in the two volumes of Herbert Simon's *Models of Bounded Rationality* (1982) constitute, in the author's words, 'a reasonably complete collection of my economic works that have not been published elsewhere in book form' (1982, 1: p.xviii). In this chapter I propose to use this collection as a single body of evidence to illuminate not only Simon's view of economics, but also his view of the human situation. It is always dangerous to consider a set of pieces published over a period of more than forty years without reference to their temporal sequence, but neither in his general nor in his sectional introductions does Simon suggest that he has discarded any of his earlier ideas. There are some qualifications and some changes of emphasis, but not many even of these. In appraising Simon's work, time does not seem to be important: as we shall see later, that statement bears more than one interpretation. Whereas Hahn's attitude to equilibrium, which we examined in Chapter 8, appears to be undergoing a process of change, Simon's view of processes appears to be in stable equilibrium. This attempt to summarize and comment on what one might call Simon's decision premises (to use his own terminology) may help us to understand not only his own work but also the reaction – or lack of reaction – to it by economists of various persuasions.

Complexity and pragmatism
Let us start with an article of 1971 which bears a characteristic title: 'Designing organizations for an information-rich world' (1982, 2: pp.171–85). Here Simon argues forcefully that plentiful information will not resolve the difficulties which we face in trying to behave reasonably. The abundance of information accentuates the scarcity of our means of handling it. Although we must attempt to recognize externalities and interdependencies, we must also recognize that:

> . . . the dream of thinking everything out before we act, of making certain we have all the facts and know all the consequences, is a sick Hamlet's dream. It is the dream of someone with no appreciation of the seamless web

*An earlier version of this chapter was presented at George Mason University, Virginia, in May 1985

of causation, the limits of human thinking, or the scarcity of human attention. (1982, 2: p.180)

That the complexity of our environment, natural and artificial, extends far beyond the bounds of our rationality is the central fact with which Simon has been trying to deal throughout his career. One obvious consequence is that we must expect to make mistakes, sometimes serious mistakes.

> The world will always remain the largest laboratory, the largest information store. . . . Of course it is costly to learn from experience; but it is also costly, and frequently much less reliable, to try through research and analysis to anticipate experience. (1982, 2: p.180)

In other words, don't expect too much from any model – and don't claim too much for it either. Nevertheless, there is no need to worry.

> We must assume, as mankind has always assumed, that a reasonable allocation of our limited attention and powers of thought will solve the crucial problems facing us at least as fast as new ones arise. (1982, 2: p.181)

Before turning to the implications of this assumption, let us briefly consider the parenthesis, 'as mankind has always assumed'. As an assertion about human history, this is obviously false; but it tells us a great deal about Simon. First, it demonstrates that his recognition of the central fact of bounded rationality is matched with a central belief: a belief in the capacity of human reason (and perhaps, like Einstein, in the fairness of God) which is so fundamental that Simon simply assumes that it must be shared by all reasonable men. That belief sets unrecognized bounds to his own rationality: and it may serve to remind us that our own systems of thought almost certainly contain basic elements which we have just never thought of as open to question. Second, such an assertion could hardly have been made by someone who is deeply interested in history: Simon looks back only to draw the lessons of immediate experience, and then quickly forward to the next problem. Third, he is a pragmatist, who gives little attention to philosophical issues. As with Oliver Edwards, who (in Boswell's *Life of Johnson*) had often tried to be a philosopher, cheerfulness is always breaking in.

Life is a succession of problems, to be tackled successively. It appears to embody no grand theories, no opportunities for global optimization. Nevertheless, the challenge of new problems, and their successful resolution, makes life an intellectual adventure (1982, 2: p.132). I am reminded of a saying by Charles Suckling (a research chemist who became General Manager, Research and Technology, in ICI) that 'the best things we can leave to our children are unsolved problems'. If this is to be a message of hope, then we must assume that we can solve crucial problems as fast as new ones arise – but preferably not much faster.

Simon's central assumption implies an interest in processes rather than equilibrium, but, since all models are incomplete representations of the phenomena to which they are applied, equilibrium concepts may be used on occasion. It implies a systems view which is, in some respects, almost the opposite of that taken by general equilibrium theorists. First, the overall system is not to be regarded as complete: there are transactions across its boundaries which are not fully modelled. Second, the behaviour of this overall system is explained in terms of the aggregate behaviour of its subsystems, each of which is explained in turn by the aggregate behaviour of its own subsystems; there is no attempt to relate overall system performance directly to its basic elements. Third, the usual problem addressed is the ongoing management of the system in response to extraneous data, rather than the calculation of equilibrium states or equilibrium flows. Finally (and particularly for Simon), the problem of system management often causes interest to be focused not on the 'real world' elements – the usual variables of economic models – but on the organizational arrangements and decision routines by which these variables are handled.

A combination of these last two elements is implied by the title of Simon's essay 'From substantive to procedural rationality' (1982, 2: pp.424–43). Instead of seeking to derive from axioms and data the values which would be ascribed to the relevant variables by an optimal decision, attention is turned to the processes by which reasonable decisions might be made. The complexity of the decision environment places optimality beyond reach, and often beyond definition; what is sought is a feasible procedure for achieving satisfactory results, and ways of checking on experience as a possible guide to doing better.

This concern for effective means of handling complexity sometimes leads Simon to argue that the progress of management science permits increasing centralization of decision-making in partial replacement of the market and that, since this centralization allows us to handle more interactions, it will improve the quality of decisions (1982, 2: pp.61–2). Although he reminds town planners that what happens in a city depends on the behaviour of its citizens, who have no intention of surrendering their freedom of action to those who have been given 'certain very limited powers to modify the design' (1982, 2: p.52), he does not appear to recognize the effects of centralization on the quality of the information supplied; he tends to be absorbed by the technology of information processing and the challenge of the conscious design of institutions. What preserves him from the advocacy of any kind of system of central planning is his continuing conviction that, for all our technical advances, the scale and complexity of the problems cannot be sensibly handled in that way. We need rather to look for means of coupling together partial decision rules – for example, through the price mechanism – or even sometimes to content ourselves with securing 'compatibility requirements', so that one decision procedure will not produce results which actually impede the effectiveness of another (1982, 1: p.191).

Loose coupling of partial systems (which is exemplified in Cyert and March's (1963) analysis of organizational behaviour) implies a set of objectives rather than any kind of single objective function, however complicated. What we do not find in these papers is a recognition of the potential value of incompatible systems: insistence on compatibility may prevent certain kinds of exploration which do not fit in with present ideas or present practices. But Simon does not consciously envisage the intellectual adventure of solving human problems as a competitive discovery procedure – although this is clearly what it is, even in several areas of pure science. Though he favours a competitive economy, he does not explain why. Neither entrepreneurship nor spontaneous organization are significant concepts in Simon's work.

Whether the fundamental cause of the difficulties which we face is to be found in our inadequate ability to cope with complexity or because at least part of the future is unknowable is not an issue which he ever raises. Unlike Shackle, he is not very interested in the philosophical issues. His continuing fascination with chess, computers, and artificial intelligence suggests that he believes the cause to be complexity: although, as we shall see later, he recognizes the indeterminacy of interdependent decisions, he does sometimes give the impression that we do live in a fully defined system, if only we had the wit to understand it. But his understanding of computers and of artificial intelligence do not give him any hope that we shall ever acquire the wit fully to understand complexity; and perhaps his interest is attracted by the belief that there are more usefully solvable problems in complexity than in ignorance. (Neoclassical economists, in his view, too often make their problems soluble by making the solutions useless.) He has no expectation of constructing a comprehensive system, no ideals to match those of many physicists or economists. His business is piecemeal social engineering.

Optimization

In some respects Simon appears very conventional. He is an enthusiast
of mathematical analysis and welcomes the increasing mathematization
of the social sciences. He is obviously pleased (1982, 2: p.3) at his
success at translating into mathematical form the theory of group interaction proposed by the sociologist G.C. Homans (1982, 2: p.33–42), to
which he applies the standard economic method of deriving comparative
static equilibria. At the end of an article entitled 'Some economic effects
of technical change', after acknowledging the unrealism of the models
presented, he offers an argument which we might expect to hear from
another author.

> If such models have no other value, they are of use in permitting a precise
> statement of the Malthusian hypothesis, and an examination of the
> conditions under which that hypothesis holds. (1982, 1: p.305)

In what ways this examination might be useful he does not say.
However, he insists that mathematical social science should be applied
mathematics: the language of mathematics should be used to say something about its nominal subject-matter, and not merely about the
language itself. Logical coherence is no substitute for empirical validity
(1982, 2: p.209). As we observed in Chapter 8, Hahn (1984, p.312)
characteristically stresses the converse proposition.

Neoclassical methods are justified, Simon argues (1982, 1: p.xix), if
the assumptions which are made are not too far removed from the real
world to invalidate the conclusions – a question to be settled by examining the assumptions, not (as with Friedman, 1953) the conclusions –
and also if the data required are obtainable and the computations
feasible. When he judges that these conditions are met, he has had no
hesitation in using neoclassical techniques. Indeed, a study undertaken
in the late 1940s of the likely impact of nuclear power on US national
income (1982, 1: pp. 325–53) anticipates both the methods and the
results of the 'new economic history' – the methods in comparing the
projected nuclear economy with an optimally adapted non-nuclear
economy, and the results in the conclusion that, in a world full of
alternatives, nothing actually matters very much.

More instructive is his attitude to the extensive collaborative work
which he undertook on production scheduling and inventory control,
in which optimization techniques were freely applied to quadratic cost
functions which were acknowledged to be false. He makes no use of
Friedman's arguments, to which he strongly objects elsewhere (1982,
2: p.369–71). The use of false assumptions is justified on two grounds:

first, they make the problem manageable, by requiring managers to supply relatively few estimates which need not be very accurate and which can be used in fairly straightforward computations (1982, 2: pp.386–8); second, as is argued in some detail (1982, 1: pp.202–11), each is a reasonably good approximation to the likely truth within the range of variation to which the decision rules are meant to apply.

It is this reasonable, and usable, approximation which, he asserts (1982, 2: p.371), is far more significant for the acceptability of data than the significance which statisticians emphasize. The best-fitting equation is not necessarily the most useful. The limits of acceptability may then be tested by sensitivity analysis, which sometimes assures us of the robustness of our conclusions, and at other times warns us of their vulnerability to estimates which have no sure foundation (1982, 1:p.264).

As Simon (1982, 2: p.486) has observed, this work has had an ironic sequel: one of his collaborators, John Muth, impressed by their success in calculating apparently optimal actions from the expected values of probability distributions, proposed that such expected values, each derived from the relevant economic theory, should be taken as the basis of rational decisions. To Simon, of course, the optimizing procedure which they had devised was itself an example of satisficing, not to be generalized without detailed examination: the optimization of artificially simplified models is not, he reminds us, a good strategy for solving problems in chess (1982, 2: p.414). But, even if we can assume that the world supplies us with probability distributions which allow us to make unbiased forecasts, and that the cost of obtaining the necessary information does not render the acceptance of possible bias optimal, the derivation of rational decisions from rational expectations is straightforward only if the loss function is quadratic (as was assumed for the original study). 'Unbiased estimation can be a component of all sorts of rational and irrational behavior rules' (1982, 2: p.438).

If Simon is sceptical about the merits of rational expectations, aggregate Cobb–Douglas production functions are dismissed with scorn. The apparent evidence in favour of such functions and of their success in predicting labour's share of output is declared to be vitiated by faulty econometric method (1982, 1: pp.444–59): 'these results are a statistical artifact without economic significance' (1982, 1: p.405). 'The data say no more than that the value of product is approximately equal to the wage bill plus the cost of capital services' (1982, 1: p.454); and since the latter explanation is adequate and simpler, it should be preferred (1982, 1: p.458). In making this recommendation, it has to be said that Simon reveals a failure to understand the purpose of Cobb–Douglas functions, or indeed of production functions as a class: Simon's preferred explanation is very far from adequate for the issues which neoclassical economists deem important. We shall return to this issue at the end of this chapter.

Aggregate production functions are under some suspicion because of the dangers of aggregation. These dangers engendered a spirited and notorious dispute between Cambridge, England and Cambridge, Massachusetts; but the reluctance of the disputants to look beyond the problems of capital aggregation suggests that the dispute was ideological, and not empirical – perhaps the reason why Simon seems never to have referred to it. The plausibility of aggregation and decomposition in the analysis of complex systems is an obvious issue for him to investigate, and it is no surprise to find him giving his paper on that subject in this collection a very high place among 'scientific publications of which I am proud' (1982, 1: p.404). It is no surprise, either, to find that it is a technical inquiry into a practical problem, not a philosophical discussion (1982, 1: pp.411–41). In *The Sciences of the Artificial* (1969), he is less technical, but still emphasizes the practical issues.

The great majority of economists still do not appear to find the issues of aggregation and decomposability of either practical or philosophical importance, even though they are central to the present confusion over what used to be called macroeconomics. Simon's own analysis no doubt helps to buttress his belief in our ability to solve problems at least as fast as they are created; but although he recognizes the practical importance of the varying speeds with which different interactions take effect, nevertheless for one who prefers process to equilibrium as an organizing principle, he seems to have very little sense of the significance of time in human affairs. Compare his writings with those of Marshall, Shackle, or the later Hicks, and one is immediately conscious of a great difference in attitude and style.

Rationality

With the increasing focus on choice, rationality has become almost the distinguishing characteristic of economic analysis; but it is rationality in a sense not recognized in the other social sciences. Simon (1982, 2: p.383) points to the contrast with psychology.

> It is only a slight exaggeration to say that what an economist or statistical theorist regards as a 'rational decision process' is what a psychologist might regard as 'habitual behavior'; while what a psychologist regards as 'rational choice', an economist would refuse to regard as 'rational' at all.

But economists have great difficulty in pursuing rigorously their

rational programme – although they are often unaware of the difficulties. Neither the objectives nor the limiting conditions within which
economic agents optimize can themselves be derived on the rational
principles which the economist wishes to use. Boundary conditions must
be imposed – and often they are imposed unconsciously. But the
analysis of constrained optimization implies a shadow price for each
constraint, and the fully rational optimizer would redefine his problem
to include the optimization of these constraints. The standard specification of the economic problem, with resources, technology and preferences all given, is necessarily an exercise in bounded rationality, whatever its practitioners may think, and the decision – if it is a decision,
and not the result of unconsidered habit – to pose the problem in this
form cannot be explained by optimization, whatever recourse may be
had to search costs and the economics of information. It also excludes
some of the most important questions, as economists as different as
Marshall and Schumpeter well realized.

The current fascination of many theorists with the concept of games
is surely due in part to the delusion that the rules of whatever game is
being modelled have the same status that such theorists implicitly
(though dubiously) accord to natural laws. But we might remember
that the game of rugby football was created by a player of association
football who broke the rules; and more-or-less orderly revision of the
rules is not uncommon in sport. Some revisions, such as the introduction
of the tie-break in lawn tennis, result directly from a redefinition of
system boundaries. Shackle has frequently drawn attention to the limitations imposed on the applicability of game theory by its exclusion of
surprise; these limitations are characteristically underrated because only
by placing all surprises out of bounds can theorists preserve the rationality of the players. Simon is well aware of the fallibility of human
decisions, and of our ability to generate unexpected problems: yet
surprise is not a concept which belongs in his pattern of thought.

Even with no surprises, as is well known, rationality may prove an
elusive goal. The search for rational solutions to the oligopoly problem
can probably continue for as long as anyone thinks it worthwhile. The
Cournot model, which has come back into favour in recent years, does
possess a quasi-rational equilibrium (reached by an irrational process);
but, as Simon (1982, 2: p.216) observes, it does not achieve fully
informed rationality since, if one agent were correctly to predict the
others' decision rules, then he could do better by changing his own.
The unpalatable fact is that it is impossible to define an equilibrium of
interdependent optimizing agents unless 'we can assume that not more
than one participant is unlimitedly clever in predicting the reactions of

the other participants to his behavior' (1982, 2: p.217). Simon here anticipates Coddington's (1975b) dictum that there can be at most one omniscient being.

The case is actually stronger than Simon realizes. He appears to accept (1982, 2: pp.215–16) that the assumptions of perfect competition, however empirically dubious, do allow every economic agent rationally to treat the actions of every other in the same way that he is supposed to treat the conventional 'givens' of the environment – 'as some kind of responsive or unresponsive mechanism'. But as Richardson (1960) has shown, this is not so: even in perfect competition, the consequences of any one person's action depend on the actions of others. The familiar cobweb theorem, whatever its deficiencies in other respects, suffices to demonstrate that the usual assumptions of perfect competition are not enough to guarantee even the (unconsciously bounded) rationality which is sought.

Determinate solutions are attainable by the axiomatic method only for problems which have been defined by non-rational constraints. Fully rational optimization within limits arbitrarily defined is one response to the unavoidable phenomenon of bounded rationality; as Simon makes clear in many places, this is sometimes a perfectly satisfactory response (and, I would add, often one useful component of a satisfactory response). The other response is to accept limits, not on the definition of the problem, but on the rationality of the procedure used to cope with it. It is the second approach which is characteristic of the study of organizational behaviour (which is to be distinguished sharply from almost everything that economists call industrial organization or the theory of the firm) and of the work of psychologists on human decision-making; and it is in the study of organizations and in psychology that Simon has primarily sought to improve our understanding of the ways in which human beings may solve problems at least as fast as new ones are created.

Institutions
If actions are to be based on reason – not, of course, to be demonstrably optimal in the way that many economists would like – then the knowledge requirements must be reduced. Decomposability of the systems within which decisions are made is a principal means of reducing these requirements, and one particularly important kind of decomposability is that which allows the actions of other people to be tolerably well predicted most of the time by the patterns of behaviour which correspond to their roles. Economies are stabilized by their institutions, in the widest sense of that word: by the recognizable sets of decision

premises which are embodied in the roles and conventions of the social (including of course the industrial) system (Simon, 1982, 2: pp.390–1). Although Simon does not go so far, his position is compatible with that of Richardson: the atomistic and anonymous competition beloved of economic theorists imposes information requirements which are impossible to satisfy; although it may, under certain assumptions, be formally compatible with a general equilibrium, it has no means of achieving or maintaining coherence. The perfectly competitive model is not appropriate for an enquiry into the working of a competitive economy.

The contrary idea, that the predominance of programmed behaviour is necessary for the combination of coherence and originative choice, is not without its supporters; among economists, we may point to Schumpeter (1934), and Kirzner (1973), in addition to Simon and Richardson. Schumpeter's theory of development depends on the ability of innovators to base their novel calculations on the routines of the circular flow – when the routines are thrown into confusion by innovation, the innovators find that they have destroyed the conditions of their own success – while Kirzner's entrepreneurs profit from their less alert contemporaries' persistence in error.

Perhaps more significant – yet never mentioned in this collection – is the similar position taken by some of those who have approached the problems of human knowledge more directly, through the philosophy of science. We have seen in Chapter 2 that both Kuhn and Lakatos set bounds to scientific rationality; and Popper, though rejecting the idea that paradigms or research programmes prevent wider thought, nevertheless affirms that the process of scientific enquiry can only be carried out within a framework which, for a time, must be placed beyond question. He even begins *The Logic of Scientific Discovery* (1972, p.13), by observing that scientists have an important advantage over philosophers of science in their ability (almost always) to work within an already defined problem-situation. That rational decision-making is easier in a substantially programmed environment is precisely what Simon argues (1982, 2: p.390).

As Simon points out (1982, 2: p.391), the stability of institutions is therefore a critical issue, although it is one that he deals with somewhat inadequately. He is not, as we have previously noted, much bothered about general problems such as this, although he has, of course, given much attention to the question of stability within formal organizations. Practitioners of institution-free economics are not likely to pay much attention to what they have decided to ignore; but the consequences of their neglect can be dangerous. It is not surprising, for example, that such economists have found it hard to discover any significant costs of inflation – even those who are most insistent that we must follow a monetary policy which will avoid (or cure) it. This failure gives us no reason for confidence in their policy prescriptions, whatever they may be. Leijonhufvud's (1975) anger was thoroughly justified.

Whereas Richardson's inquiry into the possible institutional framework for rational decision focused on relations between firms, Simon's attention has been concentrated on formal and informal organization – following Barnard (1938) in giving attention to the link between the two. (Both these research strategies rely on the decomposability of a multi-level system.) Organizational structures, and the relationships which develop within them, determine roles (1982, 2: p.308), each of which is to be understood (1982, 2: p.345) as '*a social prescription of some, but not all, of the premises that enter into an individual's choice of behaviors*'. The prescription of some of the decision premises assists prediction by others who need a reasonable basis for their own decisions; that not all are prescribed leaves some room for the exercise of reasoning power, and the making, on occasion, of novel choices. In addition to decision premises, organizations store information, and the contents of both stores change with experience (1982, 2: p.441); indeed, 'a technology exists largely in the minds of its labour force' (1982, 2: p.144).

This view of organizations has been effectively developed by Nelson and Winter (1982), who draw attention to the difficulty of defining precisely the content of any individual's knowledge and of any organization's capabilities (or programmes), and explain how institutions drift over time. This drift, as successive events are construed by individuals in terms of their own interpretative frameworks (Kelly, 1963), can help to stabilize institutions through adaptation; it may also undermine them, if the expectations of interdependent groups diverge – and that is not impossible, even if (which is unlikely) they are all exposed to the same set of phenomena.

Nelson and Winter also develop Simon's (1982, 2: p.397) observation that 'the interdependence of organization units is a strong force toward conservatism'; each unit has a strong interest in preserving the stability of its environment in order to facilitate the formation of confident expectations, and that implies a reluctance to disturb established decision programmes among its neighbours. Organizations may be stable because their members fear that they will not prove resilient. There is thus a strong tendency to try to fit innovations into existing systems; and indeed we see that innovations which typically require extensive reconstruction of existing institutions meet with great resistance and are accomplished only slowly, if at all. They may succeed only by circumventing existing structures and developing in new locations or in new industries. Schumpeter's emphasis on the necessarily destructive consequences of creativity can be justified in Simon's terms; so, in a different way, can Marshall's emphasis on the cumulative importance of incremental change, occurring in a large population of freely competing firms, each with its own established customers and competitors, but each with its own slightly idiosyncratic set of decision programmes, which facilitates particular and localized types of beneficial adjustments.

Perception and theory
In considering the role of institutions we should recognize (even though he himself does not) the warning implicit in Simon's insistence that 'the decision-maker's information about his environment is much less than an approximation to the real environment. . . . In actual fact the perceived world is fantastically different from the "real" world' (1982, 2: p.306). Because of the limitations of the human brain, selection and distortion are inevitable both in perception (the acquisition of information) and inference (the processing of the information acquired). Although Simon (1982, 2: p.307) insists that the filtering which takes place is an active process, he does not go on to point out that this process necessarily implies the imposition of a conjectural framework as a means of selection and interpretation. This is mildly surprising, not only because of his substantial interest in psychology, but also because he observes (1982, 2: p.391) that, for any individual decision-maker, 'the "facts" on which he acts obtain their status as facts by a social process of legitimation, and have only a very tenuous and indirect connection with the evidence of his senses'.

He appears to imply that such a social process is necessarily beneficial when he claims (1982, 2: p.399) that the need for stable expectations makes it 'more important, in some circumstances, to have *agreement* on the facts than to be certain that what is agreed upon is really fact. Hence we often find that the procedures for fact finding and for legitimating facts are themselves institutionalized.' The processes of social legitimation of facts are certainly important, and their neglect by economists a source of serious error; but Simon seems to have no sense of the potential fragility of the structures based on such 'pretty, polite techniques'. The stability and resilience of institutions, and of the expectations which they support, remains problematic. Leijonhufvud's (1973) 'corridor hypothesis' still awaits development, even within its original macroeconomic context. But Simon must be given full credit for recognizing that such stability ought to be – though it is not – a central concern of economics.

The significance of institutions is not diminished by the increasing availability of information. Greater information makes more acute the need to economize on attention, and increases the significance for decision-making of the means of economizing. Information-processing systems are of no value unless they are net absorbers of information (1982, 2: p.175). Among the most efficient information-processing systems is science, which exploits the redundancy of facts in a world which appears to obey natural laws by substituting the laws, which are few, for the facts, of which there are very many. 'With each important advance in scientific theory, we can reduce the volume of explicitly stored knowledge without losing any information whatsoever' (1982, 2: p.178). Thus, scientific advance simplifies our problems. 'To become a research chemist should involve less learning today than it did fifty years ago, because physical chemistry and quantum mechanics have provided such powerful tools for organizing facts, and indeed making them derivable from theory' (1982, 2: p.142).

Organizations have theories too, sometimes set out in detailed principles of corporate strategy, sometimes the result of imposing simple structures on their past record. For example, the research director of a chemical business which had lost money trying to develop self-assembly furniture, for which they produced only the bulk filler, not the surface laminates, defined his research strategy thereafter as 'no more bloody flat things' – certainly an efficient information-processing rule! But Simon does not explicitly consider the processes by which organizations acquire and amend their theories; nor do Nelson and Winter, although they do focus on the issue of knowledge within organizations. None of them recognizes that theories (or any other information-processing system) may impose misleading patterns. There can be no way of guaranteeing that an active filtering process will not lead its users astray; and to argue that no-one will persist in error (a proposition which can itself be misleading) is not sufficient reason to pay attention only to those situations in which no errors are made. Simon's own failure to recognize the possibility of faulty decisions arising from misleading theories is particularly striking when we recall that his criticism of conventional economics is precisely that the theoretical filters which it employs are inappropriate for many of its purposes. Unfortunately, his analyses of information processing are not founded on any adequate theory of the growth of knowledge.

Simon versus neoclassical economics
Simon fails to use his own (incomplete) theories of institutional conservatism and data absorption to explain the resistance of the great

majority of economists to his ideas. His own explanation (1982, 2: p.401) is one of the weakest elements in the book: 'Now I learned that behavior was of interest to economists . . . only if it had important implications for matters of policy at the level of the economy, or at least of the industry.' The proposition that the prime concern of economists is economic policy, primarily macro-policy, is an active filter which destroys more information than it absorbs.

Let us apply a little of Simon's analytical apparatus. Economists, like other people, face the problem of information overload, and they recognize the value of science in making 'facts derivable from theory'. What, then, could possibly be better than the well developed structure of microeconomics: 'deductive theory which requires almost no contact with empirical data – once the underlying assumptions are accepted or verified – to establish its propositions' (1982, 2: p.321)? Although Simon (1982, 2: p.476) points out that Occam's razor is double-edged, so that the 'much stronger assumptions . . . about the human cognitive system' which are required for theories of utility or profit maximization than for satisficing might be deemed a disqualification, succinctness is likely to be a far more powerful argument for anyone conscious of the need to absorb information. It is indeed an argument which Simon himself employs to justify the use of such theories when he deems them appropriate.

In moving from models of fully informed optimization to models of bounded rationality, one accepts increasing complexity in the specification of the decision procedure. Moreover, complexity is not the only cost: 'At each step we have (at least potentially) gained realism, but lost certainty' (1982, 2: p.235). Perfect competition 'is an essential condition for unambiguous prediction of behavior from the classical assumptions of economic rationality' (1982, 2: p.339). Although these two observations are intended as criticisms of conventional economics, they may also be used as a defence. The analyst's bounded rationality leads him to use models which generate clear outcomes. The certainty may have been false, but its disappearance is still perceived as a loss.

Moreover, let us remember that 'it may be more important to have agreement on the facts than to be certain that what is agreed upon is really fact'. Agreement on the 'fact' that the established structure of economics is broadly appropriate for economists' purposes is important in that it permits them to work within an agreed framework, and therefore to work (in some sense) more effectively. Economics is a fairly well-ordered intellectual adventure in which problems can be solved as fast as new ones are created, as long as the structure is protected by its interdependencies. The interdependence of economic theories, mutually reinforced by their derivation from a small set of ideas and assumptions, provide them with an armour which is not easily penetrated. It is this interdependence which protects Cobb–Douglas production functions and allows Occam's razor to be deployed in their defence – and in defence of every other part of the structure in turn.

This application of Simon's own arguments needs to be supplemented by the philosophical argument – which is actually psychological – supplied by Adam Smith (1980) and Shackle (1967), and set out in Chapter 1. A single, apparently well integrated theory is much more comfortable than a set of partial theories which are not readily commensurable; for it not only provides a means of accommodating all phenomena, but leaves no doubts about the relationship between the particular explanations which are employed on different occasions. If we rely on a cluster of theories which clearly do not fit together very well, then the more sensitive we are to the problems of the human condition, the more concerned we are likely to be that such obviously incomplete theories may be inadequate or misleading – and therefore unreliable as a basis for expectations and for decisions. Even if we can quieten our doubts by pretending to more assurance than we feel, nevertheless contemplation of the future brings, in Shackle's (1967, p.288) words, 'the uneasy consciousness of mystery and a threatening unknown'.

It is perhaps the most remarkable feature of Simon's work that it appears to be the product of a man who is prepared to face the unknown without a general theory, but with a faith that, despite the bounds on their rationality, human beings can display enough flexibility and imagination to recognize and to solve their problems fast enough to maintain, and even to improve their situation. If his faith is justified, few people will have done more to help us realize it.

10 A subjective appraisal of Austrian economics*

Declining confidence in the adequacy of neoclassical economic analysis has provided an opportunity for advocates of other approaches to compete in the intellectual market; and in this chapter I propose to consider the style of analysis which is usually marketed under the brand-label of 'Austrian economics'. Recent developments in Austrian economics have generated some differences of view between its practitioners, so that it is no longer easy – or perhaps possible – to define a comprehensive standard Austrian position. On the assumption that readers are less interested in an attempt at such a definition than in deciding whether any Austrian ideas or methods can be helpful in their own concerns, I shall be selective, paying rather more attention to what I believe are the stronger points of Austrian economics and avoiding, for example, any discussion of the *a priori* method, to which Professor Hutchison (1981, pp.203–32) has so forcefully objected.

The central focus of Austrian economics is on individual human action – action which depends on the objectives, perceptions, and expectations of the actor. But instead of taking the standard neoclassical short-cut of enquiring what sets of actions by individuals would be mutually consistent, so that no-one would ever need to think again, Austrians assume that perceptions, expectations, and objectives too, are subject to change – sometimes resulting from the recognition of past mistakes – as each of us tries to act sensibly in a world which is beyond our comprehension. They then endeavour to understand – rather than predict – what might comprise sensible action, and how patterns of behaviour develop and are modified. Austrian economics, according to O'Driscoll and Rizzo (1985), is the economics of time and ignorance, in which knowledge is always incomplete and in which one of the few things that we do know is that the future will, in some ways, be different from what we now expect. We have a rational expectation of being surprised. The Newtonian conception of time as another kind of space, which is the basis of models of intertemporal equilibrium, misrepresents our situation, and the principles of rational choice may

*An earlier version of this chapter was presented at the Scottish Economic Society Conference, Heriot-Watt University, in March 1987.

be good enough for playing noughts and crosses, but not for the business of living. As Herbert Simon has often reminded us, they cannot generate optimal strategies for chess, even though the game is completely specified. The choice of contingent future commodities, from a list known to be complete, is not a typical human activity.

Value, choice, and cost

Carl Menger, the founder of the Austrian School, is quite properly linked with Jevons and Walras as an originator of subjective value theory; but he differed sharply from them over what sort of theory it should be. Indeed, the casual association of Menger with the 'marginal revolution' is as misleading as the casual association of Marshall with perfect competition. Menger believed, quite plausibly, that subjective theory leads naturally not towards, but away from, formalism. Value is a relationship between a human being and an object; it cannot exist without such a relationship, and the attribution of value is part of the economic process. The list of economic goods is generated by the economic system and cannot be part of its specification. Neither the analyst nor the individual economic agent can be provided with the lists of (even potential) products, resources, technologies, and preferences which are essential to neoclassical analysis. Every choice is an experiment – and not a Bayesian experiment, which simply improves our assessment of probabilities. The fundamental Austrian complaint against neoclassical economics is that its concept of equilibrium already assumes the solution of the economic problem, which is the problem of discovering – or inventing – possibilities and making good use of them.

Every choice is a choice between the alternatives as perceived by the chooser, each valued according to the chooser's own preferences and understanding of what that alternative has to offer. Any or all of these components of choice may be the subject of mistakes by the chooser – although there are important incentives to get them right – and are not to be second-guessed by the analyst.

Every choice entails a cost, and only choices can reveal costs. The idea that cost is to be measured by the value attached to the most highly rated of the rejected alternatives is familiar enough, but Austrians seem to have been most rigorous in pursuing its implications. Valuation exists only at the moment of choice; but choice depends on private assessments and on private perceptions of the alternatives available. Now, it is supposedly a prime virtue of a perfectly competitive general equilibrium that it converts these private assessments into publicly observable costs – that is why the theory of value is so closely tied to perfectly competitive equilibrium. Unfortunately, it is precisely in equilibrium that there are no choices to be made. The process of valuation necessarily takes place out of equilibrium – where public and private values do not coincide – and we know that perfect competition cannot exist outside equilibrium.

It cannot therefore be assumed that recorded costs are a reliable measure of either the public or private value of the opportunities forgone. Austrians and some of their sympathizers have seized on this argument to demonstrate the obstacles to effective control of state-owned business. A loss of £300 million by British Coal does not tell us whether any better policies were actually available; nor are large surpluses in electricity supply reliable evidence that its managers are missing no opportunities. Decision rules and targets for such businesses may be much less important than the perception and assessment of alternatives. An injunction to price electricity at long-run marginal cost is not a solution but the statement of a problem, both for those who set the prices and for those who attempt to judge their performance.

Now, these difficulties are in no sense confined to state-owned industries. It is now no easier to assess the performance of British Gas than it was before privatization. Shareholders attempting to evaluate management, and also senior managers attempting to evaluate their subordinates, are trying to envisage choices as they appeared to those whose decisions they are evaluating, and also to determine whether all the promising alternatives were properly considered: and those being evaluated, let us observe, have been entrusted with those decisions precisely because they were thought to have skills and specific knowledge which are not possessed by those who seek to evaluate them. The most perfect system of accounting controls will not resolve the problem, since discarded alternatives generate no transactions for the accounting system to record.

Much the best source of information is likely to be found in the choices of other businesses in similar situations; moreover the choices of other comparable businesses, and their consequences, also increase the knowledge of the decision-makers themselves. Thus, Austrians are likely to agree with those who argue that the failure to break up monopolies before privatization is a serious error of policy. Control and discovery are joint products of competition; if competition is emasculated, both will be weaker. Austrians have not given much attention to private-sector monopoly, tending to claim that without government support there can be no serious impediments to free entry. As we shall see later, the behaviour of large firms is a neglected area of Austrian economics.

Macroeconomics
Austrian objections to macroeconomics may be summarized in the charge that it replaces human decisions with the manipulation of meaningless aggregates. Austrians have never been much impressed by welfare economics, but even those who are must admit that the use of national income statistics to measure changes in welfare depends formally on the assumption that the economy is in a perfectly competitive equilibrium. Capital likewise can be unambiguously aggregated only in equilibrium. On this point Austrians are in full agreement with the UK Cambridge side of the capital controversy, but since neither party called into question the other components of the aggregate production function, which are no better founded, the resolution of the controversy is of minor importance. But if the aggregates can only be computed in equilibrium – and a very special equilibrium too – then a rigorous theorist will not employ them in an explanation of how an economy reaches, or fails to reach, equilibrium.

In so far as Austrians have been interested in what are usually called macroeconomic issues, they have laid emphasis on the composition of the conventional aggregates in ways which other economists are beginning to emulate. Thus, a general stimulus to aggregate demand is not now widely thought to be an adequate response to Britain's unemployment problem, and there is general support for the idea that some reshaping of the components of aggregate supply is highly desirable. Again, few people now seem very sure what is meant by the money supply, movements in which might be used to explain (or perhaps just predict) movements in the price level – another aggregate which is not favoured by Austrian economists.

We are perhaps beginning to realize that Hayek's (1931) monetary theory is much more sophisticated, and much more clearly related to human action, than Freidman's. Friedman's distribution of money by helicopter (1969, p.4) not only exemplifies his contempt for truth in theoretical structures; it also demonstrates his belief that equilibrium is independent of process. In Hayek's analysis, it is of crucial importance who receives the extra money, because their decisions on its use will determine how relative prices change, and thus precipitate particular kinds of further decisions. Among the results will be changes in the distribution of income and in the composition of capital, which will not be easy to reverse. As O'Driscoll and Rizzo demonstrate (1985, pp.223–5), perfect anticipation will not eliminate these effects.

It has never been very easy to see why one should be bothered about inflation in Friedman's world: monetary expansion might fail to solve the unemployment problem, but it would not do much positive harm.

But in Hayek's world it can lead to expensive mistakes. Later versions of monetarist doctrine have attempted to introduce real losses as a consequence of misguided policy, and to do so have found it necessary also to introduce ignorance, but only in a facile manner: to postulate, for example, groups of economic agents on separate islands hardly counts as rigorous economics. Hayek's theory of monetary influences is embedded in a theory of market processes, which seems more appropriate to conditions of ignorance than theories which are constrained by the concept of equilibrium.

Market processes
With the passage of time, agents' subjective assessments are informed by their own particular skills and experience: thus a world of widespread – but not uniform – ignorance is necessarily also a world full of potential comparative advantages. Here too, it is not ignorance in the aggregate that is important, but its composition. A fundamental assumption which Austrians share with neoclassical economists is that at least some people will seek to pursue their own advantage – although Austrians do not translate this assumption into a principle of maximization, which is simply inapplicable in this setting (O'Driscoll and Rizzo, 1985, p.6). In their attempts to improve their own situation, agents change the configuration of the economy, the perceptions of others, and also, frequently, their own. Knowledge may be deliberately produced, but it may also arise as an externality.

Austrians assume that this pursuit of individual advantage is channelled into the market, for reasons which do not appear to be very clear: the primacy of markets seems to be accepted as equally self-evident as the incompleteness and dispersion of knowledge. This is not a point on which neoclassical economists have any right to be critical, for they too do not question the primacy of markets, and their assumptions about knowledge are evidently false; but since we nowadays observe advancement pursued so often within both private and governmental organizations, and through political processes, the relative attractions of the market and other structures might be thought to deserve a prominent place on the research agenda of Austrian (and other) economists. I shall return to this question at the end of the chapter.

The analysis of processes does not lead easily to elegant general conclusions; by assuming that processes are rapid, effective, and neutral, it is possible to divert attention to their end-states, which is the method of equilibrium theory. Unquestioning acceptance of such a problematic set of assumptions, however, leaves one with no particular reason for accepting the relevance of equilibrium analysis, which then has to be defended by instrumentalist arguments rather than appeals to logical coherence, and opens the possibility of endless debate with those post-Keynesians who argue that the attainment of equilibrium is impossible, and the concept irrelevant.

The status of equilibrium among Austrian economists seems currently a matter of some dispute. In the absence of government intervention, the market process is clearly perceived as tending to promote the coherence of economic activity; but how strong is this tendency, and what internal disturbances may deflect it, is not agreed. Kirzner (1973; 1985a) believes that there is a strong and reliable process of equilibration; but O'Driscoll and Rizzo (1985) are not so sure; and Lachmann (1986) clearly believes in the possibility of serious discoordination. Although rejecting Keynesian doctrine, these three are very sympathetic to some of Keynes's ideas, and reserve their major objections for the neoclassical synthesis. Since the possibilities and problems of coordination through markets is one of the central questions – for some, the single most important question – in economics, the issue merits some consideration.

Kirzner's *Competition and Entrepreneurship* (1973) has become the primary exposition of equilibration through entrepreneurial competition. It is a theory of arbitrage. Out of equilibrium there are necessarily, and by definition, unexploited gains from trade; and they are unexploited because they are unnoticed. The entrepreneur (who may be an entrepreneur on one occasion only, or at irregular intervals) is the person who, because of his alertness to his particular circumstances, becomes aware of such an opportunity and exploits it. Since we may think of him as concluding two contracts, for purchase and sale, he requires no resources, and has no financing problem; moreover since he observes what already exists, the knowledge on which he acts is not in doubt – he does not know the whole truth, but what he does know is nothing but the truth. As a result of his actions, the price in one particular market is brought closer to equilibrium, and other people are better-informed about the opportunities available; knowledge is the dual of equilibration.

One possible objection is that unexploited gains from trade, which may be obtained with no resources, offer a general profit opportunity; and as Richardson (1960, p.57) has pointed out, 'a general profit opportunity ... is ... a profit opportunity for no one in particular'. A reasonable reply to this objection is that, since the theoretical framework is defined as one of incomplete and differentiated knowledge, then general opportunities will not be generally noticed and the profit will be available only to a few. However, although this theoretical framework is at least as plausible as neoclassical assumptions about knowledge, one might expect Austrians to be especially interested in exploring the relationship between particular knowledge and specific circumstances. But, although Kirzner (1985a, p.28) asserts that '*human beings tend to notice that which it is in their interest to notice*', and that differences beween perceptions within a given environment can be partly ascribed to differences in those interests, he makes no attempt to explain these differences in interest, presumably because he considers them as unanalysable differences in preference, rather than the result, in part, of particular patterns of education, experience and situation.

Kirzner has sought to extend his theoretical structure without apparently appreciating the problems which these extensions entail. As well as arbitrage to remove existing gaps in coordination (thus correcting perceived error), entrepreneurs speculate on the basis of an anticipated failure of intertemporal coordination, and even create new products, processes, or patterns of coordination (1985a, pp.84–5). This third category, of entrepreneurial innovation, brings Kirzner much closer to Schumpeter's view from which he had been at some pains to distance himself in his earlier work in order to emphasize the equilibrating role of the entrepreneur. But while one might be prepared to grant, with some misgivings, that present opportunities are facts, the anticipation of future coordination failures and the 'imaginative, bold leaps of faith, and determination' by which the entrepreneur can '*create* the future for which his present acts are designed' (1985a, p.56) must surely open up the possibility that the entrepreneur will generate, rather than correct, error.

Yet Kirzner insists that all these activities promote coordination; although the future is unknown, 'man is *motivated* to formulate the future as he envisages it, as accurately as possible' (1985a, p.55) and this motivation is assumed to be sufficient to ensure general success. It is assumed to be sufficient even though 'a correct perception of one's situation calls for a perception not only of physical possibilities and constraints, but also of the possibilities and constraints imposed by the actions, present and prospective, of others' (1985a, p.83). The problems of interdependency, to which Richardson (1960) attempted to draw our attention, are hardly more regarded by Kirzner than in neoclassical competitive theory. Nor does Kirzner fully recognize that speculation and innovation, unlike arbitrage, need resources: judgements have to be backed with money, as Richardson has also pointed out, and entrepreneurship is not open to everyone on equal terms.

O'Driscoll and Rizzo are aware of these problems and are more cautious in their claims for the performance of markets. They insist on the fundamental assumption that individuals will learn something from the passage of time and the stream of events (1985, p.38). What they learn may be beyond our ability to predict: indeed the critical advantage of the competitive market process through which individuals learn is that at least some of its results are unexpected (1985, p.110). Uncertainty is endogenous to the process (1985, p.71); society is not a stochastic system (1985, p.126) and the outcome cannot be calculated from initial data but must be discovered by letting the process run.

What, then, can be said about the results of competition? Certainly not that they are optimal, by conventional standards – but conventional standards are falsely based. Will it result in effective coordination of the knowledge that it produces? O'Driscoll and Rizzo (1985, pp.85–6) argue for 'pattern coordination', in which plans are compatible in their general features but, being open-ended, may conflict in detail and be the subject of revision, which may continue indefinitely. Kirzner (1985b) has objected that the concept of pattern coordination seriously underestimates the achievement of the market process, which, in the absence of extraneous disturbance (which, of course, never is absent for long enough) would arrive at a full equilibrium.

By contrast, Lachman (1986, p.5) emphasizes that every piece of entrepreneurial coordination disrupts some previously satisfactory plan, and he is not prepared, as Kirzner is, to assume that a better plan can readily be produced. Refutations do not automatically evoke better conjectures. Competition necessarily results in some discoordination as a joint product of coordination, and sometimes (as with Schumpeterian innovation) the discoordination may be severe and long-lasting. Many people may be bewildered by the disintegration of established routines, as Schumpeter (1934, pp.79–80) asserted. Lachman (1986, pp.9–14) argues that much greater attention should be paid to inter-market processes, especially those in which plans necessarily extend over a substantial period of time and are therefore vulnerable to the generation of new knowledge. Like Richardson (1960), Lachmann (1986, p.74) recognizes that, in such conditions, coordination will rarely be achieved by price alone. In his view, such inter-market processes provide the most appropriate focus for the analysis of macroeconomic problems, which are thus to be handled by characteristic Austrian methods: not aggregates, but their composition; not investment or consumption functions, but human decisions in the face of changing knowledge and expectations – which are themselves, of course, not to be mechanically treated.

The growth of knowledge

To me, what most distinguishes Austrian economics from neoclassical theory, especially in the recent books by O'Driscoll and Rizzo and by Lachmann, is its much more intelligent (not to say scientific) treatment of problems of knowledge. Hayek's sketch, presented in his 1937 essay 'Economics and knowledge', of the possibilities of coherent action based on local decisions which rest on incomplete, and possibly erroneous, perceptions relies on a process of subjective conjecture and exposure to refutation analogous to that propounded three years earlier, in Hayek's native language, by Karl Popper whose *Logik der Forschung* is indeed cited on the first page.

The intellectual relationship between Hayek and Popper surely deserves a major study; what I wish to emphasize here is that the relationship between scientific and market processes is not just that of analogy, for the growth of knowledge is the subject of both. It is not then surprising that the problems and limitations of Popper's analysis (considered in Chapter 2) are mirrored in Austrian economics – most clearly in Kirzner's work. The central difficulty, which Popper (1972) himself emphasizes, is that there is no way to establish the final truth of any proposition, however well corroborated. Thus any decision, including decisions by economic agents, may be wrong. Furthermore, no hypothesis can be tested without assuming the truth of many more; if any of these assumptions are wrong, then the apparent result of the test, whether it indicates acceptance or rejection, may be misleading.

One piece of false knowledge may infect a body of knowledge, and lead scientists systematically astray. Similarly, one false piece of knowledge in the market process may result in a well coordinated set of activities which is nevertheless fundamentally flawed and unsustainable. This, in essence, is Hayek's theory of the business cycle, which is initiated by false monetary signals. But false monetary signals are not the only possible origin of the sequence which Hayek analyses; there is no reason why such a cycle should not result from false perceptions – even indeed false scientific perceptions about, for example, the effects of large-scale combustion of fossil fuels, or the reliability of automatic control systems. Kirzner's endeavours to demonstrate that the market process must work well cannot succeed, just as there is no way of proving that our scientific processes – or any conceivable scientific process – must produce true knowledge. What can be argued is that both market and scientific processes may reasonably be expected to produce reliable knowledge, to use Ziman's (1978) term. The quality of knowledge depends primarily on the quality of the process which produced it. So does the performance of an economic system.

Science and the market require the interaction of ideas, criticism, and tests. Efficient interaction requires some agreement (usually tacit) on an agenda; but if there is no certain knowledge, any proposition may be challenged at any time. From the first, Popper emphasized that scientific progress required a set of conventions to provide a framework for exploration, a proposition which Lakatos (1970) later developed into the concept of a scientific research programme. Markets need research programmes too, and their investigation seems a natural task for Austrian economists. Lachmann seems most conscious of this task, for he emphasizes (1986, pp.53–4) that action, and even the evaluation of the consequences of previous action, depends upon interpretation which is an active process. 'Those who speak of the "decoding of messages" lay claim to the existence of a comprehensive code book no mortal man ever possessed' (1986, p.46). Kirzner's 'alertness' cannot simply be a recognition of facts; nor is it enough for him to argue (1985a, p.50) that the entrepreneur corrects error, for the identification of error is inherently ambiguous.

In contrast to Kirzner's alertness to objective data, Lachmann brings perception into the orbit of subjective judgement – as characteristic an example of the use of a research programme as the introduction of information sets into general equilibrium theory. Events need to be interpreted, and the interpretation depends on the individual (Lachmann, 1986, p.4). But subjective interpretation, in a world of interdependent decisions based on incomplete and ever-changing knowledge, poses its own problems. 'It means that A's knowledge of B's knowledge, however indispensable to the success of A's action, must always remain problematical in a sense in which A's knowledge of molecules, machines or the human body is not' (Lachmann, 1986, p.29). (Knowledge of molecules, machines, and the human body is also forever problematical, but these subjects of knowledge do not change of their own volition.) As Lachmann observes, this is not only an obstacle to economic generalizations about human action, but also to the prospects for coordination through entrepreneurial competition. It suggests the possibility of a case for indicative planning.

Institutions
For Austrians who reject any kind of planning, and wish to remain within their tradition, it suggests much more attention to another part of Menger's (1963) conception of economics, which we can perhaps now clearly see is complementary to subjectivism – namely the importance of institutions.

Social life is made possible by the fact that we do not all continuously use our imagination to devise and try out new plans of action, but for the most part unquestioningly accept current conventions, all of which are questionable, and some of which are doubtless defensible only on the grounds that any convention is better than none, and that change is difficult. Institutions at once facilitate and constrain. In science – including economics – they promote the efficient investigation of problems as they are presently defined, and impede redefinition. (Economists should not be surprised, or dismayed, to discover that the methods which they use in their own discipline always entail opportunity costs.) In markets, they promote coordination by furnishing a common basis of decision, while discouraging inquiry into the soundness of that basis.

Institutions are themselves the result of human action, and may be explained in terms of the objectives, knowledge, and expectations of human actors. But, although they may be carefully crafted (to use a characteristic expression of Oliver Williamson), we should not assume that the results are always and only what was intended – as Williamson far too readily does. Since they evolve through human interaction, the major institutions at any time, like the prices, products, and scientific theories of that time, embody more human knowledge than can possibly be recovered by any individual. Moreover, institutions (particularly when they can be interpreted as rules) may be best explained by the absence of sufficient knowledge to make rational choices in specific instances (O'Driscoll and Rizzo, 1985, p.119; see also Heiner, 1983); they help us to act sensibly beyond the bounds of our rationality.

For these reasons, rational appraisal of existing institutions is not easy: to apply analytical techniques it may be necessary to operate on a parody of the institution in a caricature of its environment. Thus it may be foolish, or even dangerous, to reject an institution because it cannot be reduced to rationality. We could easily reject every accepted method of doing economics on that basis. This does not mean that institutions should not be subjected to criticism; no doubt there are many that could be discarded with advantage, and few that could not be improved. But the criticism should be undertaken in the realization, at the least, that they exist primarily in order to cope with the problems which are simply denied existence in neoclassical economics. The appraisal of institutions is not a task only for Austrians, but it is essential to them.

The most obvious deficiency in Austrian economics, as Lachmann (1986, p.131) points out, lies in the market process itself. Austrians have nothing to say about the relationship between price-takers and price-setters, nor about the changes over time in the roles of market participants. Lachmann does not, however, seem to appreciate that the study of price formation entails a study of market institutions. Indeed, it seems impossible to go much further in the analysis either of intra-market or inter-market processes without focusing on the evolution and effects of the institutional framework. The market is a process which can exist only by happening. It cannot exist without some rules or conventions created – not always intentionally – by human action. In particular, the situation and actions of the entrepreneur become much more intelligible when we consider which market institutions help, which hinder, and which appear capable of being successfully and profitably challenged.

Finally, I suggest that Austrians ought to challenge one of their own institutions: their almost total lack of interest in organizations as an arena for human action. Mises (1945; 1949) is the obvious exception, although he is more concerned with problems than possibilities. An organization may be regarded as a set of institutions which imposes a framework on the discovery and use of dispersed and local knowledge, as an alternative to the set of market institutions which might perform a similar function. Perhaps it is because Austrians tend to assume that only profit can act as an adequate incentive that they do not enquire how organizations may generate and use knowledge; but in the philosophical value theory which was being developed among Menger's colleagues and contemporaries there was no such restriction on effective motives to human action (Grassl and Smith, 1986). O'Driscoll and Rizzo (1985, pp.124–5) are clearly attracted by Nelson and Winter's (1982) theory of changes within firms, mediated by market competition, and recognize the major elements which it shares with Austrian concepts. They appear ready to take an interest in organizations, but are perhaps less ready than Lachmann to recognize that the working of markets is also problematic. All of them are less ready than Richardson (1972) to recognize that the boundaries between organization and market are themselves ill-defined and as subject as other parts of the system to entrepreneurial initiative.

Conclusion

The prime inherent virtue of Austrian economics, with its emphasis on subjective assessments and incompletable knowledge, is that it is intellectually an open system. Not everyone likes open systems (not even Austrian economists) and there have been attempts by Austrians to force closure in order to achieve certainty – notably about the necessary superiority of market processes over planning. But it is inherently impossible to use Austrian methods to prove that planning cannot work – just as there is no way of proving that economics will not progress most rapidly if we all agree henceforth to obey the instructions of, say, Robert Lucas? Wynne Godley? Frank Hahn? The inherent tendency of neoclassical economics, by contrast, is to force closure, and reach determinateness, or at least the near-determinateness of stationary distributions. The reward is an immensely superior technical apparatus to anything the Austrians have produced. Is the reward worth the cost? I cannot say, because value is determined by the customer; the appraisal must be subjective.

11 Disequilibrium states and adjustment processes

Coordination failure in general equilibrium

As Hahn (1984, p.65) has pointed out, Arrow–Debreu models of general equilibrium lack any of those features which give rise to Keynesian problems; and short-period Walrasian models appear to show that 'almost everything, and not just the unemployment theory, in Keynes is wrong' (Hahn, 1984, p.177). If there is to be any general equilibrium approach to the theory of unemployment, it cannot therefore be Walrasian. One simple theoretical stratagem, which is exemplified by Malinvaud (1977; 1985), is the imposition of price vectors on an otherwise standard model of atomistic rational behaviour. When the prices thus imposed fail to clear markets, non-Walrasian equilibria can be defined by the specification of analytically suitable rationing schemes; and, by judicious choice of price vectors, it is possible to produce examples of such equilibria which variously exhibit the principal features of Keynesian unemployment, classical unemployment, or suppressed inflation.

However, this apparently simple modification of the general equilibrium method should leave us theoretically uncomfortable. One of the great attractions of an Arrow–Debreu model is that it is all of a piece: everything is derived from a few basic axioms of preference and technology. Short-period Walrasian models introduce some unexplained constraints, but within those constraints everything proceeds as before. However, a model such as Malinvaud's violates this harmony: far from exhibiting the consequences of tastes and technology, its price vectors have no origins other than the desire of the analyst to produce the phenomena which he seeks to interpret; and the rationing schemes which are applied have little better justification.

This analytical scheme requires an economy of well-informed maximizing agents – firms as well as households – to acquiesce in a situation where many of them might reasonably, even rationally, expect to better their position by undertaking trades at prices other than those imposed. But these agents are not, one must assume, entirely quiescent, for there is only a single price for each commodity. Thus, agents are all energetic and skilful enough to ensure that no-one can obtain an especially favourable deal on price, but not energetic and skilful enough to change prices which leave many of them dissatisfied.

One may ask whether the goal of displaying an economy with coordination failures has been achieved only by abandoning, at crucial points, the axiomatic method which many of us have been led to believe is a prime virtue of the general equilibrium research programme. Such models do help to emphasize the connection between macroeconomic coordination problems and the failure of the price system to reflect accurately the basic data of the economy. But, of course, we all know that these problems arise because, in some sense, prices are wrong. What this analytical method cannot even attempt to explain, by the very principles of its construction, is *why* prices might be wrong. As Coddington (1978, p.1017) has observed, without such an explanation it may not be easy to choose effective remedies.

Adjustment and the auctioneer

Although the imposition of non-market clearing prices for the theoretical purpose of producing a quantity-constrained equilibrium seems hard to reconcile with the assumption of an economy composed of maximizing agents, there is nevertheless an impregnable defence of this procedure – although it is not one likely to commend itself to most general equilibrium theorists. The defence is simply this. If all agents are defined to be price-takers, then *any* price vector is adequate to sustain an equilibrium, simply because every agent is constrained by that definition to take as a datum whatever price vector is imposed. Is it, indeed, any more unreasonable to require every economic agent to accept without question a set of prices than fixed lists of goods and techniques of production? Marshall, of course, imposed none of these requirements. Nor did Schumpeter on his innovators. By contrast, in both Walrasian and non-Walrasian models of competitive equilibrium there are no forces *within* the economy making for change. Walrasian excess demand equations are not themselves forces, but only signals which may lead to action; that action must come from some agent or agency which will respond to these signals, and respond in the appropriate way. If there is no such agent or agency (and if everyone is defined to be a price-taker, there is no-one left to adjust prices), then the actors in the economy must seek to optimize their situation by quantity-adjustment, subject to whatever price vectors happen to exist.

The attainment of a Walrasian equilibrium depends not only on the existence of an auctioneer, but also on the auctioneer's willingness to follow a set of instructions provided by the economic theorist who is analysing the economy. In other words, a Walrasian system can be relied on to attain its logical equilibrium only if it is being analysed.

At this point some readers may recall the Oxford limerick satirizing the philosophical doctrine of idealism.

> There once was a man who said 'God
> Must think it exceedingly odd
> If he finds that this tree
> Continues to be
> When there's no one about in the Quad.'

They may also recall the reply.

> Dear Sir, your astonishment's odd:
> *I* am always about in the Quad.
> And that's why the tree
> Will continue to be,
> Since observed by Yours faithfully, God.

Now, although the particular economic theorist who acts as God to any specific Walrasian system may not always be around, he is certainly always there when needed; no Walrasian system has ever been observed that was not being analysed throughout the period of observation. But one may reasonably wonder what lessons can be drawn from the study of the self-regulating properties of a system which has been so designed as to be incapable of self-regulation.

Out-of-equilibrium behaviour is no less dependent on the auctioneer as long as all agents are required to be price-takers. It is therefore quite natural in this class of model that the law of the single price should hold throughout any period of adjustment; for the auctioneer would make his own task quite unnecessarily difficult if he were to call out a range of prices for a single commodity at each round. However, since we need an auctioneer, it appears perverse to use him to produce a series of price vectors which will map out a path between equilibria – which can only be done after discovering the configuration of the new equilibrium – rather than simply announcing that configuration once it is discovered. If he does announce such a path, only the requirement that all agents be price-takers can ensure that this path is followed; otherwise there are profit opportunities in anticipating published price changes. So the auctioneer has also to act as a price commissioner.

Quantity-constrained equilibria do not dispense with the auctioneer; they too transform him into a price commissioner. But his authority cannot be limited to price-fixing. When markets fail to clear, many potential transactions must be frustrated; therefore we require some explanation of what transactions take place. Leaving this to the agents' initiative cannot be relied on to produce the allocation computed by theorists, who therefore insist on a rationing scheme which is logically very wide-ranging. Now, as all those with any experience of rationing know, an effective and extensive scheme needs not only to be carefully devised, but also efficiently administered and policed. Since the auctioneer appears to be the only costless resource available, he seems to be the only plausible candidate for the job. But this model of a highly regimented economy does not seem particularly well suited to explore the possibilities of coordination failure among well-informed, self-seeking and active individuals in a market system.

It is only by such questionable means that a fixprice, quantity-adjustment method of analysis, which as Hicks (1982, p.232) has emphasized is a disequilibrium method, can be presented as a means of defining equilibrium. But, even if converted into equilibrium, the method belongs to economic dynamics: it therefore requires a '*continuation theory*', which is concerned with the effect of the events of a first period upon the expectations and plans which themselves determine the events of its successors' (Hicks, 1982, p.223). The fixprice method does not dispense with the need for a theory of price; but it does separate, in the language of Popper, the formation of conjectures from their exposure to possible refutation. The short-period equilibrium shows whether the prices were well chosen or whether they need to be revised. Our attitude to a present situation of Keynesian unemployment, or suppressed inflation, or whatever, should be influenced by our expectations about what may happen next. That may depend on how the present situation came about, and how that history is interpreted by economic agents. A model of disequilibrium transformed into equilibrium is not enough; we need to know something about the processes of adjustment. General equilibrium theories are not strong on adjustment; and the imposition of non-market clearing prices and of rationing confers no additional strength.

Now, of course, an analytical procedure which imposes constraints on the behaviour of agents, and then relies on external control to produce its results, may have predictive value; if, in addition, it is simpler or more tractable than alternative procedures there may be a good case for sometimes using it. Such a procedure might also be justified as a stage en route to something better. But it certainly cannot be plausibly claimed that the procedure offers an explanation of the way in which the system works – or ever could work; and if it is used as a basis for recommendations on system design the results could be disastrous. To analyse the working of a competitive system, and the ways in which it might get into trouble, we need to consider more carefully the behaviour over time of economic agents who are acting within a particular structure and subject to particular experiences. In the remainder of this chapter I propose to consider several approaches to the analysis of disequilibrium and adjustment.

The market process
It is convenient to start with the theory of the competitive, or market, process put forward by Kirzner (1973), since this can be readily compared with general equilibrium. For Kirzner, as for other members of the Austrian school of economics, equilibrium is a state in which the market process has come to an end, and is therefore of interest only in describing precisely what would have to be the case if it were to cease. Moreover, the specification of a terminal state by the analyst is not a necessary precursor to the tracing of a disequilibrium path. The path is traced forward from the starting-point, with the aid of expectations; and since the analyst claims no ability to specify the set of possible states of the world, these expectations cannot be analytically derived from any calculated equilibrium.

In the face of limited knowledge, the idea that rational behaviour implies maximization loses its force. It is still possible to suggest that an agent might choose to maximize the expected value of some subjective probability distribution, but there are other formulations which are just as plausible. Kirzner has adopted von Mises's broad concept of 'human action', motivated by the desire to improve one's position. The process of market adjustment is then set in motion by an entrepreneur's perception of an apparent opportunity to make a profit by changing the set of market offers – which may simply mean offering to buy or sell an existing commodity or factor service at a price other than that currently quoted.

One might indeed argue that neoclassical models are very special cases of Austrianism. Certainly, were an Austrian-type economic agent to find himself in a perfectly competitive market, and unable to think of any way of making his product or services especially attractive to customers or his custom especially attractive to suppliers, one might expect him to choose to be a price-taker, since he would see no advantage in being anything else; but if circumstances changed so that prices failed to clear markets, then the very same agent might reasonably be expected to show some price initiative. Not inevitably so, however; his estimates of the consequences of shifting his prices may lead him to believe, for reasons such as those offered by Marshall (1961) and

Andrews (1949), that he will be better off where he is. Such estimates should not be lightly construed as rational conjectures.

There is a warning to theorists here. In a perfectly competitive equilibrium, all agents freely choose to be price-takers. Because the assumption that all agents are price-takers is so plausible in that situation and so convenient analytically, it is very easy to carry it over into situations of disequilibrium, when the conditions which validate it have disappeared. This is the real justification for our original unease with quantity-rationed general equilibrium models. When markets do not clear, an assumption of atomistic competition is not sufficient to justify treating all agents as price-takers.

Kirzner's model might indeed be represented as one of atomistic competition in a situation where markets have not cleared – or, perhaps, to incorporate the incomplete knowledge which is essential to the model, where entrepreneurs believe that some markets have not cleared. Kirzner concentrates on those human actors who are seeking to improve their position by making profits, and on the opportunities which are created by changes in tastes or technology. These changes are external to his model, as in standard microtheory.

Now opportunities for profit might appear to arise whenever an economy is out of market-clearing equilibrium; but, as Richardson (1960, p.57) has pointed out, if this opportunity is both obvious to and open to everyone, it is hardly an opportunity for anyone in particular. So these profit opportunities arise out of the imperfections of knowledge – indeed out of differential valuations, as Shackle (1972, pp.409–21) has argued. In fact, profit is just what the accountants say it is; the difference between the net asset values at the beginning and at the end of a period. Given perfect foresight, the asset values at the beginning of an accounting period would reflect their known earning power; thus their value would not increase, and there would be no profit. In full Walrasian competitive equilibrium profits are, of course, zero.

In addition to differentially imperfect knowledge, Kirzner's market process depends on false trading. It is traditional to derive equilibrium values from original conditions; the process of seeking equilibrium is supposed not to affect the configuration of the equilibrium which is found. Where it does, notoriously in the case of oligopoly, both prediction and evaluation become far more difficult. Game theorists' approaches can lead to the definition of a core only if the results of the game do not depend on the skill of the players – and not always even then. Now, the market processes described by Kirzner are motivated precisely by the desire to change the final configuration – in particular, the final distribution of income – by exploiting superior knowledge.

If that configuration were ineluctably determined by preferences and technology, as theoretical convenience would prescribe, then the market process would not occur. Profit opportunities depend on false trading, and false trading upsets the equilibrium. We have to send for the auctioneer.

It follows from this conception of profit-seeking behaviour in circumstances of limited knowledge that one might expect more than one price to be quoted for a single commodity at one time: the law of one price would effectively impede the market process described by Kirzner, if it could be enforced. In addition, while adjustment is taking place, we would expect to find a good deal of rationing, and even the coexistence of quantity-constrained buyers and quantity-constrained sellers in different parts of the same market. Kirzner does not discuss how the rationing problem is resolved while the economy is in disequilibrium during the process of adjustment; to him what matters is that this problem is the source of entrepreneurial opportunity, which keeps the process going. Unemployment, for example, is a sign of potential gains from trade, and indicates that the market process has not yet run its course.

It may not be inappropriate to apply a version of Hicks's fixprice model. Each entrepreneur chooses a price, or set of prices, as part of his plan; these plans are tested in the market, and quantities are (typically) adjusted by changing stock levels. If the plan is not fully realized, the resulting stock disequilibrium provides a basis for choosing next period's price. This market process of conjecture and refutation continues until the profit opportunities are exhausted. We are then in an equilibrium as defined by Hahn (1973; 1984, p.59), in which all agents' theories and policies are corroborated and are therefore unchanged.

In Kirzner's world, the entrepreneur serves as the agent of change. (We may just note in passing the similarities with Romney Robinson's (1971) interpretation of Chamberlin and also with Mrs Penrose's (1959) concept of a firm's 'productive opportunity'.) Now, if what had to be discovered were no more than a set of preferences and of technologies that the analyst had hidden, as it were, for the economic agents to find, then this process might be worth some study, but sooner or later it would come to an end and we should be left with equilibrium. Our interest in market processes would then be in observing the ability of economic agents to discover what we have 'hidden'. This is characteristic of the literature on search theory. But search theorists might perhaps take note of a psychologist's comments on the equivalent assumptions underlying psychological learning experiments:

When a subject fails to meet the experimenter's expectations, it may be inappropriate to say that 'he has not learned'; rather, one might say that what the subject learned was not what the experimenter expected him to learn. . . . If we are to have a productive science of psychology [or economics?] let us put the burden of discovery on the experimenter rather than on the subject. Let the experimenter find out what the subject is thinking about, rather than asking the subject to find out what the experimenter is thinking about. (Kelly, 1963, p.77)

An economic system's ability to arrive at an equilibrium state which has been prescribed by an outside observer is of much less significance than is commonly assumed. It is of even less significance if the practical question is of the system's ability to respond to new situations and to create new opportunities.

Monetary disorder
The Austrian theory of the market process does not in itself provide any explanation of unemployment: at best it shows how unemployment triggers its own cure. But it does provide a starting-point for an explanation – in fact, for the explanation put forward by Hayek in *Prices and Production*, first published in 1931. The great virtue of the market process as a method for tackling the coordination problem is its economy of information; agents apparently have no need to know the reasons for scarcities or surpluses, but only that prices are relatively high or relatively low. (As we have seen in Chapter 6, that is not quite adequate.) But this virtue depends crucially on the reliability of the price signals; the working of the market process is desperately vulnerable to false prices. This is why Austrians are opposed to government intervention in pricing; it also explains why Hayek has long been concerned with the dangers of monetary disorder.

Hayek rejects the traditional, and still prevalent, distinction between value theory, which seeks to explain the pattern of relative prices, and monetary theory, which seeks to explain the general level of prices. Austrians share the distaste of general equilibrium theorists for analysis in terms of aggregates and averages, arguing that aggregates and averages may be calculated from the results of individual decisions but cannot help to explain them. For Hayek, changes in the quantity of money are important not because they affect the general level of prices but because they affect intertemporal price relativities, and therefore offer profit opportunities which must prove spurious.

Now it was observed earlier that all the standard theories, whether they be varieties of Keynesianism or derived from general equilibrium concepts, attribute unemployment to a wrong pattern of prices. But, in these theories, the trouble always lies in the present pattern of prices which, for one reason or another, cannot be got right. What sets Hayek's model apart is that present unemployment is the consequence of wrong relative prices in the past, and any short-run solution can only be at the expense of postponing (Hayek would say aggravating) problems in the future.

Hayek argues that a theory of unemployment should show how unemployment can arise from a situation of full employment equilibrium. Let us then begin with an example of successful coordination. Suppose there is a substantial shift of preferences in favour of future consumption. In a Walrasian production economy, this would generate a new equilibrium configuration in which future prices were higher relatively to present prices and some present resources were diverted to future production.

Given the existence of an appropriate range of technologies, some of these diverted resources would, in equilibrium, be used in the early stages of longer, but more productive, processes: the average period of production, if one is willing to use that dangerous metaphor, would be longer. Such a change in production methods would require a different outfit of capital goods, and there would be a fairly lengthy adjustment process, during which a series of interconnected investments would be undertaken. One may imagine spectacular examples such as the development of a major new oilfield, entailing sequential expenditure on production equipment, new refineries, petrochemical plant and multifarious downstream installations, or a railway electrification scheme, which requires the rebuilding of bridges, realignment of track, new signalling systems, new locomotives and new rolling stock; but even quite simple developments may require a sequence of investments extending over several years.

Suppose now that, while these investment projects are in mid-course, the pattern of preferences reverts to its former state. We would be left with a partly-finished capital outfit which was unusable in its present state but no longer worth finishing. Capital goods industries which had expanded to meet the new demands would be faced with large-scale cancellation of orders, and there would be no way in which they could provide full employment for their workers.

Such arbitrary shifts in preferences offer a theory of unemployment very similar to that of Keynes, at least as interpreted by Shackle. But Hayek's argument is different: it is that monetary expansion can create the illusion of a shift of preferences, an illusion which cannot be sustained. An expansion of credit will increase the supply of loans and reduce the rate of interest, in the same way as an increase in savings deposited with financial institutions; and it is no business of the potential borrower to enquire into the origin of the increased funds. That two very different causes could produce the same signals had been a major concern of Robertson (1926).

Cheaper and easier credit gives entrepreneurs command over greater resources and increases the present value of future output; it thus induces them to undertake a series of investments designed to lengthen the period of production. As in the previous case, resources are diverted from present to future goods. However, in this instance, the extra resources claimed by the entrepreneurs for the production of future goods have not been voluntarily relinquished by consumers. If the economy was originally in equilibrium, it is now suffering from an excess demand for present goods. This excess demand provides profit opportunities for those selling present goods, so that their prices rise relatively to the prices of future goods, thus invalidating the assumption on which the new investment projects were launched. Continued expansion of credit may revalidate them for a time, but as soon as the expansion of credit stops – it does not need to be reversed – there is a crisis.

This is the process which Hayek has more recently described as catching a tiger by the tail. Short of an accommodating shift in preferences, it is impossible to return to equilibrium except by abandoning a capital outfit which is appropriate only for a period of credit expansion. No auctioneer can solve the pricing problem for an economy in this situation. The basic cause of unemployment is structural, although it may well be aggravated by what are now called multiplier effects (the existence of which was widely if loosely recognized before 1931). The extent of the dislocation depends on the specificity of the misallocated resources: the more easily plant and people can be switched to goods in current demand, the smaller the scale of unavoidable unemployment. It is a serious weakness of Hayek's theory that it accounts for the specificity of capital but not of labour; however, the practicality of structural unemployment has been long recognized. A general stimulus to demand will not cure unemployment, except by creating inflation.

We may note a certain similarity between this analysis and the multiplier–accelerator models of the trade cycle. In these models the peak demand for investment goods, being related to the unsustainable rate of growth during the upswing, is necessarily higher, and possibly very much higher, than the demand appropriate to a full-employment steady growth rate of the economy; so if the capital goods industries are equipped to cope with this peak demand, or anything like it, the achievement of full employment equilibrium entails a reduction in the capacity of these industries and a corresponding redeployment of labour.

Growth and cycles

The combined impression left by Kirzner and Hayek is of a competitive – but not, of course, perfectly competitive – economy which adjusts fairly smoothly to external change, but which can be diverted by monetary mismanagement into a cycle of boom and recession. The recession is necessary in order to allow the economy to regain a path of sustainable development; resources are unemployed because they are unemployable in the form into which they have been moulded. When unemployment appears, it is already too late for remedies, for the only effective remedy is to avoid the misallocation which is created by the preceding boom. Thus the trade cycle, with its accompanying unemployment, is a monetary phenomenon.

One famous Austrian economist took a very different view. For Schumpeter (1934) the trade cycle, although its features might be exaggerated by monetary mismanagement, was the form inevitably taken by economic development in a capitalist economy. The Schumpeterian trade cycle embodies a process of adjustment in response to the beneficial disequilibrium which the system itself creates.

The relationships between Schumpeter's model and general equilibrium are worth noting. The fundamental difference is that the exogenous features of general equilibrium analysis – resources, technology, products, even preferences – are themselves the subject of entrepreneurial action: economic development requires innovation in all these areas, and this innovation is brought about by profit-seeking entrepreneurs. Whereas Kirzner's entrepreneurs respond to changing data, Schumpeter's cause the data to change. It necessarily follows that Schumpeter does not assume perfect competition: indeed, in his most famous later exposition (1943), he placed considerable emphasis on the beneficial activities of large firms, and the encouragement given to innovation by perishable monopoly.

Innovations are the product of entrepreneurial imagination; but entrepreneurs are profit-seekers and therefore wish to undertake credible appraisals of their projects. In Schumpeter's (1934, p.141) theory, animal spirits are not enough. Credible appraisals require credible data – in particular credible prices of inputs and of both complementary and competitive outputs. To provide these prices, Schumpeter invokes the stable pattern of a fully adjusted circular flow – something very like a Walrasian equilibrium. This provides the price signals which the entrepreneurs need in order to calculate the prospective profitability of innovations which will first disturb and eventually destroy that equilibrium. The initial innovations attract imitators, and also create opportunities for other entrepreneurs; and the original equilibrium has not yet been sufficiently disturbed to cast much doubt on their investment appraisals. The expansion accelerates into a boom.

This boom shares with Hayek's the characteristics of a diversion of resources to investment and a consequent rise in the price of consumer goods. It is also, like Hayek's, unsustainable, but for different reasons. In Hayek's story, the new production facilities never come into use, as the calculations on which they are based are shown to be false; in Schumpeter's version, the original calculations were sound enough, but they were used to justify a particular investment project (a railway, say, or a steelworks), and when that project is completed the investment demand comes to an end and is succeeded by a supply of new goods. Now, in principle, new investment projects might replace the old; but, with new products flooding onto the market, the original equilibrium price vector is destroyed and, with it, the basis of calculation which is essential for further innovation (Schumpeter, 1934, pp.235–6). Moreover, the non-entrepreneurs, who are competent to follow the routines which characterize equilibrium, are thrown into disarray by the disintegration of the price patterns on which those routines are based. The next wave of development must await the emergence of a new circular flow, or Walrasian equilibrium, and that, in the absence of a helpful auctioneer, must take some time.

So for Schumpeter, as for Hayek, the boom inevitably leads to recession; unemployment can be avoided only by preventing the boom. But preventing the boom is now not a matter of sound management: it entails the prevention of economic development. For Schumpeter, development implies discontinuity; discontinuity creates disequilibrium, and a new equilibrium has to be found by trial and error. But, even while it lasts, the period of disequilibrium is much less painful than in Hayek's model: the economy is now more productive than in the preceding equilibrium, so even if a significant proportion of the increased capacity is unused, most people are likely to be better-off than they have ever been before.

However, the process of adjustment to a new equilibrium is problematic in Schumpeter's theory, since there appears to be no individual or group competent to undertake it. The non-entrepreneurs are pure price-takers, well-fitted to support an established equilibrium, but unable to generate their own conjectures; the entrepreneurs possess the imagination to make conjectures, but will not act on them unless they can calculate the likely profit, which requires the prior existence of an equilibrium framework of the kind which needs to be established. One might suggest calling in Kirzner's entrepreneurs to do the job, since equilibration is their business; but Kirzner's model appears to deal with the problem of local adjustments within a generally stable system, not with the disruptive consequences of Schumpeterian enterprise. In Kirzner's world, the principle of continuity holds sway.

Marshall's short period

The principle of continuity inevitably calls to mind Alfred Marshall, but simultaneously warns us not to expect him to resolve all our analytical problems. For a relevant treatment of disequilibrium and consequent adjustment, we may consider his discussion of short-period normal price. Now, Marshall argues throughout his analysis that there will be a tendency towards a single price for each commodity, provided both that competition is free from the restraints of inertia and unquestioned custom and that each agent's 'knowledge of what others are doing is supposed to be generally sufficient to prevent him from taking a lower or paying a higher price than others are doing' (1961, p.341). As was demonstrated in Chapter 4, Marshall was well aware both of the importance of market structure and experience to generate knowledge, and of the profit incentive to seek it out. Marshall's model of competition works precisely because it is *not* perfect competition.

This context is especially important in considering short-period behaviour. The pattern of established custom and of established competition is one necessary part of the explanation why 'the true marginal supply price for short periods . . . is nearly always above, and generally very much above the special or prime cost for raw materials, labour and wear-and-tear of plant' (Marshall, 1961, p.374). The other part is the relationship between short-period and long-period behaviour.

In an important sense, Marshall reverses the modern sequence of textbook analysis. Nowadays we begin by considering the short-run consequences of a demand shift, and go on to the long-run effects only after establishing the short-run equilibrium; and we can do this because we make the implicit assumption that the new demand curve contains all the information about demand conditions which agents need. In particular we assume that, even though this demand shift was totally unexpected (an assumption which is necessary to preserve the logic of the comparative equilibrium method) agents should ignore the possibility of any further surprises of this kind – which implies that the expectations embodied in the new demand curve are, at best, boundedly rational. But, in Marshall's scheme, the long period comes first, in the sense that it establishes the conditions in which short-period adjustments are made.

Thus a short-period fall in demand need not create expectations of any long-run fall; and if it does not, both buyers and sellers will cling to their very similar notions of normal price, and of the normal quantities which accompany them. Because they expect demand to revive, sellers are unwilling to supply goods at low prices now which can probably be sold at higher prices later; and because they too anticipate a future revival, buyers wish to preserve their suppliers' business. Although Marshall is not explicit, it is reasonable to suppose that times of boom would exhibit corresponding price restraint and priority to regular customers, thereby strengthening the business connections to which he attached so much importance. However, such quantity-adjusted equilibria cannot last, since the adjustments are based on the expectation that demand will revert to its normal level. If it does, the need for quantity-adjustment disappears; if it does not, then some more fundamental changes are required.

Marshall's model, which has been revived and elaborated by Okun (1981), explains quantity-adjustment in the goods markets, and, with the simple addition of short-term labour contracts, it also explains unemployment – although not persistent unemployment. Furthermore, the unemployment is due to a deficiency of demand. The origins of this deficiency are less obvious; but it does seem plausible that one kind of fall in demand that would be judged temporary is a fall which is common to many industries and apparently attributable to a temporary depression of trade. So short-period quantity-adjustment, and its associated worker lay-offs, may be considered as most obviously characteristic of trade depression.

Marshall's explanation of trade depression in his *Principles* is very brief: it is loss of confidence by customers.

> For when confidence has been shaken by failures, capital cannot be got to start new companies or extend old ones. Projects for new railways meet with no favour, ships lie idle, and there are no orders for new ships. . . .
> The greater part [of the evil] could be removed almost in an instant if confidence could return, touch all industries with her magic wand, and make them continue their production and their demand for the wares of others. (Marshall, 1961, pp.710–11)

This explanation, which persists unchanged through all the editions of the *Principles*, dates back to the *Economics of Industry* of 1879; if it seems less than satisfactory, one should remember that it epitomizes the argument of Chapter 12 of Keynes's *General Theory*.

Keynes's revolution

But Marshall's model is not as close to that of Keynes as this comparison suggests. Their perspectives on the coordination problem are very different. Consider the following two sentences. 'Since we claim to have shown in the preceding chapters what determines the volume of employment at any time, it follows, if we are right, that our theory must be capable of explaining the phenomena of the Trade Cycle.' 'Since we claim to have shown in the preceding chapters what determines the phenomena of the Trade Cycle at any time, it follows, if we are right, that our theory must be capable of explaining the volume of employment.' The first sentence, of course, is from Keynes (1973a, p.313) and nowadays seems platitudinous. But before 1936 one would have expected the second statement. Unemployment occurred in a slump, and a slump was one stage in a process known as a business cycle. One looked to business cycle theorists for explanations of unemployment, rather than to employment theorists for explanations of the business cycle. (New classical macroeconomics appears to be taking us once more round this cycle of theory construction.) Both the title ('Notes on the trade cycle') of the single chapter in which he discusses business cycles, and its placing – 22nd out of 24, and in Book VI, headed, 'Short notes suggested by the General Theory' – are symptomatic of Keynes's abandonment of a cyclical theory of unemployment.

This abandonment of the generally accepted framework for the analysis of unemployment was one reason why many found the new doctrine hard to accept. For, instead of a process which leads to a slump, we are offered an explanation of a particular situation, in terms of the current state of:

> (1) the three fundamental psychological factors, namely, the psychological propensity to consume, the psychological attitude to liquidity and the psychological expectation of future yield from capital-assets, (2) the wage-unit as determined by the bargains reached between employers and employed, and (3) the quantity of money as determined by the action of the central bank. (Keynes, 1973a, pp.246–7)

and the adjective 'psychological' is a warning not to seek any further explanation.

Like Marshall's quantity-adjustment model, Keynes offers a short-period analysis; but unlike Marshall's, Keynes's short period is shorn of all reference to long-period equilibrium. Whereas Marshall envisages a situation in which capital stock and expectations of normal demand are roughly in line, and the problem is how to adapt to a fall in demand which is generally agreed to be temporary, in Keynes's scheme capital-

stock, long-run expectations and present demand are each simply whatever they happen to be, and bear no particular relation to each other,
since liquidity preference, the marginal efficiency of capital and the
propensity to save are each based on necessarily unstable guesses about
an unknowable future. If, as Hicks (1982, pp.288–9) argues, liquidity
preference and the marginal efficiency of capital are unquestionably 'in
time', this is because of their dependence on expectations: but there is
no *reliable* inter-temporal link – indeed that is an essential feature of
the analysis.

On liquidity preference, it is true, Keynes is ambiguous. In one
passage the trouble seems to be that liquidity preference is perversely
insensitive to changes in the news or in public policy:

> The difficulties in the way of maintaining effective demand at a level high
> enough to provide full employment, which ensue from the association of a
> conventional and fairly stable long-term rate of interest with a fickle and
> highly unstable marginal efficiency of capital, should be, by now, obvious
> to the reader. (Keynes, 1973a, p.204)

Yet at other times – even indeed on the same page – it is the suscepti-
bility of the liquidity preference function to such influences which is
emphasized.

In Shackle's (1967, p.182) vivid metaphor, Keynes offers us a series
of tableaux, in each of which some particular combination of functions
leads to a determinate level of employment; but all the action – all the
changes in these functions – takes place while the curtains are closed,
and none of it is ever explained to the audience. Not only is there no
movement to be seen; no path is suggested by which one short period
might lead to another. One does not, as Shackle (1974, pp.76–7) also
observes, seek to explain the relationship between the series of patterns
produced by successive shakes of a kaleidoscope. Everything in
Marshall is deeply penetrated by the effects of time; the formal part of
Keynes's model, as Hicks (1982, p.289) emphasizes, is strictly timeless.
One observes the consequences of arbitrarily imposed patterns, which
are not allowed to be modified within the model. That is how the
temporary disequilibrium of the slump is turned into an unemployment
equilibrium. In these respects, Keynes is much closer to quantity-
rationed general equilibrium than to Marshall. He also finally parts
company from D.H. Robertson.

Hayek and Marshall both refer present behaviour to the past and the
future; but whereas Marshall explains how firms' confidence in the long-
run validity of their plans would lead them in the short period to hold
prices and cut output, in Hayek's model past errors must be liquidated

before full equilibrium can be restored. In a Hayekian slump it is the capital-stock, including the stock of skills, and not current demand, which is out of line with long-run normal demand, and therefore it is capital-stock rather than current output which needs to be adjusted. In a Schumpeterian recession, too, the composition of capital and skills is at fault, but not (primarily) because it was based on expectations distorted by credit inflation – although that can happen too: it was, for the most part, correctly designed for a situation which has now irretrievably passed away. Unlike Keynes, Marshall and Hayek and Schumpeter all offer microeconomic theories of unemployment which are embedded in time.

In an important sense, in Keynes's *General Theory* history doesn't matter; and it doesn't matter because he works in aggregates. (The trouble with so much macroeconomics is that it is not sufficiently micro.) Although the division between capital and consumption goods is crucial, the composition of the capital-stock itself is of no importance; it can accommodate itself to any pattern of effective demand. That this characteristic of his theory limited its applicability was tacitly recognized by Keynes (1937a) in his *Times* articles of 1937.

> So long as surplus resources were widely diffused between industries and localities it was no great matter at what point in the economic structure the impulse of an increased demand was applied. But the evidence grows that – for several reasons into which there is no space to enter here – the economic structure is unfortunately rigid. . . . We are in more need today of a rightly distributed demand than of a greater aggregate demand. (Keynes, 1982, p.385)

The unemployment rate was then over 12 per cent; thus the 'several reasons' for structured rigidity might constitute an empirically important theory of unemployment, which might resemble Hayek's, Schumpeter's or indeed a microkaleidic Shackle model.

Keynes's distinction, in the passage just quoted, between total demand and its distribution is natural and effective; but it may offer a misleading guide to policy, since it implies that structural as well as general problems of unemployment are problems of demand, to be met by more detailed schemes of demand management. But such detailed schemes may be not merely unnecessary, but unwise. Marshallian short-run unemployment is likely to be quite heavily concentrated on the instrumental trades, but does not need any sectoral remedy. Hayekian and Schumpeterian unemployment is concentrated in trades whose output is not and will not be required – in the former case because the apparent demand was always an illusion, in the latter because demand has shifted in the process of economic development. In both cases, the problem is not of inadequate sectoral demand but of inappropriate sectoral supply – so long, that is, as we consider that the overriding purpose of an economy is to satisfy its members' wants, rather than to provide jobs. There is an analytical basis for arguing that jobs which might be created by government intervention in Hayekian and Schumpeterian depressed industries could properly be designated 'not real jobs'.

Coordination and partial ignorance

Although Hayek's analysis of the way in which money affects the economic system is distinctive, his work is nevertheless orthodox in the more fundamental sense of showing how monetary disorders can infect a system which otherwise would work well. Schumpeterian capitalism gives us a rougher ride, but the incidental discomfort of the journey is the price for a rate of progress which can be attained in no other way and by no other system. So long as they are soundly based on the preceding general equilibrium – and without this basis they will not occur – Schumpeterian innovations embody what turns out to be the truth (Schumpeter, 1934, p.85). The entrepreneur's conjectures are seldom refuted.

But if, as the Austrians, like Keynes, often choose to emphasize, our knowledge of the future is incomplete, we may guess wrong: after all, scientific conjectures are usually refuted, and indeed most new products fail. How then are we to distinguish between false investments due to credit creation and false investments due to forecasting failures? Perhaps we should not try. Certainly Hayek's analysis of the consequences of false investments can be applied to situations such as have faced, for example, the world shipbuilding and steel industries and the European synthetic fibre industry in recent years. We might disagree about the relative weight to be given to cheap credit and to optimistic forecasts of the growth of world industry and trade; but if we agree that there is now long-run excess capacity, we face the Hayekian dilemma. For example, we might offer special subsidies to shipowners to replace ships long before their scrapping dates; but unless the new ships are in turn to be scrapped very early in their lives, we have then postponed the problem at the expense of aggravating it.

There is another sense in which perhaps we should not try too hard to distinguish between 'monetary' and 'real' problems; for such a distinction encourages us to persist with two classes of model, in one of which market coordination works, and in the other it does not. Leijonhufvud (1973) may well be right in his suggestion that what we really need to model are fallible systems, and fallible systems must surely be based on partial ignorance. It has repeatedly been shown how difficult it is, starting with a high degree of knowledge, even in a probabilistic sense, to explain a failure of coordination. In models of quantity-rationed general equilibrium, failure is imposed on the system by compelling it to work with the wrong prices. On the other hand, if the future is unknown, what do we even mean by successful coordination in a system which is making substantial forward commitments? And why should the strivings of Kirzner's entrepreneurs, each reflecting his own view of the future, ever add up? This, of course, was one of Joan Robinson's favourite questions. Apparently, only a properly planned economy can be coherent: there is absolutely no reason to believe that the planners will guess right, but they might be consistent.

Now, coherence in the face of partial ignorance is a real problem which standard analysis has done very little to elucidate. But, as we have seen in Chapter 2, post-Einstein science, having been forced to abandon the notion of certainty in scientific knowledge, faces the same problem. If we accept the Popperian idea of scientific knowledge as a structure of corroborated hypotheses, any of which might yet conceivably be falsified – including all those hypotheses which must be assumed true in order that any one may be tested – then the question of what to do when faced with an apparent experimental disproof is wide open. We can choose to regard the result as disproving any single item within the enormous body of 'knowledge' which lies behind any experiment. Similarly, recognition of a coordination failure in an economy is insufficient to establish exactly what has failed.

In practice, however, there is normally a large measure of agreement within a particular branch of science as to the kind of response which is appropriate. That degree of agreement still leaves room for displays of (sometimes dazzling) initiative in choosing the precise response. This pattern of human action within an agreed framework is what Lakatos (1970) had in mind in writing of 'scientific research programmes'; but frameworks, of a more permeable kind, are characteristic of Popper's analysis too.

Since a great deal of human behaviour can be pictured as the formulation and testing of hypotheses (sometimes in a very ill-structured way) and since, in particular, the idea of agents' plans can be so pictured, it may not be unreasonable to make use of the concept of 'research programmes' in trying to understand how an economy works. Agents' plans, like scientists' hypotheses, will usually be modified only in certain ways – a measure of consensus which obviously makes coherence easier to achieve. Research programmes, in Lakatos's analysis, have the interesting property that they usually lead to progress but can sometimes go badly wrong. Internal coherence does not guarantee continued success in predicting real world phenomena; and there may occasionally be nothing for it but to abandon a set of interconnected hypotheses or a set of interconnected plans. Unemployment might then be explained as one of the consequences of a failed research programme.

A failed research programme, in Schumpeter's terms, implies a failure either of entrepreneurial imagination, or of the calculations by which that imagination is converted into policy. Neither can be excluded by invoking the incentive to seek profits – it is not uncommon for individuals or teams to lose contests which they were trying hard to win – and Schumpeter offers no argument to persuade us that the price vector of a Walrasian equilibrium, which reflects a particular constellation of data and expectations, should prove a good predictor for circumstances in which that constellation is to be radically altered by actions which are deemed profitable on the basis of these prices. Indeed, there is no sign that he recognized the inconsistency within his own theory. Keynes's pessimism about the possibility of such rational calculation is not obviously less justifiable than Schumpeter's optimism. But if the programme has failed rather than succeeded – or even failed in part – then the process of rallying the economic system, which is a precondition of further advance (Schumpeter, 1934, p.217) is made even more difficult; and, as we have noted, Schumpeter does not tell us how it is to be done. Nor is it clear how alternative, and more successful, research programmes may be built up, especially when the markets in which plans are to be tested are known to be in disequilibrium. Entrepreneurs may simply not know what to do.

Government intervention
The theoretical frameworks which we have been considering leave ample room for the suspicion that competitive (is it necessary to add, not perfectly competitive?) economies can get into difficulties which are not easy for them to get out of. It is therefore appropriate to consider the case for government intervention. There is no intention of doing so here, but it is important to recognize that a theory of government intervention is as necessary as a theory of economic development and disequilibrium. To treat the government as the equivalent of the auctioneer, but calling quantities instead of prices, does not aid our understanding.

To postulate the maximization of social welfare as a governmental objective is less plausible than the attribution of profit maximization to firms: the political and administrative processes, the personal and professional interests of ministers, civil servants, advisers and lobbyists cannot be so simply summarized. As well as being less plausible, it is even less operational. How does one discover what actions are implied? Can the structural disequilibrium be identified, and if so, how is it to be dealt with? How is the government to identify new lines of development which are worth pursuing? In Britain, major government development programmes have not been notably better-founded than attempts to preserve obsolete structures and methods.

Furthermore, government activity changes both the environment in which entrepreneurs work and the data on which they base their calculations. It is intended to, of course; but the results may include a diversion of entrepreneurial energies into securing government support for schemes which, with such support, promise substantial profit but dubious utility. If government seeks to influence firms, we should expect firms to seek to influence government, and thus to reinforce the effects of the sectional interests analysed by Olson (1982). Moreover, the problem of forecasting government action – especially when government policy is seen to be inconsistent or subject to reversal, with or without a change of administration – is likely to foster an increasing realization of the fragility of all forecasts, and of the risks entailed in undertaking any substantial forward commitment. That attempts at governmental stimulus might discourage private investment, not through crowding-out but through its effects on business confidence, was a common fear in the 1930s.

No one was more critical of governmental error than Keynes; but the most disturbing feature of Keynes's attitude was his tendency to conclude such criticisms by proposing to increase the power and responsibilities of those criticized. Presumably all would be well were they to follow the right advice. Would they, and how do we know if the advice is right? The advisers, it is plain to see, are not in agreement. Keynes appears to display an intellectual arrogance which has long been a characteristic tradition of Cambridge – perhaps traceable to Alfred Marshall, who believed in the University's mission to send out into the world graduates with warm hearts and cool heads to benefit mankind (Pigou, 1925, p.174). Are the theories with which we cool our heads better than 'the pretty, polite techniques' which Keynes tells us entrepreneurs use? Is it true of economists, as of others, that, in Keynes's (1937b, p.113) words, 'we have, as a rule, only the vaguest idea of any but the most direct consequences of our acts'?

12 One firm spot on which to stand*

The problem of foundations

'Give me one firm spot on which to stand and I will move the world.'
So claimed Archimedes, impressed with the power of a single principle,
the principle of the lever. Modern theories of cosmology tell us that
Archimedes's simple condition is impossible to meet: nowhere in the
universe is there a spot which is itself immovable. Nevertheless, there
are many spots which may be assumed to be firm enough to make
effective use of the principle of the lever – although the assumption is
sometimes falsified, both in major engineering projects and in little jobs
around the home.

Similarly, we now realize that there is no single fact or synthetic
proposition which can provide an absolutely assured basis on which to
build our knowledge. Nevertheless, there have been facts and propositions which have proved sufficiently firm to provide the leverage
necessary for many scientific investigations – including investigations by
economists – and for many reasoned decisions – including decisions by
economic agents – although in mental, as in engineering, operations
the fulcrum on which we depend may crumble or slide under the weight
that we put on it.

It is not possible to predict with certainty when any spot will cease
to be firm, or indeed to be sure that we have identified all the implicit
assumptions that underlie our belief in its firmness. Nevertheless, some
forewarning is possible, and some assumptions can be uncovered and
examined. In the first part of this chapter we shall examine the limitations of rational choice theory as a firm basis for our operations;
and in the second part we shall explore the possibility of a rational
alternative.

This alternative is closely linked to a second issue. In social organizations, such as scientific communities, firms, and markets, it is often
necessary to have agreement on the basis of operations: and if our firm
spot is not a unique natural given but a matter of assumption, we then
face the requirement that this assumption be agreed among the relevant

*This chapter is a revised and extended version of a paper presented to the Scottish
Economists' Conference at the Burn, Edzell, in September 1986, and has benefited from
discussion there.

189

people. Who are the relevant people, and how do they come to agree? This, in a slightly different guise, is the central economic problem of coordination; but its solution does not lie in an equilibrium of rational optimizers – even when the relevant people are an invisible college of economists. Agreement implies the acceptance of a set of conventions, rules, procedures, criteria – what are collectively known by the not entirely unambiguous term 'institution'. (Indeed, this use of the word 'institution' is itself an institution.) An organization, such as a firm, may be characterized as a particular set of institutions: this is one tolerably firm spot on which one may attempt to construct a theory of the firm, and Nelson and Winter (1982) have already demonstrated that it provides some leverage.

The principal argument of this chapter is that institutions are necessary components for constructing both a theory of the growth of knowledge, including a theory of the development of economic analysis, and also a theory of the behaviour of economic agents – especially behaviour in interdependent systems, which is normally the object of our interests. Since assumptions (sometimes implicit) about agents' knowledge are crucial to our analyses, this correspondence should not be surprising; but perhaps a little less obvious is the proposition that institutions are necessary to the working of markets. Indeed, it is a striking paradox that a microeconomic theory which is overwhelmingly a theory of markets has so little to tell us about the conditions for the successful operation of markets. A market and its operations are far more problematic than most economists appear to realize. This spot is not at all firm.

Before proceeding further it seems only just to acknowledge Carl Menger's (1963, Book 3) recognition of the importance of institutions in human affairs. His views appear remarkably well balanced. Although some of the institutions which we observe may accurately reflect the intentions of their creators, and therefore are explicable by the direct application of rational choice theory, others do not. Such institutions are not, however, incapable of rational explanation; for Menger appears to anticipate Popper's (1969, p.342) assertion that 'the *main task of the theoretical social sciences . . . is to trace the unintended social repercussions of intentional human actions*'. In Simon's language, people are intendedly rational, but not completely so, and so the results, especially the remoter results, of their actions are not always what they expect; indeed, according to Popper (1969, p.124) 'it is one of the striking things about social life that *nothing ever comes off exactly as intended*'. Sometimes people simply make mistakes; but sometimes their actions have consequences which they have never even thought of. Unlisted consequences are incompatible with strictly rational choice, as economists understand it; but, as Hutchison (1981, p.182–3) has pointed out, Menger was well aware that theories of rational action made implausible demands on the knowledge of the actors. Although he did not make the link himself, incomplete knowledge not only explains why many institutions evolve in ways which were not intended; it also explains why people need institutions – to limit the requirements of rationality.

Menger was critical of Benthamite rationalism, which was liable to destroy what it did not understand and to create what would not serve its own intended purposes. But he also objected (1963, p.181) to Burke's insistence on the necessary superiority of tradition, and the historical jurists' veneration of the common law and of other undesigned institutions (1963, p.233). What was required was, first, an attempt to analyse the processes by which a particular institution had evolved, and second, an appraisal of its present effects: 'never . . . may science dispense with testing for their suitability those institutions which have come about "organically"' (Menger, 1963, p.234). Spontaneous order is often preferable to designed structures, but not necessarily so, as Olson (1982) has convincingly shown. This is not quite the dominant research programme of contemporary economic analysis. But, as we have seen in earlier chapters, the institutions of economics have themselves evolved in ways which were not always intended, and they too should be tested for their suitability.

Rational choice theory
The central convention – indeed, virtually definition – of orthodox economic theory is that of optimizing agents whose actions are determined by applying to the natural givens of their situation (endowments, technologies, future states of nature) preference functions which are also naturally given. Adam Smith would have thoroughly understood the psychological appeal of the 'connecting principles' of such a coherent rationality; and Shackle, having recorded in *The Years of High Theory* (1967) the collapse of what he called the Great Theory, and the consequent discomfort among practitioners of the subject, was able to note in his preface to the second edition (1983) how the edifice has been reconstructed on an even grander plan. Becker (1976) has claimed that this principle of coherent rationality not only provides a unified framework for the analysis of all human behaviour – itself a claim of astonishing ambition, if not arrogance – but that it is the only such basis – the only firm spot on which to stand. The annexation of this uniquely firm spot by economists has, of course, the happy effect of

ensuring for all time the superiority of economics over every other social science.

One need not, however, explain the dominance of this analytical principle purely by its psychological appeal. It is also a very effective institution, as we observed in Chapter 3. But it has problems on both counts; for its coherence is seriously flawed. A universal theory of rational action requires a matching theory of rational belief, but no such theory is possible. It is astonishing how readily analysts of rational choice assume that beliefs are well-founded, presumably (for they are not always explicit) on some rules of inference, derived from a principle of induction which has been known to be invalid for at least two centuries.

Decision theorists regularly use the rules of inference which are embodied in Bayesian learning; but a Bayesian process must begin with the imposition of subjective probabilities on a list of possible outcomes which is known to be complete. How is the completeness of the list to be established? Calculating the value of information within such a framework can sometimes be useful, but the framework – and the concept of information – is severely restricted. There is no conception of the possibility of discovering unsuspected opportunities or unanticipated outcomes: there is no novelty. Instead there is a pretence of knowledge.

It is still possible to make effective use of decision theory to display a network of choices and the possible consequences of each, and to calculate the action which is most completely consistent with a particular set of preferences and a particular set of expectations. This calculation may be very useful as a means of testing whether a proposed course of action is in line with purported objectives and declared views about the likelihood of various future events, whether for an individual or for a decision-making group. When no more than this is claimed one should have no objection – except that the application of decision theory may sometimes pre-empt attention from making provision for the unexpected.

Yet there would not be much merit in aligning actions with expectations if expectations were often seriously awry. Even those who most emphasize the subjective basis of conventional decision theory like to argue that subjective estimates are based on individual knowledge, which is generally well-founded; and economists, whose aim is to analyse, and often to appraise, the working of an economic system, can hardly ignore the question of agents' knowledge. It is perfectly possible to construct a temporary equilibrium which rests on wildly inaccurate expectations, but that is not a good basis for predicting future states of the economy; and longer-run concepts of equilibrium depend on the absence of contradiction between expectations and outcomes. Although it is often enlightening to enquire whether a past situation can be reasonably characterized as a long-run equilibrium, there is no way of telling whether present expectations will support a future equilibrium – except in the mind of the analyst. The equilibrium method of economics, as we all know, has a choice-theoretic basis, and any weakness in that basis is liable to weaken the method.

However, if agents' knowledge were indeed secure enough to validate our equilibrium models, then those models would be of very little use, since the course of history would have already been decided. It does not seem to be generally appreciated how completely a rigorous adherence to the concept of rational choice equilibria inhibits the analysis of any kind of change which is not merely the performance of a predetermined script. By definition, a perfect foresight model is protected from anything unexpected. An Arrow–Debreu system allows for many possible futures, together with a set of contracts appropriate to each; but the emergence of one or other of these futures simply triggers the relevant contracts, and permits no further choice. Thus, it is illegitimate to enquire how such a system would adjust to a contingency not provided for; such a contingency would demonstrate that it was never a properly constituted Arrow–Debreu system after all.

Examining the consequences of shocks is a staple of rational expectations macroeconomics; but can shocks be combined with the concept of rationality employed? Since these shocks are deemed to be quite impossible to foresee and to follow no discernible pattern, it is assumed that they call for no revision of the model which is used to form expectations. But the impossibility of using such events to improve the forecasting model does not mean that they convey no useful information; and even the weakest version of rational expectations assumes that all useful information will indeed be used. The information conveyed by unpredictable shocks is that the strongest form of rational expectations is invalid: the best model available for forming expectations cannot be the correct model of the economy, since it ignores something important – namely, unpredictability.

Although it is hardly possible to forecast the unpredictable, it is possible to take some precautions. Indeed, a world in which some part of the future is known to be unpredictable (not reducible to probability distributions) is, in some important respects, very different from a predictable world. Hicks (1982, pp.287–8) gives Menger credit for recognizing that the search for liquidity is just one aspect of a general pattern of rational provision for unforeseeable contingencies. Much recent writing on management has taken exactly the opposite line to rational expectations theory, proclaiming that the ability to forecast is a dangerous illusion, and that organizational structures and attitudes need to be flexible and imaginative. Rational management requires something more than what economists call rational choice.

Economists' concern with interdependent systems introduces a second order of difficulty with coherent rationality. In addition to knowledge about the natural world, rational agents now need to be able to predict the choices of other rational agents. Unfortunately, as Simon (1982, 2: p.217) has observed, in an interdependent system not more than one person can be unlimitedly clever: an economy of interdependent coherent optimizers is itself incoherent. This dilemma is well recognized in the study of oligopoly, where the objective of many theorists is to minimize the damage done to the concept of rationality by the expedients necessary to produce a determinate outcome; but the dilemma is pervasive. A perfectly competitive economy, which was thought to be exempt from this difficulty, possesses no means of adjustment to any change in circumstances, as Richardson (1960) has explained.

Indeed, Arrow (1959) had recognized that the conditions of perfect competition cannot exist outside equilibrium, since any excess demand or supply is incompatible with the ability of all agents to carry out their plans at current prices. Price theory in economics is actually a theory of response to prices which have somehow been set by others. Even monopoly is studied in terms of equilibrium prices. Our theory of rational choice does not produce a theory of price-setting. We have no true theory of price; and that is because we have no theory of markets.

Even an equilibrium of competitive markets imposes certain requirements, such as a law of contract, together with certain measures to police it, some system of weights and measures, and a unit of account: agents require a firm spot on which to be rational. It also appears to require an auctioneer. As we saw in Chapter 11, fixprice models with rationing, far from dispensing with the auctioneer, require of him a double duty: he has not only to set, and maintain, the 'wrong' prices, but also to administer, and police, the rationing scheme. None of these conditions can plausibly be treated either as a natural given or as a consequence of optimizing choice.

Game theory might appear to offer a way out of the problems of interdependencies; but the exit is blocked. Non-cooperative games, notoriously exemplified by the prisoner's dilemma, often yield solutions which are clearly inferior to other possible outcomes; and these solutions have been interpreted as challenges to the concept of coherent rationality. Social norms or moral codes have sometimes been invoked to induce more desirable outcomes (Elster, 1986), but it has not been clear how these were themselves to be rationally explained. Cooperative games generate more attractive solutions, but where do the rules of cooperative games come from? Nash (1951) proposed that the rules of any cooperative game should be derived as the solution of a prior bargaining game, which would be non-cooperative; but why should agents decide to proceed in this way, and if they do, how are the rules of the bargaining game to be set? Game theory is boundedly rational. Indeed, it should be recognized that the terms of the prisoner's dilemma, as it is usually presented, are the product of statute law and legal procedures (including the American practice of plea bargaining, which is not universal), which are clearly not naturally given nor at all obviously the result of optimizing choice. They are institutions.

Faced with these difficulties of explaining the knowledge basis of rational choice, it is not surprising that economists so often seek to abolish choice altogether, by postulating conditions in which agents are tightly constrained – a stratagem which is usually labelled either situational determinism or the use of single-exit models. In perfect markets it does not matter what any agent wants, or what he believes: there is only one thing to be done. It is encouraging to learn that not all markets need to be perfect: perfect capital markets appear to impose very effective constraints in other markets. They ensure that monopoly price is not chosen, but imposed, like all other prices. How they are imposed, and by whom, no-one can tell us – unless we believe in the auctioneer, which is hardly evidence of rationality. An alternative expedient is to appeal to predictive success as the crucial test, sometimes in terms which suggest that, in building a model, anything goes. Rational choice theory is thus emptied of content, and becomes a mechanical device for generating predictions. This expedient, as was suggested in Chapter 2, is not a very satisfactory basis for scientific activity, or for economic agents to improve their knowledge.

The focus on equilibrium avoids the problems of learning, which is a threat to rational choice theory. To allow a process of learning is to lose control of the analysis, as some economists have realized: individual rational choice is then not enough to fix the behaviour of the system, and indeed is not always easy to specify. Hahn's (1973; 1984, p.59) definition of equilibrium as a situation in which the economy generates messages which do not cause agents to change the theories which they hold or the policies which they pursue, is explicitly a definition of a situation in which learning has ceased. It is not necessarily a situation in which agents have discovered the correct theory, or even a situation in which they have no reason to believe their theories are in error; for in a real, rather than Bayesian, world they might know that something is wrong without seeing how it might be put right. That is not an unfamiliar situation, even for professional economists. The world of equilibrium appears to offer protection from knowledge problems, but enough theoretical challenges to keep economists busy; if one wishes to make predictions or to give policy advice, all that is necessary is to assume that the economy is somewhere near equilibrium, offering, if one feels the need, the justification that, if agents are optimizing, then this must be so.

Nevertheless, there are serious difficulties with the cavalier treatment of knowledge in rational choice theory, and serious problems with the pretence of knowledge in the predominant method of economic analysis. It seems appropriate to look for help in theories of the growth of knowledge. Indeed, we gain a new perspective on economists' revealed preference for rational choice by considering the predominant methods as a set of institutions – a particular example of the institutions of science.

The institutions of knowledge
The central difficulty in the theory of knowledge, which we first encountered in Chapter 2, is the logical impossibility of verifying any general statement. The evidence that can be brought to bear on any general law is only a small part – usually an infinitesimally small part – of the evidence that is relevant. As Popper has frequently emphasized, the statistical probability that an important theory is true is very low indeed: indeed, that is effectively his definition of an important theory. None of us can ever know that we have the correct model of any phenomenon; we may have, but all that we can say with certainty is that our model has not yet failed. Our experience provides no adequate basis for probabilistic assessments of future success, although it may, if we are willing, lead to a choice of action on the basis of equivalent gambles. A probabilistic assessment, just as much as a single-valued prediction, is a conjecture which is exposed to refutation.

Unfortunately, refutation is not straightforward. The impossibility of proving the truth of a general law paradoxically entails the impossibility of proving its falsity; for in order to test one hypothesis, many others must be assumed correct – and any one of these assumptions may be false. This difficulty, which was discussed in Chapter 2, is generally labelled the Duhem–Quine problem: what is refuted is a particular conjunction of hypotheses (including, notably, all the hypotheses which underlie the test procedure), and thus all that we know is that the set is not consistent. Even a specification of the set is, in general, impossble to complete.

If we map out a programme of formulating and testing hypotheses on a decision tree, we must recognize that a refutation is not an event but a decision. How is this decision to be made? If there is to be any kind of systematic acquisition of knowledge, even for an individual, then there must be some methodological rules. The logic of scientific discovery (the title of Popper's first book (1972)) is a logic of the application of rules, not of their selection: indeed, Popper's celebrated demarcation criterion for science is explicitly proposed as a convention (1972, p.37). Such conventions may be the subject of reasoned argument – as Popper and others have demonstrated – but not of rational choice.

Although science may be practised in isolation, it is subject to economies of specialization and scale: the process of conjecture, criticism, and experiment is much more effective as a social activity. But this social activity requires a substantial degree of conformity in the methodological rules that are applied: that is, a more or less orderly framework. Popper (1972, p.13) opens his *Logic of Scientific Discovery* with a contrast between science and philosophy: in most areas of science the practitioner can get down to work straightaway on a well-defined problem-situation, whereas philosophers are far from agreeing on how their problems should be defined. But the framework of scientific activity is not determined by facts or by first principles. It cannot be the direct product of rational choice, as defined in rational choice theory, since the object is to produce novelty – ideas not yet conceived. Nor is it created by a formal hierarchy, although this may be true in research teams or even research centres. It is built, and changed, by a series of individual decisions to accept, reject, or modify current practitioners' conceptions of problems and ways of tackling them. Sometimes the changes are abrupt, sometimes gradual; sometimes they are readily accepted, sometimes they are accompanied by much controversy – as we see in the history of economics, of political parties, and of major companies.

Public science – the science of universities, research institutes and of individuals, linked by the journals of the subject area – produces public knowledge (although what is publicly available is not always readily assimilable by non-specialists): as we have seen in Chapter 3, it proceeds towards open agreements, openly arrived at, within a broadly agreed but permeable framework, using broadly agreed concepts and methods, although the agreement may be tacit and is never completely specified. Ziman (1968, p.9) characterizes scientific method as the search for consensus over the widest possible field. It is a social process which is carried on within the social structures of science and helps to shape them. This search for consensus is likely to be assisted by a framework of wide scope and intellectual appeal, such as is offered by the rational choice model. Rational choice theory is significant, not so much as an intendedly correct theory, but as a set of institutions which help to guide conjecture and focus debate.

Science cannot produce certain knowledge, any more than any other human activity; what it does produce, according to Ziman, is generally reliable knowledge, and this reliability, which is far from complete, is a consequence of the process which generates it. This process of conjecture, testing and criticism is not impersonal but interpersonal, not objective but intersubjective; it is a process of competition between theories and between scientists. In the early stages of this competition, reliability is not high: Ziman (1978, p.40) estimates that 90 per cent of the contents of the physics textbooks is correct – a non-negligible margin of error on which to base rational expectations – but that 90 per cent of the contents of the physics research journals is false.

The creation of public knowledge has obvious similarities with the operation of competitive – not, of course, perfectly competitive – markets, which Hayek (1978, pp.179–90) has characterized as a discovery and control process. Here too the outcomes are validated (so far as they can be) by the process which produces them – as indeed are the outcomes of sporting contests; and here too, as is often forgotten, the process is dependent on an institutional framework. Markets generate and test knowledge about technologies, preferences, and commodities – the givens of standard equilibrium theory – by a process of conjecture, testing and criticism: voice and exit are both characteristic of markets as well as organizations (Hirschman, 1970). Innovations may obviously be regarded as conjectures, but so too may prices: to consider the setting of price as a conjecture offers some promise of liberating price theory from its dependence – which is as great in fixed-price rationing models as in market-clearing models – on some unanalysable external agency to perform what appears to be the most critical function within orthodox microeconomics.

As we have seen in Chapter 3, sociologists sometimes regard science as a reputational system: that is entirely appropriate, provided that we recognize that reputations are created in the scientific market much more than by hierarchical judgements. Heads of scientific departments may be able to decide who gets appointed to what position; they cannot decide what piece of theory will be assimilated into the body of reliable knowledge, and what will be discarded. Nor can a scientific reputation, gained in the scientific market-place, be used to maintain a judgemental monopoly. To be sure, such a reputation can gain a hearing for a hypothesis, or a line of criticism, that would receive little attention if propounded by an unknown; but if the hypothesis or criticism has little value the consequence will be not the triumph of this view but the eclipse of the reputation.

Reputations are very important also to the functioning of markets: in Hayek's (1949, p.97) words, 'the function of competition is here precisely to teach us *who* will serve us well'. The attempt to exploit a market reputation by offering lower-quality merchandise may be compared with the attempt to exploit a scientific reputation by offering lower-quality ideas: it may achieve some success, but will not last. This does not mean that no damage will be done, nor that the attempt cannot yield sufficient gains for it to be considered as intelligent, if regrettable, behaviour, just as a policy of high prices which incites successful entry may sometimes be the most profitable. No-one can impose judgements of value, either of commodities or of ideas, in a competitive system. But the market, like science, is not impersonal, but interpersonal, not objective, but intersubjective: it scarcely resembles the model of perfectly competitive equilibrium.

A unified framework facilitates the process of scientific discovery by increasing the efficiency of the communication system. It does so by constraining thought; this is essential, but dangerous. Constraints are chosen rather than imposed, and even within a well developed science there is some variety of practice, as well as some mavericks. It is notable that the two best known attempts to explain the constrained choices of science, by Kuhn (1962; 1970a) and Lakatos (1970), fail to define any agreed set of constraints, or even to define their concepts, of paradigm and research programme in such a way as to suggest that any precise definition is possible. Kuhn was, indeed, taken to task for the multiplicity of meanings which he implicitly gave to the word 'paradigm' (Masterman, 1970).

Both writers might have been more positive in stressing the necessary ambiguities of any general research framework. Just like the firm and for the same basic reason, a research programme or paradigm embodies an imperfectly specified contract. These ambiguities, though often producing misunderstandings and delaying progress in one particular direction, are important in facilitating shifts of direction. Even inconsistencies may sometimes be very helpful; for boundedly rational humans might cut themselves off from valuable sources of knowledge if they insisted on coherence within the bounds of their comprehension.

The inconsistency of choice behaviour frequently revealed by posing formally equivalent options in different decision frames (Tversky and Kahneman, 1981) may be part of the price we pay in order to leave ourselves open to new knowledge; and the importance of pattern-recognition in science (Ziman, 1978, pp.43–56) may explain attempts by experimental subjects to impose patterns on what are declared to be randomly generated data. The human propensity to impose patterns may historically have had survival value: false identification of the presence of a prey or predator from what are wrongly taken to be significant clues may be much less costly than failure to identify either by treating clues as coincidences. In modern society, too, patterns help to foster conjectures; and we seem to need many conjectures before we find one which is corroborated. Thus 'we expect regularities everywhere and attempt to find them even where there are none' (Popper, 1969, p.49). If the propensity to make patterns is so useful, why should people abandon such behaviour when faced with the transparent and transient artificiality of these choice experiments? Those economists who will look at nothing but an equilibrium of rational optimizers may preserve the coherence of the ideas of their imagination; but it is a dangerous game. What is consistent to human perception is also incomplete.

Economic institutions
Simon (1982, 2: p.383) has observed that, whereas economists tend to regard the psychologists' conception of rationality as quite inadequate, psychologists tend to characterize the economists' model of rational choice as programmed behaviour which exhibits no features of human decision. The study of economic institutions needs the psychologists' conception if it is to be fully effective. The developing analysis of markets and hierarchies, predominantly associated with Oliver Williamson (1975; 1985; 1986), has brought such phenomena as transactions costs, asset specificity, information impactedness, and opportunism within the scope of economics, and has provided us with a framework for the analysis of organizational scope. Because the form of organization is rationally chosen, it is, moreover, a framework that appears plausibly consistent with the comprehensive scheme of rational choice; and it allows us to compare the information and incentive structures of markets with those of formal organizations.

Yet, for anyone who has pondered Coase's (1937) article, to which Williamson pays frequent tribute, the form of analysis is not entirely satisfactory. For Coase was arguing not that in certain, rather common, circumstances the firm provided a more efficient means of optimization – a view developed, notably by Fama (1980), into the general proposition that the firm is a nexus of markets – but that the firm offered a means of escape from optimization when prospects were too uncertain to make any rational choice algorithm credible. Imperfectly specified contracts are a means of postponing choice and avoiding commitment – a form of liquidity.

It is not surprising that Williamson says very little about the way firms operate; his analysis does not allow him to. The effects of future operations are embodied in the specification of the present choice, thus collapsing the future into the present as effectively as Debreu's contingent markets. It is even less surprising that he has nothing to say about the ways in which markets operate; the factors which make markets inefficient simply lead to their supersession by firms. He does recognize, and indeed emphasize, that the practical choice is between imperfect systems; yet the logic of his argument – the logic of fully specified rational choice – which keeps him in touch with the neoclassical method drives the analysis towards the conclusion that the allocation of activities between markets and firms is an efficient allocation. But this logic gives inadequate recognition to the institutions of the market.

Williamson has never adequately grappled with Richardson's (1972) analysis of the structure of industry in which he demonstrated that many relationships of close interdependence, which Williamson later argued could only be efficiently handled by vertical integration, were in practice continuously managed by members of separate organizations. On the one hand, Williamson has not given enough weight to the problems of managing activities which, though closely complementary, are not similar (to be fair, on the evidence of some recent divestments, neither have a number of managing directors and company presidents); on the other hand and like almost all industrial economists, he has not allowed for the institutions of the market.

In the remainder of this chapter, I will try to indicate some ways of looking at institutions within organizations and in markets, emphasizing the common features in the hope of finding one firm spot that will serve for both analyses, and thus also for institutional comparisons. I shall rely principally on the work of Nelson and Winter (1982), who appear to have gone further than other economists in developing an institutional theory of organizational behaviour. An evolutionary theory of economic change, which they are seeking to produce, must be both a theory of the development of institutions and a theory of development within an institutional framework.

Organizational knowledge and routines

Unlike rational choice theorists, Nelson and Winter (1982) recognize that knowledge is problematic. Much of it is tacit, and therefore inexpressible in forms, such as words or symbols, which render it amenable to formal analysis. Its scope is ambiguous, not only because its claims are always subject to refutation, but also because the scope of those claims is not usually specified with care: knowledge is likely to be wrong in some respects, and almost certainly not fully understood. (Even the contents of the physics textbooks, remember, are judged by Ziman to be 10 per cent false; and he makes no claim to know which 10 per cent.) Coherence is imposed, but is not often well articulated. Since so much is learned by doing, and often in a way which is not easily expressed and even less accurately remembered, the experiential basis of individual knowledge is only partly known and cannot be fully recovered. Reliance on what can be rationally explicated, in the sense of rational choice theory, entails denying oneself access to a great deal of tolerably reliable knowledge.

This is still more true of both formal and informal organizations which attempt to bring together the knowledge of many individuals: it is not possible to provide adequate reasons for many of the conventions and procedures which characterize them. As Menger argued, they should not therefore be exempt from criticism, but criticism requires more than a logical argument derived from the critic's own premises and what he regards as relevant evidence. Hayek (1949) has claimed that competitive markets utilize the knowledge of individuals in ways which none of them, or no combination of them, would be capable of achieving by any nominally rational process; his argument is well taken, but we should recognize that something similar may be achieved within an organization, if its institutions are appropriate.

Nelson and Winter (1982, pp.96–136) devote a chapter – perhaps the most valuable in their book – to organizational routines. In this, they note the importance not only of patterns of behaviour but of the cues that trigger them, many of which are neither written down nor even spoken, and which may differ substantially between organizations even in the same industry. I have myself observed an experienced consultant, newly arrived in another consultancy organization, unable to understand how the new system worked, while his new colleagues found his bewilderment equally baffling.

These emergent differences are a natural consequence of the role of practice in maintaining the organization's memory: skills are created by performance and lost by non-performance. If there is learning by doing – as there surely is – there is forgetting by not doing. The firm's production function is not a set of blueprints, but a bundle of possibilities which wax and wane, usually both at one time. In particular, an organization will not be flexible unless it frequently changes its patterns of behaviour within its claimed flexible range, whether these patterns relate to production, marketing, financial, personnel, or any other skills. This may help to explain why organizations sometimes come to grief through a failure in what had been widely regarded as their strength. There are also other reasons, as we shall see.

Particular interest attaches to those routines which link organizational sub-units, especially the control systems which define the degree of sub-unit independence and which therefore tend to limit superiors' formal knowledge of what goes on inside them and of the range and limitations of the skills which are currently available – hence the importance attached to informal contacts, sometimes known as 'management by walking about', in many organizations which seek to prepare themselves for the unexpected. Any organizational design seeks to decompose what is an imperfectly decomposable system, and the pattern of decomposition shapes the routines by which it operates; these routines usually tend to reinforce the scheme of decomposition – but not always, because there may be attempts to frustrate or undermine the official design. If the design is well adapted to the current situation, the members of the organization will become habituated to it: their plans are tested within the organization, and their conjectures are not refuted. The price of this adaptation is the difficulty that is likely to be encountered in shifting to another pattern of behaviour.

Routines evolve over time. Some changes result from accidental variation, the results of which are thought to be worth preserving. One common source of accidental variation is a change in personnel; for knowledge and routines, as Nelson and Winter envisage them, are not capable of complete articulation, and thus even elaborate schemes of training (which are hardly standard practice) cannot ensure the replication of existing routines among new people. Change in personnel may be associated with deliberate change, either because the newcomers are selected for that purpose, or because they bring with them ideas and routines which they wish to use in their new environment. Those appointed to make changes do not always make the changes which those who appointed them had in mind; and 'white knights', called in to save the incumbent management from an unwelcome takeover, often appear less amenable on closer acquaintance.

Change, with or without changes in personnel, may be a response to changes in the environment. Of particular interest are those changes, discussed by Pfeffer and Salancik (1978), in the relative importance of various kinds of transactions across the organizational boundary. Shifts in the power or policies of trade unions, new environmental pressure groups, safety legislation, the arrival or departure of government as a major customer, are all examples of redefinitions of the critical areas to be managed, and are likely to lead to significant shifts in the influence of functions within the organization, of the people who perform these functions, and of the routines employed.

Some of these changes are likely to be experienced as discontinuities, calling for the creation of new routines. That may be difficult if an organization has not developed institutions which are suited to this purpose. Both the width and the content of the repertoire of behaviour may be important. The more easily new operating patterns can be accepted as a new application of familiar principles (such as surface coating technology, the leisure market, or rational choice theory) the more likely they are to be accepted; but the currently available skills within that principle may still be seriously inadequate to the new tasks – most obviously because the extension may create a conflict with another, hitherto harmonious principle. For example, Levitt's (1962) advice that businesses should be defined in terms of market substitution may lead companies into areas of technological ignorance and disaster just as surely as following the logic of technology may bring companies into markets which they do not understand. Unrecognized ignorance is a major explanation of failure to construct appropriate routines.

The contemporary fashion in management literature for seeking 'excellence' appears to embody a search for routines which will produce innovation within a particular range of abilities. What is particularly interesting is the apparent perception that opening up an organization to change, loosening many of the administrative routines embodied in reporting relationships and schemes of management control, places emphasis on the need for much wider agreement on a coherent framework. If an organization is to become more like a scientific community, then it needs to adopt more of the conventions and procedures (including perhaps the system of reputational control) of that community. Otherwise, as some economists fear about their own subject, the attempt to embrace learning may lead to disintegration.

A further characteristic of routines to which Nelson and Winter devote attention is their contribution to organizational truce. This is a development of the proposition by Cyert and March (1963) that organizations typically avoid the apparent need to arrive at an agreed objective function (the formidable difficulties of which have been decisively demonstrated by Arrow) through such patterns of behaviour as sequential attention to goals, local rationality, and the use of budgets to allocate resources and to provide limited independence and protection from incursions. Well established routines likewise provide security and help to stabilize the organization.

But the more important this function becomes, the more difficult it may be to change these routines: if custom and practice are the only protection against the erosion of our position, then custom and practice must be inviolate. (Consider the attitudes of printing workers in Fleet Street.) Thus, even changes which in themselves are totally unobjectionable may be resisted because acceptance might appear to indicate willingness to acquiesce in other changes. Moreover, as Nelson and Winter note, if this is recognized by those who would like to change, they may make no attempt to introduce it, either because they value the truce or because they estimate that the cost of a battle outweighs the likely benefits. (Change in Fleet Street awaited the arrival of proprietors who were social as well as business outsiders.) What appears to be a Pareto-improvement is forgone – although it is not a Pareto-improvement if the choice set and constraints are correctly specified.

As my former colleague M.S. Common has observed of some ecological systems, stability is an alternative to resilience. Stability is economical, but potentially fatal: organizations may dissolve rather than adapt their routines, even when the necessary skills appear to be available. It was because Schumpeter expected this to happen that he thought lengthy depressions were inevitable. Effective routines, for the great majority who are capable of no more than routine, will emerge only 'if things have time to hammer logic into men' (Schumpeter, 1934, p.80), but, before a new logic can be hammered in, the old, outdated, logic has to be erased, and that may take some time. It is not easy to take Popper's advice to let our ideas die instead of ourselves – especially if whatever ideas we use have to be compatible with those of other people within a formal organization or an informal network.

One further complication which Nelson and Winter do not mention is that most of us belong to several organizations or networks of varying degrees of formality, and therefore operate within several institutional frameworks. For most of us, a modest degree of inconsistency between frameworks is tolerable, although the degree of tolerance is not uniform; but some coherence there must be, and if the response which is apparently necessary to keep our firm in business is hard to reconcile with our behaviour in our union, our family, our profession, our church, our social club, or whatever, then that response may be unacceptable. At one extreme, the result may be the triumph of integrity over expediency; at another, the destruction of many people's hopes through obstinacy.

Market routines

Let us consider some parallels with the operation of markets. Markets rarely work on a basis of anonymity, but normally involve relationships which persist over some time. These relationships depend on patterns of experience and on conventions of collaboration – even among competitors – which are often implicit and poorly specified. Among these conventions are certain shared assumptions about knowledge (described by Keynes, 1937b; 1973c, p.114). The institutional basis of markets, including shared assumptions about knowledge, permeates Marshall's (1961) analysis, as was emphasized in Chapter 4. The achievement of temporary equilibrium in the corn-market depends not just on preferences and endowments, but on the shared experiences of regular traders, with the expectation that they will continue to trade in that market in future weeks. The maintenance of price above short-run costs in the face of depressed demand depends not only on regular patterns of purchase but also on a shared belief that the depression will not persist; if this belief is not shared, there will be trouble, as indeed there sometimes is. The long-run improvement in technique and organization takes place, in contrast to Schumpeter's vision, against a continuing, yet evolving, network of relationships.

Richardson's (1972) discussion of market institutions is the most Marshallian of all modern treatments – perhaps, indeed, the only Marshallian modern treatment: in notable contrast to Williamson, he explores the institutional structures which permit the close collaboration between companies which are entirely separate in ownership and control. The institutional structures may not always work; indeed the continuing concentration of the grocery business into the hands of a very few giant chains is already raising questions about the persistence of present arrangements with their suppliers – although one can see why the supermarket operators should be reluctant to get involved in manufacturing in which they have no experience and which exhibit much less attractive patterns of cash flow. Supermarkets can thrive on negative current assets, selling most of their stocks long before they have to pay for them. The pattern of trade credit developed long ago by manufacturers as a crucial part of their strategy for gaining control over retailers has financed the growth of quick-turnover chains, and thus eventually had the unintended consequence of undermining the manufacturers' bargaining power.

The study of the evolution of market institutions might seek to apply Nelson and Winter's ideas on routines, their drift, the difficulties of replication, and even their importance in maintaining a truce between market participants. Perhaps of particular interest is the paradoxical position of the entrepreneur – at once a beneficiary and breaker of routines (a combination nicely encapsulated in Casson's (1982, pp.1–6) fable of Jack Brash). Such questions appear to be particularly appropriate to business historians who wish to go beyond studies of single enterprises to consider interactions between firms.

For those concerned less with the efficient allocation of activities between firms and markets at a particular conjuncture – the focus of the comparative institutions approach – than with the possibilities of effective adaptation, a central, and highly topical question is that of the relative potential of adaptation at different levels. In what circumstances is adaptation most effectively practised within the firm, in what circumstances through the displacement of one firm by another? One must expect that the answers will depend not only on the circumstances – which may themselves reflect some other institutional pattern, such as that of a government agency, a scientific community, or a trade union – but also on the particular institutional characteristics of the particular firm or market. There may sometimes be a case for direct intervention to change these characteristics, although that is not a course to be lightly advocated. What are the institutions which guide the evolution of market relationships? I suspect that Klein's (1977) hypothesis that micro-stability always undermines macro-stability is far too simple; but it may provide a useful framework for organizing thought among those seeking to investigate the problem.

Conclusion

In this chapter I have been critical of the present dependence of most economic analysis on the concept of rational choice, though not unmindful of the value of that concept as an institution in the development of tolerably reliable knowledge. My guess is that the proportion of truth in economic textbooks is much less than 90 per cent, but well above 10 per cent; the greater the reliance on what Nelson and Winter call 'appreciative theory' the higher the percentage. Some of the important problems in economics, notably the operations of organizations and of markets, cannot be adequately handled without an institutional framework. That certainly does not call for the abandonment of the concept of deliberate choice; but it does require the recognition of the limitations on human choice, and of the need to take seriously the problem of human knowledge.

What I am suggesting is a modification of the institutions of economics, to focus on knowledge rather than choice, and to exploit as far as possible the similarities between the growth and decay of knowledge, the evolution of organizations, and the operation of markets. Both organizations and markets are instruments for the generation, diffusion, and testing of knowledge, and all operate within an institutional framework which is never completely explicit and modified by the processes which it guides. My proposition, adapted from Kelly (1963), is that rational economic agents follow not the dictates of rational choice, but the rules of scientific method: man is not an optimizer but a scientist. Rational choice, in its special economic sense, is not expelled but, like other once-general theories, becomes an analytical structure which is invaluable for certain, quite extensive, purposes: the invocation of scientific method allows rationality to be more generously interpreted.

There is no one spot sufficiently firm to allow us to apply sufficient leverage on all our problems. There are several spots each of which will serve very well for more modest ambitions. I believe there are enough 'connecting principles', to use Adam Smith's phrase, to support a reasonably coherent, though imperfectly specified, system of thought which allows for shifts between them, both by economic analysts and by economic agents.

References

Andrews, P.W.S. (1949), *Manufacturing Business*, Macmillan, London.

Andrews, P.W.S. (1951), 'Industrial analysis in economics' in T. Wilson and P.W.S. Andrews (eds), *Oxford Studies in the Price Mechanism*, Oxford University Press, London, pp.139–72.

Andrews, P.W.S. (1964), *On Competition in Economic Theory*, Macmillan, London.

Andrews, P.W.S. and Brunner, E. (1975), *Studies in Pricing*, Macmillan, London.

Ansoff, H.J. (1965), *Corporate Strategy*, McGraw-Hill, New York.

Arrow, K. (1959), 'Towards a theory of price adjustment' in M. Abramovitz *et al.*, *The Allocation of Economic Resources*, Stanford University Press, Stanford, Calif., pp.41–51.

Barnard, C.I. (1938), *The Functions of the Executive*, Harvard University Press, Cambridge, Mass.

Baumol, W.J. (1959, 1967), *Business Behavior, Value and Growth* (1st edn.), Macmillan, New York; rev. edn, Harcourt, Brace and World, New York. (References are to 1967 edn.)

Becker, G. (1976), *The Economic Approach to Human Behavior*, Chicago University Press, Chicago.

Bharadwaj, K. (1972), 'Marshall on Pigou's *Wealth and Welfare*', *Economica*, NS, **39**, pp.32–46.

Blaug, M. (1976), 'Kuhn versus Lakatos or Paradigms versus research programmes in the history of economics' in S.J. Latsis (ed.), *Method and Appraisal in Economics*, Cambridge University Press, Cambridge, pp.147–80.

Blaug, M. (1980), *The Methodology of Economics*, Cambridge University Press, Cambridge.

Burns, T. and Stalker, G.M. (1961), *The Management of Innovation*, Tavistock, London.

Caldwell, B. (1984), *Appraisal and Criticism in Economics*, Allen and Unwin, Boston.

Casson, M. (1982), *The Entrepreneur: An Economic Theory*, Martin Robertson, Oxford.

Chamberlin, E.H. (1933), *The Theory of Monopolistic Competition*, Harvard University Press, Cambridge, Mass.

Chamberlin, E.H. (1961), 'The origin and early development of monopolistic competition theory', *Quarterly Journal of Economics*, pp.515–43.

Chasse, J.D. (1984), 'Marshall, the human agent and economic growth: wants and activities revisited', *History of Political Economy*, **16**, pp.381–404.

Clapham, J.H. (1922) 'Of empty economic boxes', *Economic Journal*, **32**, pp.305–14; reprinted in Stigler and Boulding (1953), pp.119–30.

Coase, R. (1937), 'The nature of the firm', *Economica*, NS, **4**, pp.386–405; reprinted in Stigler and Boulding (1953), pp.331–51.

Coase, R.H. (1984), 'Alfred Marshall's mother and father', *History of Political Economy*, **16**, pp.519–28.

Coddington, A. (1975a), 'The rationale of general equilibrium theory', *Economic Inquiry*, **13**, pp.539–58.

Coddington, A. (1975b), 'Creaking semaphore and beyond', *British Journal for the Philosophy of Science*, **26**, pp.151–63.

Coddington, A. (1978), Review of E. Malinvaud 'The theory of unemployment reconsidered', *Journal of Economic Literature*, **16**, pp.1012–18.

Cyert, R.M. and March, J.G. (1963), *A Behavioral Theory of the Firm*, Prentice-Hall, Englewood Cliffs, NJ.

Debreu, G. (1959), *Theory of Value*, Wiley, New York.

Debreu, G. (1984), 'Economic theory in the mathematical mode', *American Economic Review*, **74**, pp.267–78.

Demsetz, H. (1969), 'Information and efficiency: another viewpoint', *Journal of Law and Economics*, **12**, pp.1–22.

Dorfman, R., Samuelson, P.A. and Solow, R.M. (1958), *Linear Programming and Economic Analysis*, McGraw-Hill, New York.

Drucker, P.F. (1955), *The Practice of Management*, Heinemann, London.

Ellis, H.S. and Fellner, W. (1943), 'External economies and diseconomies', *American Economic Review*, **33**, pp.493–511.

Elster, J. (ed.) (1986), *Rational Choice*, Blackwell, Oxford.

Fama, E.F. (1980), 'Agency problems and the theory of the firm', *Journal of Political Economy*, **88**, pp.288–307.

Friedman, M. (1953), 'The methodology of positive economics,' in M. Friedman, *Essays in Positive Economics*, University of Chicago Press, Chicago.

Friedman, M. (1969), *The Optimum Quantity of Money and Other Essays*, Macmillan, London.

Grassl, W. and Smith, B. (1986), *Austrian Economics: Historical and Philosophical Background*, Croom Helm, London and Sydney.

Hahn, F.H. (1973), *On the Notion of Equilibrium in Economics*,

Cambridge University Press, Cambridge; reprinted in Hahn (1984), pp.43–71. (References are to this reprint.)

Hahn, F.H. (1982), *Money and Inflation*, Basil Blackwell, Oxford.

Hahn, F.H. (1984), *Equilibrium and Macroeconomics*, Basil Blackwell, Oxford.

Hall, R.L. and Hitch, C.J. (1939), 'Price theory and business behaviour', *Oxford Economic Papers*, no.2, pp.12–45; reprinted in Wilson and Andrews (1951), pp.107–38.

Harrod, R. (1969), *Money*, Macmillan, London.

Hawkins, C.J. (1970), 'The revenue maximization oligopoly model: comment, *American Economic Review*, **60**, pp.429–32.

Hayek, F.A. (1931), *Prices and Production*, Routledge, London.

Hayek, F.A. (1937), 'Economics and knowledge', *Economica*, NS, **4**, pp.33–54; reprinted in Hayek (1948), pp.33–56.

Hayek, F.A. (1945), 'The use of knowledge in society', *American Economic Review*, **35**, 519–30; reprinted in Hayek (1948), pp.77–91.

Hayek, F.A. (1948, 1949), *Individualism and Economic Order*, University of Chicago Press, Chicago; Routledge and Kegan Paul, London.

Hayek, F.A. (1975), 'The pretence of knowledge', *Swedish Journal of Economics*, **77**, pp.433–42.

Hayek, F.A. (1978), *New Studies in Philosophy, Politics, Economics and the History of Ideas*, Routledge and Kegan Paul, London.

Heiner, R.A. (1983), 'The origin of predictable behavior', *American Economic Review*, **75**, pp.560–95.

Hicks, J.R. (1935), 'A suggestion for simplifying the theory of money', *Economica*, NS, **5(2)**, pp.1–19; reprinted in Hicks (1982), pp.46–63.

Hicks, J.R. (1939), *Value and Capital*, Oxford University Press, Oxford.

Hicks, J.R. (1976), 'Some questions of time in economics' in A.M. Tang, F.M. Westfield and J.S. Worley (eds.), *Evolution, Welfare and Time in Economics*, Lexington Books, Lexington, Mass., pp.135–51; reprinted in Hicks (1982), pp.282–300. (References are to this reprint.)

Hicks, J.R. (1982), *Collected Essays on Economic Theory. Volume II: Money, Interest and Wages*, Basil Blackwell, Oxford.

Hirschman, A.O. (1970), *Exit, Voice and Loyalty*, Harvard University Press, Cambridge, Mass.

Hobson, J.A. (1914), *Work and Wealth: A Human Valuation*, Macmillan, London.

Hutchison, T.W. (1981), *The Politics and Philosophy of Economics: Marxians, Keynesians and Austrians*, Blackwell, Oxford.

Kaldor, N. (1934), 'A classificatory note on the determinateness of equilibrium', *Review of Economic Studies*, **1**, pp.122–36.

Kaldor, N. (1939), 'Speculation and economic stability', *Review of Economic Studies*, **7**, pp.1–27.

Kelly, G.A. (1963), *A Theory of Personality*, W.W. Norton, New York.

Keynes, J.M. (1937a), 'How to avoid a slump', *The Times*, 12, 13, 14 January, 1937: reprinted in Keynes (1982), pp.384–95.

Keynes, J.M. (1937b), 'The general theory of employment', *Quarterly Journal of Economics*, **51**; reprinted in Keynes (1973c), pp.109–23. (References are to this reprint.)

Keynes, J.M. (1972), (ed.) D.E. Moggridge, *Essays in Biography*, vol. 10, *Collected Writings*, Macmillan, London.

Keynes, J.M. (1973a), (ed.) D.E. Moggridge, *The General Theory of Employment, Interest and Money*, vol. 7, *Collected Writings*, Macmillan, London.

Keynes, J.M. (1973b), (ed.) D.E. Moggridge, *A treatise on probability*, vol. 8, *Collected Writings*, Macmillan, London.

Keynes, J.M. (1973c), (ed.) D.E. Moggridge, *The General Theory and after: Part II: Defence and development*, vol. 14, *Collected Writings*, Macmillan, London.

Keynes, J.M. (1982), (ed.) D.E. Moggridge, *Activities, 1931–39. World Crises and Policies in Britain and America*, vol. 21, *Collected Writings*, Macmillan, London.

Kirzner, I.M. (1973), *Competition and Entrepreneurship*, University of Chicago Press, Chicago.

Kirzner, I.M. (1985a), *Discovery and the Capitalist Process*, University of Chicago Press, Chicago.

Kirzner, I.M. (1985b), 'Review of O'Driscoll and Rizzo (1985)' in *Market Process*, **3(2)**, Center for the Study of Market Processes, Fairfax, Va.

Klein, B. (1977), *Dynamic Economics*, Harvard University Press, Cambridge, Mass.

Knight, F.H. (1921), *Risk, Uncertainty and Profit*, Houghton Mifflin, Boston, Mass.

Knight, F.H. (1924), 'Some fallacies in the interpretation of social cost', *Quarterly Journal of Economics*, **38**, pp.582–606; reprinted in Boulding and Stigler (1953), pp.160–79.

Koutsoyiannis, A. (1979), *Modern Microeconomics*, (2nd edn.) Macmillan, London.

Kuhn, T.S. (1962, 1970a), *The Structure of Scientific Revolutions*, University of Chicago Press, Chicago.

Kuhn, T.S. (1970b), 'Reflections on my critics' in I. Lakatos and A. Musgrave (eds), *Criticism and the Growth of Knowledge*, Cambridge University Press, Cambridge, pp.231–78.

Lachmann, L.M. (1986), *The Market as an Economic Process*, Basil Blackwell, Oxford.

Lakatos, I. (1970), 'Falsification and the methodology of scientific research programmes' in Lakatos I. and Musgrave A. (eds), *Criticism and the Growth of Knowledge*, Cambridge University Press, Cambridge, pp.91–195.

Lakatos, I. and Musgrave, A. (eds) (1970), *Criticism and the Growth of Knowledge*, Cambridge University Press, Cambridge.

Lancaster, K.J. (1966), 'A new approach to consumer theory', *Journal of Political Economy*, **74**, pp.132–57.

Leibenstein, H. (1966), 'Allocative efficiency vs X-efficiency', *American Economic Review*, **56**, pp.392–415.

Leibenstein, H. (1976), *Beyond Economic Man. A New Foundation for Microeconomics*, Harvard University Press, Cambridge, Mass.

Leijonhufvud, A. (1973), 'Effective demand failures', *Swedish Journal of Economics*, **75**, pp.27–48; reprinted in Leijonhufvud (1981), pp.103–29.

Leijonhufvud, A. (1975), 'Costs and consequences of inflation' in G.C. Harcourt (ed.), *The Microeconomic Foundations of Macroeconomics*, Macmillan, London; reprinted in Leijonhufvud (1981), pp.227–69.

Leijonhufvud, A. (1981), *Information and Co-ordination*, Oxford University Press, New York and Oxford.

Levitt, T. (1962), *Innovation in Marketing*, McGraw-Hill, New York.

Loasby, B.J. (1966), 'The substance of management education', *District Bank Review*, **160**, pp.41–56.

Loasby, B.J. (1967), 'The organic life of Little', *Management Today*, September.

Loasby, B.J. (1971), 'Hypothesis and paradigm in the theory of the firm', *Economic Journal*, **81**, pp.863–85.

Loasby, B.J. (1976), *Choice, Complexity and Ignorance*, Cambridge University Press, Cambridge.

Machlup, F. (1974), 'Situational determinism in economics', *British Journal for the Philosophy of Science*, **25**, pp.271–84.

Malinvaud, E. (1977, 1985), *The Theory of Unemployment Reconsidered*, Basil Blackwell, Oxford.

Marris, R.L. (1964), *The Economic Theory of 'Managerial' Capitalism*, Macmillan, London.

Marshall, A. (1907), 'The social possibilities of economic chivalry', *Economic Journal*, **17**, pp.7–29; reprinted in Pigou (1925), pp.323–46.

Marshall, A. (1919), *Industry and Trade*, Macmillan, London.

Marshall, A. (1961), *Principles of Economics*, (9th (variorum) edn.), 2 vols. Macmillan, London. (References are to Volume I unless otherwise identified.)

Masterman, M. (1970), 'The nature of a paradigm' in I. Lakatos and A. Musgrave (eds), *Criticism and the Growth of Knowledge*, Cambridge University Press, Cambridge, pp.59–88.

McCloskey, D.N. (1983), 'The rhetoric of economics', *Journal of Economic Literature*, **21**, pp.481–517.

Meade, J.E. (1936), *An Introduction to Economic Analysis and Policy*, Oxford University Press, Oxford.

Medawar, P.B. (1982), *Pluto's Republic*, Oxford University Press, Oxford.

Menger, C. (1963), *Problems of Economics and Sociology*, University of Illinois Press, Urbana, Ill.

Mises, L. von (1945), *Bureaucracy*, Hodge, London.

Mises, L. von (1949), *Human Action*, Hodge, London.

Moss, S. (1984), 'O'Brien's "The Evolution of the Theory of the Firm": a discussion' in F.H. Stephen (ed.), *Firms, Organization and Labour*, Macmillan, London, pp.63–8.

Nash, J.F. (1951), 'Non-cooperative games', *Annals of Mathematics*, **54**, pp.286–95.

Nelson, R.R. and Winter, S.G. (1982), *An Evolutionary Theory of Economic Change*, Harvard University Press, Cambridge, Mass.

O'Brien, D.P. (1974), 'The development of economics', *Scottish Journal of Political Economy*, **21**, pp.187–99.

O'Brien, D.P. (1984a), 'The evolution of the theory of the firm' in F.H. Stephen (ed.), *Firms, Organization and Labour*, Macmillan, London, pp.25–62.

O'Brien, D.P. (1984b), 'Research programmes in competitive structure', *Journal of Economic Studies*, **10**, pp.29–51.

O'Driscoll, G.P. Jr. and Rizzo, M.J. (1985), *The Economics of Time and Ignorance*, Basil Blackwell, Oxford.

Okun, A.M. (1981), *Prices and Quantities*, Basil Blackwell, Oxford.

Olson, M. (1982), *The Rise and Decline of Nations*, Yale University Press, London.

Parsons, T. (1931), 'Wants and activities in Marshall', *Quarterly Journal of Economics*, **66**, pp.101–40.

Penrose, E.T. (1959), *The Theory of the Growth of the Firm*, Oxford University Press, Oxford.

Pfeffer, J. and Salancik, G.R. (1978), *The External Control of Organisations*, Harper and Row, New York.

Pigou, A.C. (1912), *Wealth and Welfare*, Macmillan, London.

Pigou, A.C. (1920, 1924, 1929), *The Economics of Welfare*, Macmillan, London.

Pigou, A.C. (ed.) (1925), *Memorials of Alfred Marshall*, Macmillan, London.

Pigou, A.C. (1928), 'An analysis of supply', *Economic Journal*, **38**, pp.238–57.

Polanyi, M. (1958), *Personal Knowledge*, Routledge and Kegan Paul, London.

Popper, K.R. (1966), *The Open Society and its Enemies* (5th edn.), Routledge and Kegan Paul, London.

Popper, K.R. (1969), *Conjectures and Refutations* (3rd edn.), Routledge and Kegan Paul, London.

Popper, K.R. (1970), 'Normal science and its dangers' in I. Lakatos and A. Musgrave (eds), *Criticism and the Growth of Knowledge*, Cambridge University Press, Cambridge, pp.51–8.

Popper, K.R. (1972), *The Logic of Scientific Discovery* (6th impr.), Hutchinson, London.

Pounds, W.F. (1969), 'The process of problem finding', *Industrial Management Review*, **11**, pp.1–19.

Remenyi, J.V. (1979), 'Core demi-core interaction: toward a general theory of disciplinary and subdisciplinary growth', *History of Political Economy*, **11**, pp.30–63.

Richardson, G.B. (1960), *Information and Investment*, Oxford University Press, Oxford.

Richardson, G.B. (1972), 'The organisation of industry', *Economic Journal*, **82**, pp.883–96.

Richardson, G.B. (1975), 'Adam Smith on competition and increasing returns' in A.S. Skinner and T. Wilson (eds), *Essays on Adam Smith*, Clarendon Press, Oxford University Press, Oxford, pp.350–60.

Robertson, D.H. (1924), 'Those empty boxes', *Economic Journal*, **34**, pp.16–31; reprinted in Stigler and Boulding (1953), pp.143–59.

Robertson, D.H. (1926), *Banking Policy and the Price Level*, P.S. King, London.

Robertson, D.H. (1930), 'Symposium on increasing returns and the representative firm. The trees of the forest', *Economic Journal*, **60**, pp.80–92.

Robertson, D.H. (1952), *Utility and All That and Other Essays*, Allen and Unwin, London.

Robinson, E.A.G. (1931), *The Structure of Competitive Industry*, Cambridge University Press, Cambridge.

Robinson, J.V. (1933, 1969), *The Economics of Imperfect Competition* (1st and 2nd edns), Macmillan, London.

Robinson, J.V. (1951), *Collected Economic Papers, Vol 1*, Basil Blackwell, Oxford.

Robinson, R. (1971), *Edward H. Chamberlin*, Columbia University Press, New York and London.

Russell, B. (1946), *History of Western Philosophy*, Allen and Unwin, London.

Russell, B. (1963), *Mysticism and Logic*, Allen and Unwin, London.

Samuelson, P.A. (1955), 'Comment on "Professor Samuelson on operationalism in economic theory"', *Quarterly Journal of Economics*, **69**, pp.310–14; reprinted in J.E. Stiglitz (ed.), *The Collected Scientific Papers of Paul A. Samuelson*, **2**, MIT Press, Cambridge, Mass. and London, pp.1767–71. (Reference is to this reprint.)

Samuelson, P.A. (1967), 'The monopolistic competition revolution' in R.E. Kuenne (ed.), *Monopolistic Competition Theory: Studies in Impact*, John Wiley, New York, pp.105–38; reprinted in R.K. Merton (ed.), *The Collected Scientific Papers of Paul A. Samuelson*, **2**, MIT Press, Cambridge, Mass. and London, pp.18–51. (References are to this reprint.)

Samuelson, P.A. and Nordhaus, W.D. (1985), *Economics* (12th edn.), McGraw-Hill, New York.

Schumpeter, J.A. (1934), *The Theory of Economic Development*, Harvard University Press, Cambridge, Mass.

Schumpeter, J.A. (1943), *Capitalism, Socialism and Democracy*, Allen and Unwin, London.

Shackle, G.L.S. (1967, 1983), *The Years of High Theory: Invention and Tradition in Economic Thought 1926–1939*, Cambridge University Press, Cambridge.

Shackle, G.L.S. (1972), *Epistemics and Economics*, Cambridge University Press, Cambridge.

Shackle, G.L.S. (1974), *Keynesian Kaleidics*, Edinburgh University Press, Edinburgh.

Simon, H.A. (1969), *The Sciences of the Artificial*, MIT Press, Cambridge, Mass.

Simon, H.A. (1982), *Models of Bounded Rationality*, 2 vols, MIT Press, Cambridge, Mass.

Skinner, A.S. (1979), 'Adam Smith: an aspect of modern economics?' *Scottish Journal of Political Economy*, **26**, pp.109–25.

Smith, A. (1976), *An Inquiry into the Nature and Causes of the Wealth of Nations*, ed. R.H. Campbell, A.S. Skinner and W.B. Todd, 2 vols., Oxford University Press, Oxford.

Smith, A. (1980), 'The principles which lead and direct philosophical enquiries: illustrated by the history of astronomy' in W.P.D.

Wightman, (ed.), *Essays on Philosophical Subjects* (1795), Oxford University Press, Oxford, pp.33–105.

Sraffa, P. (1926), 'The laws of return under competitive conditions', *Economic Journal*, **36**, pp.535–50; reprinted in Boulding and Stigler (1953), pp.180–97.

Stephen, F.H. (ed.) (1984), *Firms, Organization and Labour*, Macmillan, London.

Stigler, G.J. (1976), 'The existence of X-efficiency', *American Economic Review*, **66**, pp. 213–16.

Stigler, G.J. and Becker, G.S. (1977), 'De gustibus non est disputandum', *American Economic Review*, **67**, pp. 76–90.

Stigler, G.J. and Boulding, K.E. (eds) (1953), *Readings in Price Theory*, Allen and Unwin, London.

Townshend, H. (1937), 'Liquidity-premium and the theory of value', *Economic Journal*, **67**, pp.157–69.

Triffin, R. (1940), *Monopolistic Competition and General Equilibrium Theory*, Harvard University Press, Cambridge, Mass.

Tversky, A. and Kahneman, D. (1981), 'The framing of decisions and the psychology of choice', *Science*, **211**, pp.453–8; reprinted in Elster (1986) pp.123–37.

Walker, D.A. (1987), 'Walras's theories of tatonnement', *Journal of Political Economy*, **95**, pp.758–74.

Walras, L. (1874, 1900), *Elements d'Économie Politique Pure, ou Théorie de la Richesse Sociale* (1st and 4th edns), Rouge, Lausanne.

Whitaker, J. (1977), 'Some neglected aspects of Alfred Marshall's economic and social thought', *History of Political Economy*, **9**, pp.161–97.

Whitaker, J.K. (1988), 'The Cambridge background to imperfect competition' in George R. Feiwel (ed.), *The Economics of Imperfect Competition and Employment*, Macmillan, London.

Whitley, R. (1984), *The Intellectual and Social Organization of the Sciences*, Clarendon Press, Oxford University Press, New York.

Williamson, O.E. (1964), *Economics of Discretionary Behavior: Managerial Objectives in a Theory of the Firm*, Prentice-Hall, Englewood Cliffs, NJ.

Williamson, O.E. (1975), *Markets and Hierarchies: Analysis and Antitrust Implications*, Free Press, New York.

Williamson, O.E. (1985), *The Economic Institutions of Capitalism: Firms, Markets, Relational Contracting*, Free Press, New York.

Williamson, O.E. (1986), *Economic Organisation: Firms, Markets and Policy Control*, Wheatsheaf, Brighton.

Wilson, T. and Andrews, P.W.S. (eds) (1951), *Oxford Studies in the Price Mechanism*, Oxford University Press, Oxford.

Young, A. (1913), 'Pigou's wealth and welfare', *Quarterly Journal of Economics*, **27**, pp.672–86.

Ziman, J.M. (1968), *Public Knowledge*, Cambridge University Press, Cambridge.

Ziman, J.M. (1978), *Reliable Knowledge*, Cambridge University Press, Cambridge.

Name index

Subject index